7/99

D0147114

WITHDRAWN

JUNGIAN REFLECTIONS
WITHIN THE CINEMA

Jungian Reflections within the Cinema

A Psychological Analysis of Sci-Fi and Fantasy Archetypes

JAMES F. IACCINO

Westport, Connecticut
London

Library of Congress Cataloging-in-Publication Data

Iaccino, James F.
    Jungian reflections within the cinema : a psychological analysis
of sci-fi and fantasy archetypes / James F. Iaccino.
        p.   cm.
    Includes bibliographical references and index.
    ISBN 0-275-95048-4 (alk. paper)
    1. Science fiction films—History and criticism.   2. Fantastic
films—History and criticism.   3. Archetype (Psychology) in motion
pictures.   I. Title.
PN1995.9.S26I23   1998
791.43'65—dc21   97–41705

British Library Cataloguing in Publication Data is available.

Library of Congress Catalog Card Number: 97–41705
ISBN: 0-275-95048-4

First published in 1998

Praeger Publishers, 88 Post Road West, Westport, CT 06881
An imprint of Greenwood Publishing Group, Inc.

Printed in the United States of America

The paper used in this book complies with the
Permanent Paper Standard issued by the National
Information Standards Organization (Z39.48–1984).

10 9 8 7 6 5 4 3 2 1

As always:
To my archetypal companion Michele,
and our four primordial children: Jon, Nicole, Kaitlin,
and Rebecca

Contents

**Part Three
A Jungian Analysis of Television Archetypes**

Preface

When I was writing my book entitled *Psychological Reflections on Cine-matic Terror: Jungian Archetypes in Horror Films* for Praeger Publishers in 1994, I knew that I would not be able to do justice to the psychoanalytic theory by focusing on just one movie genre. Though the correlation be-tween Carl Jung's primordial images and horror story lines was a striking one, I felt that other treatments could be considered along the same lines of investigation as the first work. Thus, the purpose behind *Jungian Re-flections within the Cinema* is primarily to extend the archetypal analysis to a number of movie categories, ranging from science-fiction to fantasy films. There is even a section on television series that have tried to emulate the larger-than-life movies in plot and character development. In the proc-ess of broadening my scope, I hope that I have succeeded in providing greater substance and three-dimensional life to Jung's extensive list of ar-chetypes not only to this present generation of readers, but also to those who will follow.

The format of *Jungian Reflections within the Cinema* is similar to the previous text. Each chapter will concentrate exclusively on an archetype via a package of films that illustrate its essential contents. For instance, the Jungian shadow has been represented in various movies as an oppressive society (*Logan's Run*) or an alien race (*Battlestar: Galactica*) that is hell-bent on maintaining control and order in the universe. Archetypal heroes like Logan-5 or Commander Adama are inserted into the stories not only to fight such debilitating influences, but also to lead the people to a more democratic (and paradisiac) way of life. The perpetual struggle between the ego and its complementary dark side is a common theme which has been transmitted to every culture since the beginning of time and will not be ignored here.

Some other notable images discussed within these pages consist of the following: the space-father, the god-image, and the shadow species for the science-fiction genre (Part One); alchemic travelers, divided superheroes, grail quests, and deadly children for the fantasy genre (Part Two); and, to complete the analysis, shadow pursuers for the television genre (Part Three). A special introduction to Jung's archetypes will precede the three basic divisions to supply the reader with the necessary reference point for mastering the complex material presented later.

I am indebted to the authors listed below for helping me perform my second set of archetypal investigations: first and foremost, Carol S. Pearson, who has written several pivotal works on the subject, including *The Hero Within: Six Archetypes We Live By* (1989) and, more recently, *Awakening the Heroes Within: Twelve Archetypes to Help Us Find Ourselves and Transform Our World* (1991); also Robert H. Hopcke, who has done an excellent job in giving a layman's perspective on Jung's major concepts with his *Guided Tour of the Collected Works of C. G. Jung* (1992); and, finally, Stuart M. Kaminsky, who really started the process of applying Jung's archetypes to the cinema and television in, respectively, *American Film Genres* (1988) and *American Television Genres* (1988).

I would personally like to thank my wife, Michele, for the hours she has devoted (and continues to devote) to the rearing of our four children: Jon, Nicole, Kaitlin, and Rebecca. She has made it possible for me to read every possible source of Jung's I could find, thus allowing me to become an expert on his archetypal theory. Without my wife's assistance and support, I could never have written this companion text to *Psychological Reflections on Cinematic Terror* or, for that matter, ever begun the archetypal journey into the cinema. Thank you so much, Michele!

Let us now enter the world of primordial images and see what we can discover by examining some fairly popular films over the last two decades. I can assure you that our travels will be quite exciting. We might even open up new doors into our hidden psyche and understand a little bit better exactly who we are and what our nature is like.

Introduction to Jungian Archetypes

Carl Jung referred to his psychological theory as being strictly analytical to distinguish it from the Freudian model of psychoanalysis which prevailed at the time. However, many contemporary writers feel that the term *archetypal* is a more apt description of the Jungian approach since it is those very contents of the collective unconscious that are emphasized throughout his series of essays.[1]

According to Jung, archetypes are archaic (or primordial) images which "have existed since the remotest times."[2] They have found expression in tribal lore, mythology, fairy tales, religious systems, and primitive art. The repository for all archetypes is the collective unconscious, a part of the psyche which was the first to evolve and now provides the necessary link with humanity's ancestral past. Through the collective unconscious, the human is able to tap into these inherited forms and experience perceptions common to every member of the species. A good way of describing archetypes is that they are "racial memories" which unknowingly shape and mold our current thought processes.[3]

At this point in our discussion, we should make an important distinction between the archetypes per se and the objects to which they relate. Archetypes should not be regarded as fully developed pictures that reside in the collective unconscious; rather, they are *"forms without content* [similar to the Platonic *eidos*], representing the possibility of a certain type of perception and action."[4] One might say that each image is more like a negative, waiting for the necessary experiential influences to define it.[5] Thus, objects within the environment provide substance to the archetypes and make them more anthropomorphic and meaningful to each person.

To give an example, the godhead archetype is a transcendent spirit which superimposes itself over the life force and establishes order in the universe. It is an invisible presence, like the wind, that is more powerful than the human, yet it breathes its existence into each and every living creature.[6] To grasp the immaterial essence of a god, the individual must connect the concept to a concrete instance of reality. This will vary from person to person, but the underlying image will remain the same. In depicting the godhead, one of Jung's patients described the being as a gigantic type of father-figure that held him in huge, nurturing arms.[7] While this version might not be relevant to all people, the fact remains that we have an innate idea of what god is: a superior entity who views the human race as absolutely vital to its continued existence. Each archetype operates in much the same way, by controlling our psyches via particular situations in life that can be directly tied to the collective form.

Let us now consider some of Jung's most significant archetypes which affect our personality.

THE PARENTAL ARCHETYPES

The mother archetype is a fascinating one to begin with since Jung relates every conceivable maternal image to this concept. From earth mothers giving birth to the world to fertility goddesses feeding its people, one element stays constant: everything springs from the "maternal well" of life.[8] The archetype is not without its dark side, however. Anything that devours and swallows up its young can be treated as a mother symbol, suggesting that there are both "loving *and* terrible" qualities associated with the primordial matriarch.[9]

The mother archetype also lies at the very root of all mother complexes. Typically, it is the mother who is the first significant feminine being that the son encounters and with whom he identifies.[10] Not only does she foster love and attraction in the boy, but she might also stimulate feelings of repulsion and hatred by her refusing to let the child develop his own identity. Smothered with affection, the male cannot break away from the mother and remains forever married to the parent of the opposite sex.[11] All subsequent relationships with women are, for the most part, marred by this deleterious perception of the prime Mother.

The complementary father archetype contains many of the same ingredients as the mother archetype, including the ability to take charge and protect his charges from harm. Often pictured as a strong and powerful leader, the way the father rules is as ambivalent as any other archetype.[12] Sometimes he might discipline his subjects with a benevolent hand; other times, he might enforce his authority with an iron fist. If the more destructive form of control is chosen, the result could be an uprising on the part of the family members who want to be heard and heeded. Thus, the father runs the risk of being ousted from his select position in the kingdom by continuing to use strictness and inflexibility.

THE CHILD ARCHETYPE

In addition to the parental archetypes, the collective unconscious holds an image of the child-god (or *puer aeternus*), which serves to remind us that our development is far from complete. Jung's child is a symbol of future hopes and dreams, of something that will eventually evolve toward wholeness and unity. In its present form, the *puer* might appear helpless and operate in a fairly dependent mode; yet greatness is an essential part of its destiny.[13]

It should be pointed out that the child is more than human. Divinity radiates from its very core. The "seedling" is capable of executing superhuman feats at a young age and can cope with any danger that confronts it. Considered the youngest of heroes, this small one must move beyond its infantile impotence so that it can accomplish the "bigger than big" tasks that lie ahead in the tradition of many child-gods, such as Hercules and Christ.[14] The miracle is that the child can do so much, given its restricted stature.

THE PERSONA/SHADOW ARCHETYPES

Probably Jung is best known for his work with the persona and shadow archetypes. Many of his writings refer to these two forms, and so an explanation of each is in order at this juncture.

The word "persona" originally meant the mask that the actor put on to assume a part in a play.[15] Jung used this basic definition to describe his psychological archetype. The persona is our conscious outer face, our social mask that we put on to conceal the private self which lies within. It is necessary to maintain the persona so that we can carry out the functions that society expects of us (such as getting along with others and performing our work well). Also called the conformity archetype, the persona creates a lasting and favorable impression on society's members and will make the individual more readily acceptable in their eyes.[16] We might have more than one mask (for example, one for work, one for home, one for recreational pursuits), but collectively they constitute our persona. Each mask simply helps us to conform in various ways to a wide range of situations we must face each day in our public lives.

There is a negative side to the persona. People might come to believe who they pretend themselves to be. In other words, the ideal image with which we identify might hide the weaker and underdeveloped personality beneath it. As Jung states, persona identification can contribute to the neglect of our inner selves and lead to an assortment of psychological problems.[17] This is the price we have to pay for effectively meeting the demands and challenges of the outer world: we might never become aware of our true personalities so long as we continue to play those all-important social roles.

The shadow is one aspect of that self we tend to ignore and repress from consciousness. All our inferiorities, unacceptable impulses, and shameful behaviors constitute this dark side of our personality.[18] Many people tend to cover up their shadow with the persona, but if they look under the social guise, they will find a brutal primitive waiting to be unleashed upon the world. The shadow rarely operates in a civilized manner; instead, it uses a "pre-logical" type of thinking,[19] governed by strong desires and animalistic needs. By courageously removing the constraints and trappings of our current existence, we might be able to come to terms with that haunting past and even accept it as a vital part of our identity. The shadow, furthermore, displays a level of emotionality that is quite genuine and spontaneous. Although it might be overpowering (and even frightening) to the modern-day observer,[20] all of humankind's creativity and intuitiveness stem from this "archaic feeling" state.[21] Because the shadow represents the best *and* the worst in the human species, it is considered the most powerful archetype of the lot.

In a more cosmic sense, Jung's shadow is the absolute evil that must coexist with the absolute good of nature as well as godhood. Without the shadow (personified in Jung's writings as the devil archetype), the Christian Trinity is incomplete and provides, at best, a restricted view of the all-powerful deity. The inclusion of the devil in an expanded quaternity gives the god image a more multidimensional personality akin to the human's, with all of the associated strengths and weaknesses.[22] Jung advises us not to avoid this satanic dark side when relating with others; otherwise, all sorts of evils, such as global warfare and nuclear destruction, can be unconsciously visited upon humanity in the attempt to elevate the moral and upright trinitarian part of our character.

THE ANIMA/ANIMUS ARCHETYPES

Besides the shadow archetype, the collective unconscious contains a sub-personality of the person's complementary gender. For the man, it is the feminine "soul-image," or anima, and for the woman, it is the masculine "spirit," or animus.[23] Sometimes Jung alluded to the anima and animus as the inferior parts of each sex, not so much to downgrade their importance as to indicate just how functionally incomplete they were to the individual's more overt identity.[24] More times than not, each gender will try to deny its opposite so that the culturally imposed roles of masculinity and femininity can be maintained. It might even be said that our Western society deems it virtuous to hide this other side from the eyes of others. To express one's anima or animus openly could have a serious impact on traditional types of relationships.

Nevertheless, our invisible partner must be heard if we are ever going to attain a harmonious and total balance, or syzygy. If the anima is denied expression for too long in the male of the species, he runs the risk of losing his "manly" strength and becoming more effeminate in appearance and characteristics. The way that he associates with women also changes. A subservient, helpless mode might be chosen in order to allow the female to take charge of the situation. In a way, the anima-repressed male is hoping that his "inner woman" can be more like the external one to which he is mated. Likewise, the female might become so possessed by her restrained animus that she adopts more masculine (and very unladylike) qualities, such as stubbornness, willfulness, a lust for power, and physical aggressiveness.[25] Her overbearing demeanor and "always right" attitude can sorely test the limits of a man's patience to the point where he is driven crazy by this incredibly strong Amazon.[26]

Of course, since the time of Jung, social conceptions concerning masculinity and femininity have been modified and greatly expanded upon to the extent that the anima and animus archetypes might be considered somewhat outdated or culturally inappropriate.[27] The key idea to keep in mind is that Jung believed *both* the male and feminine elements were essential and equally important to normal personality development. If readers do not limit the anima and animus images to one gender exclusively, then they might be in a better position to see the merits of this theory and realize that not every part of their identity is actualized to the same degree.

THE FAIRY TALE ARCHETYPES

To repeat what was emphasized at the beginning of this section, Jung saw a number of archetypes reflected in the legends and folktales of various cultures. The story of the hero undertaking a quest to find a sacred object (or treasure) that will help him transform his kingdom to a more utopian paradise is a common theme that has been transmitted from generation to generation.[28] We will look at the hero's journey more closely and consider the wide assortment of archetypal figures he encounters during his exploits.

The hero himself certainly has an alluring (if not mysterious) character. Ever since childhood, he has had to contend with forces that would deny him his own independence and self-direction. The hero's first battle is with his mother, the "demon woman" who has the power to sap him of any developing strength.[29] Should he succeed in breaking away from this vindictive parent, the hero is faced with countless other struggles for the remainder of his life, all of which involve the same epic life-and-death proportions. The warrior modality is so strong in the hero that slaying others (including the primordial dragon) is considered a necessity in order to protect himself and the things he values. The outcome of each fight is more than simply good triumphing over evil; it shows how personal convictions can shape one's world, hopefully for the better, when one takes charge of his (or her) life.[30]

Sometimes the hero requires counseling since his warrioring tendencies have placed him in plenty of desperate, no-win scenarios. This is where the archetypal wise old man intervenes to lend a helping hand. The old one exemplifies the hidden strength that the hero needs to seek out and call upon before confronting the crisis; as such, this character is not part of the mainstream of society, but he is concealed from the crowd, living the lifestyle of a hermit in a secret abode. Through his wisdom and moral insight, the old man is able to induce self-reflection in the hero. Who am I, where am I going, what is the purpose of my journey—these are all questions that are posed to the hero to make him stop and think before acting.[31] For Jung, sleeping on the problem is just as important as engaging in the warrior mode; when combined, both qualities will ensure the hero's success in the upcoming battle.

The old one is certainly more than a counselor or advisor to the hero. He possesses great magical abilities, similar to the Merlin figure in the Arthurian legends. Often referred to as the white magician, the old one can communicate his intentions through dreams and can even change his shape and size from human form to elfin and animal. Although his powers are great, this ancient wizard cannot force the hero to undertake the right course of action. He can only point out the roads that lead to the intended goal or supply the means to vanquish the assorted devils and witches along the way.[32] Because the old one's sphere of influence is limited, in the final analysis it is up to the hero to decide what to do with the given information. Fortunately, in most tales, the hero follows the wizard's instructions, and, as a result, a new and more confident leader of the people is created.[33] One might speculate that without the insertion of the wise one, the heroic transformation would never take place.

The antithesis of the wise old man is the trickster, the malicious shapeshifter who loves to play his inane jokes and pranks on the hero. Once freed from his bottle, this devil is able to plague humanity with his evil, magical powers for eons to come.[34] The trickster is notorious for metamorphosing into such ominous creatures as the wolf or raven and can elude capture all too easily. Moreover, he can mesmerize his intended victims into believing they want to be with him forever. In fairy tales, the princess happens to be the trickster's most frequent prey. It is her innocence and virginity that the "black spirit" desires, and so he draws her into his netherworld to make her his own.[35] The hero is faced with the almost insurmountable task of defeating the trickster so that he can rescue the virgin before she is totally converted to the dark side.

In several of his essays, Jung equates the princess figure to the Kore archetype, or maiden, who exposes herself to all types of danger because of her youth and naiveté. Frequently, the maiden is inducted into obscene, orgiastic rites and might even drink the blood of the living before she herself is sacrificed.[36] If the girl is able to survive her passage into darkness, she is no longer the same person. The maiden might even become the "queen of the underworld"[37] and relish her new-found nature. If this is the case, the hero might not be able to rescue his beloved and so leaves empty-handed, never to hold his most precious treasure in his arms again. Not all fairy tales end on such a happy note with the warrior getting his woman; some-times, the female deviates from her traditional role of damsel-in-distress and fights the hero every step of the way in order to express her previously repressed animus as best she can without being converted back to her help-less state. The hero's task then is to accept this change and let go of his own preconceptions as to what the world should be like.[38]

THE MANDALA ARCHETYPE

This brief introduction into the Jungian archetypes will conclude with an examination of the mandala, the essential core of personality which is mainly pictured as a circle or wheel with arms extending radially from a common center. For Jung, the perfectly rounded sphere was truly represen-tative of psychic wholeness, of that god-image residing within the human soul.[39] Such symbols of completion and integration have been used most extensively in describing the creation of the world, in which all of human-kind originated from the mythological egg.[40]

However, there is one image of the mandala that has continued to fas-cinate the human race over the centuries, namely the unidentified flying object (or UFO). Pictured as a fiery disc that flashes across the skies, the UFO contains the godlike power of being anywhere at any given moment, seemingly in defiance of the normal laws of time and space.[41] Sometimes people report having seen more than one extraterrestrial craft; they envision an entire space fleet invading the planet like a horde of hungry locusts. This "plurality of UFOs"[42] might signify a fragmentation of one's personality into numerous parts. Whatever the reason for these multiple sightings, one thing is immediately apparent in Jung's writings. He speculates that the UFO (individually or collectively speaking) is a reflection of one's disturbed unconscious which feels threatened by the technological progress that the human species has attained this past century. By retreating to space, the mind finds a haven in alien worlds that offer hope for a new tomorrow.[43] Thus, angelic visions of spheres descending on the earth are functionally comforting to humanity: they serve to bridge the gap between our conscious

and hidden selves and create a unity which is sorely needed in these troubled times of global warfare and universal catastrophe.

Having provided the reader with a cursory knowledge of Jung's most
important archetypes, this author will now proceed with his investigation
of the cinema. The films which have been chosen are familiar enough to
most so that lengthy plot synopses are not required. By not becoming
bogged down by the details of each story line, we should be able to reach
our primary objective of correlating the work(s) under discussion to the
respective Jungian image in a much more efficient manner.

NOTES

1. Robert H. Hopcke, "Archetypes and the Collective Unconscious," in *A Guided Tour of the Collected Works of C. G. Jung* (Boston: Shambhala, 1992), 13.

2. Carl G. Jung, "Archetypes of the Collective Unconscious," in *The Archetypes and the Collective Unconscious: The Collected Works*, trans. R.F.C. Hull (Princeton, NJ: Princeton University Press, 1990), 5.

3. Jung, "The Concept of the Collective Unconscious," in *The Archetypes and the Collective Unconscious*, 42–43.

4. Ibid., 48.

5. Calvin S. Hall and Vernon J. Nordby, *A Primer of Jungian Psychology* (New York: New American Library, 1973), 42.

6. Jung, "The Phenomenology of the Spirit in Fairytales," in *The Archetypes and the Collective Unconscious*, 208–11.

7. Carl G. Jung, "The Relations Between the Ego and the Unconscious. Part One: The Effects of the Unconscious upon Consciousness," in *The Basic Writings of C. G. Jung*, trans. R.F.C. Hull (Princeton, NJ: Princeton University Press, 1990), 118–19.

8. Hopcke, "Mother," in *A Guided Tour of Jung*, 100.

9. Jung, "Psychological Aspects of the Mother Archetype," in *The Archetypes and the Collective Unconscious*, 81–82.

10. Ibid., 85–86.

11. Carl G. Jung, "The Syzygy: Anima and Animus," in *Aion: Researches into the Phenomenology of the Self: The Collected Works*, trans. R.F.C. Hull (Princeton, NJ: Princeton University Press, 1990), 12–14.

12. Carl G. Jung, "The Significance of the Father in the Destiny of the Individual," in *Freud and Psychoanalysis: The Collected Works*, trans. R.F.C. Hull (Princeton, NJ: Princeton University Press, 1989), 323.

13. Hopcke, "Puer/Divine Child," in *A Guided Tour of Jung*, 107.

14. Jung, "The Psychology of the Child Archetype," in *The Archetypes and the Collective Unconscious*, 165–67.

15. Carl G. Jung, "Definitions, under Soul [Psyche, personality, persona, anima]," in *Psychological Types: The Collected Works*, trans. R.F.C. Hull (Princeton, NJ: Princeton University Press, 1990), 465.

16. Hall and Nordby, *Jungian Psychology*, 44–45.

17. Hopcke, "Persona," in *A Guided Tour of Jung*, 86–87; Jung, "The Relations Between the Ego and the Unconscious. Part Two: Individuation," in *Basic Writings*, 167–69.

18. Hopcke, "Shadow," in *A Guided Tour of Jung*, 81.

19. Carl G. Jung, "Archaic Man," in *Modern Man in Search of a Soul*, trans. W. S. Dell and Cary F. Baynes (San Diego, CA: Harcourt Brace Jovanovich, 1990), 125–26.

20. Jung, "The Shadow," in *Aion*, 8–9.

21. Jung, "Archetypes of the Collective Unconscious," in *The Archetypes and the Collective Unconscious*, 20–21.

22. Edward F. Edinger, "The Trinity Archetype and the Dialectic of Development," in *Ego and Archetype: Individuation and the Religious Function of the Psyche* (London: Penguin Books, 1972), 179–84; Jung, "Psychology and Religion. Dogma and Natural Symbols," in *Basic Writings*, 541–43.

23. Carl G. Jung, "The Masculine in Women: Letter of 12 November 1957," in *Aspects of the Masculine*, trans. R.F.C. Hull (Princeton, NJ: Princeton University Press, 1989), 109.

24. Hopcke, "Anima/Animus," in *A Guided Tour of Jung*, 91; Jung, "The Anima: Lecture V, 19 February 1930, Dream [23]," in *Aspects of the Masculine*, 136.

25. Jung, "The Relations Between the Ego and the Unconscious. Part Two: Individuation," in *Basic Writings*, 168–84.

26. Frieda Fordham, *An Introduction to Jung's Psychology* (London: Penguin Books, 1966), 57–58.

27. Hopcke, "Anima/Animus," in *A Guided Tour of Jung*, 92–93.

28. Carol S. Pearson, *Awakening the Heroes Within: Twelve Archetypes to Help Us Find Ourselves and Transform Our World* (San Francisco: HarperCollins, 1991), 1–3.

29. Carl G. Jung, "The Battle for Deliverance from the Mother," in *Symbols of Transformation: The Collected Works*, trans. R.F.C. Hull (Princeton, NJ: Princeton University Press, 1990), 299–301.

30. Carol S. Pearson, *The Hero Within: Six Archetypes We Live By* (San Francisco: HarperCollins, 1989), 74–75.

31. Jung, "The Phenomenology of the Spirit in Fairytales," in *The Archetypes and the Collective Unconscious*, 220.

32. Ibid., 221–24.

33. Hopcke, "Wise Old Man," in *A Guided Tour of Jung*, 117–18.

34. Carl G. Jung, "On the Psychology of the Trickster-Figure," in *The Archetypes and the Collective Unconscious*, 255; Jung, "The Spirit Mercurius," in *Aspects of the Masculine*, 158–59.

35. Jung, "The Phenomenology of the Spirit in Fairytales," in *The Archetypes and the Collective Unconscious*, 239–40.

36. Jung, "The Psychological Aspects of the Kore," in *The Archetypes and the Collective Unconscious*, 184–85.

37. Hopcke, "Kore/The Maiden," in *A Guided Tour of Jung*, 110.

38. Pearson, *Hero Within*, 81.

39. Jung, "A Study in the Process of Individuation," in *The Archetypes and the Collective Unconscious*, 354.

40. Ibid., 293; Hopcke, "Self," in *A Guided Tour of Jung*, 95.

41. Carl G. Jung, "UFOs as Rumours," in *Flying Saucers: A Modern Myth of Things Seen in the Skies*, trans. R.F.C. Hull (Princeton, NJ: Princeton University Press, 1991), 21.

42. Jung, "UFOs in Dreams," in *Flying Saucers*, 29.

43. Jung, "Epilogue," in *Flying Saucers*, 115–18.

Part One

A Jungian Analysis of Science-Fiction Films

1

The *Star Wars* Trilogy: The Space-Father Archetype

It seems logical to start our analysis with the *Star Wars* trilogy because its roots are based in the Saturday matinee serials of the 1930s and 1940s. Just like its predecessors, the *Star Wars* story is a simple and highly entertaining one: it revolves around the heroic adventures of Luke Skywalker (portrayed by Mark Hamill) and his rag-tag team of resistance fighters, who must battle the evil forces of the Empire before the entire universe is enslaved by their dark power. Luke is aided by the "whitest" of magicians, Obi-Wan Kenobi (actor Alec Guinness), and a very spunky Princess Leia (actress Carrie Fisher) but he finds his match in the formidable trickster, Darth Vader (muscleman David Prowse with voice supplied by James Earl Jones). By the end of the trilogy, goodness prevails and justice is finally restored throughout the galaxy.

While most critics have likened *Star Wars* to a futuristic fairy tale,[1] a deeper archetype supplies most of the backbone to this fantasy (as well as the audience's attraction to it). Luke is an orphan who encounters a number of fairly interesting Jungian father-figures during his exploits. It is these parental characters that help shape the personality of the young Skywalker, for better or worse, from adolescence to his adulthood. The focus of this chapter will be on such influential, extraterrestrial fathers (or space-fathers), starting with the 1977 classic film *Star Wars*.

STAR WARS: SPACE-FATHERS WHO ABANDON THEIR OFFSPRING

When Luke is first introduced, one can sense the strained type of relationship he is having with his Uncle Owen. Apparently, Luke wants to apply to the Space Academy and fulfill his dream of becoming a pilot, but Owen has repeatedly kept the boy from fulfilling this goal, using crop harvest time as the excuse to keep Luke on the farm. After two droids (R2–D2 and C-3P0) are purchased to help out in the dry fields of Tatooine, Skywalker sees this as the perfect opportunity to bring up the subject of his departure once more. He argues that the additional mechanical hands are quite capable of carrying out all the assorted responsibilities, without his relatives risking any financial loss. Owen, however, still holds the opinion that Luke's presence is needed for at least one more year and does not want to admit that the farm can function effectively without his nephew.

Luke's uncle resembles the father archetype in that he needs to keep things the way they are, with himself in charge. The individuality which Luke is showing cannot be tolerated because it threatens the entire structure Owen has imposed over his family.[2] In addition, Owen is afraid that Luke will follow in the adventuresome footsteps of his father (who, at this point in the trilogy, is presumed to be dead). By keeping Luke on Tatooine, the uncle hopes that the young boy will emulate him and take up farming as a permanent occupation. Owen's wife, Beru, wisely suggests that the career decision should be Luke's whatever the circumstances, indicating that it might be wrong to hold the young one back from pursuing his desires. Unlike Owen, Beru realizes the negative effects of such strong parental control on the boy, among them disappointment, a sense of powerlessness, and the fear of abandonment should she and her husband both die.[3] Yet the substitute father remains steadfast in his convictions, not really caring what psychological harm befalls his kin.

As in many other orphan stories, the world of Luke Skywalker is completely destroyed after the Imperial guard tracks the two droids to Owen's farm. The troopers level the place and incinerate Luke's relatives to make sure that any plans the robots might be carrying about the Empire's ultimate weapon, the Death Star, perish with the humans in the flames. Fortunately, Luke and the droids are not on the premises since they have been searching for a Ben Kenobi who might assist them in the delivery of the Death Star blueprints to the rebel forces. After Old Ben is located, Luke returns home and painfully experiences the first major turning point in his life. He is all alone; the only parents he ever knew are now dead; and a smoldering landscape (reminiscent of the old Western frontier massacres[4]) is all that is left to remind him of a more secure past gone forever. Clearly Owen did not prepare the adolescent for coping with the realities of suffering and death. Instead, he instilled in Luke a false vision of safety and love, without considering that the dog-eat-dog universe might intrude on his fictitious paradise with disastrous consequences. (So much for paternal insight!)

As Luke adjusts to his orphan state, he comes to rely more and more on Ben Kenobi for advice and guidance. It seems only natural that Luke should gravitate toward the elderly Jedi master since Ben and his father were such close friends. Tragically, it is revealed that a pupil of Kenobi's by the name of Darth Vader had murdered Luke's father. Trying to make sense of the death and giving it some meaning is uppermost on the orphan's mind. By providing Ben the opportunity to train him in the ways of the Force, Luke sees some rescue from a pretty hopeless situation. All it takes is the support and love of one person to move the orphan out of his immobilization.[5] Ben is that individual: he is there for Luke and wants the young one to learn the Force's good side so that the world can become a better place for all that reside in it. One might say that Obi-Wan assumes the role of the space-father for the needy Luke who was deprived of such a mentor figure throughout his formative years.

While Luke's lessons progress, psuedo-father and son seek out a space smuggler, Han Solo (played by Harrison Ford), and his furry alien copilot, Chewbacca the Wookie, who transport them safely aboard the Death Star. There the resistance fighters rescue Princess Leia, the only individual who knows the location of the rebel headquarters. Before they make good their escape, Old Ben confronts his nemesis, Vader, and engages the evil knight in a light-saber duel. Acknowledging Luke with a nod of the head, Obi-Wan unexpectedly prostrates himself before Vader who mercilessly incin-erates the elder's corporeal form. Powerless to intervene, Luke can only watch the proceedings as another parent is brutally removed from his slowly shrinking world of human contacts.

This second loss is even more excruciating than the first because, through Ben, Luke had learned to hope again and place his trust in someone who would protect him from the steadily growing evils of the universe. Now Luke has to stand on his own and subsist as best he can. Interestingly, costar Guinness convinced writer/director George Lucas to allow his char-acter to die in martyr-like fashion rather than survive the climactic fight sequence.[6] This modification in the *Star Wars* story actually made it pos-sible for Luke to choose the path of the hero. Old hermit Ben knew that as long as he was physically present, the boy would never develop on his own or embrace the ways of the Force. Ben's sacrifice was, therefore, a necessary one to help Luke find himself (and his destiny), without being beholden to someone while in the orphan mode.[7]

As soon as Luke and his team arrive at the rebels' lunar base, a strike force is prepared to penetrate the Death Star's defenses and ultimately de-stroy it with photon torpedoes directed at the highly vulnerable exhaust port. Our hero succeeds in obliterating the Empire's most deadly weapon only after he hears Ben's spiritual voice directing him to use the powers of the Force at just the right moment. This is a critical scene in the movie for it shows that Luke has finally integrated a father-image (in this case, Obi-Wan) into his incomplete personality. As Robert Hopcke and Carl Jung relate, wise old men are essential to the hero's accomplishments. They represent forces in the unconscious (comparable to the all-pervading Lucas energy) which guide and fortify the savior in the midst of deadly struggles. These ancient ones might even be regarded as a particular derivative of that most powerful Father of all human history, Yahweh.[8] For Luke to recognize Ben's presence and, most important, to act upon it suggests that he has found the inner "parental" strength to continue. No longer does Luke feel abandoned or alone: now he has his space-father to help him become a true Jedi knight.

The viewer is left with a feeling that things will be all right for our hero at the close of the first *Star Wars* movie. The mood, however, drastically changes with the second entry in the space saga, *The Empire Strikes Back* (1980). A darker side to the space-father figure is revealed, imbuing the plot with even more archetypal undertones than the first installment.

THE EMPIRE STRIKES BACK: SPACE-FATHERS WHO TRY TO RECLAIM THEIR LOST OFFSPRING

Although George Lucas was able to develop his characters further in this first *Star Wars* sequel,[9] especially Solo and Leia's budding relationship, the focus was still on Skywalker and his goal of eliminating the forces of the Empire forever. As Luke makes his journey from orphan to Jedi warrior, we find that his troubles have in no way been alleviated. He comes to realize some very important, universal truths on his soul-searching path: heroes are not always fearless nor are villains always completely evil. It is these shades of grey that Luke must confront, including the ambivalent poles of the space-father archetype.

The Empire Strikes Back opens with Luke facing a ravenous snow beast on the ice planet Hoth and vanquishing it with the psychokinetic powers of the Force into which he has tapped. He braves his way through the frigid storms to return to the rebel camp but soon succumbs to the inhospitable climate. It is then that his conscious mind registers a message from the ghostly presence of Obi-Wan who urges him to continue the Jedi training under the supervision of the ancient Yoda. After Luke is rescued by his space-faring companion Han Solo, he departs on his new quest—away from his friends and the war with the Empire.

Armed only with his father's light-saber, the young warrior enters the Dagobah System in search of the mysterious Yoda. What he discovers upon his crash landing is a cynical, gnomelike creature that claims to be the Jedi master. Luke cannot believe his eyes: how can anything so small possess such powers of greatness? Jung interprets the dimensions of "small" and "big" in an entirely different way when the collective unconscious is the reference point. The strongest (and most explosive) energies can originate from the microphysical world of the mind, and so one should not be deceived into thinking that physical size is directly correlated with psychic components. Even the old ones can be "little in length/ [yet] mighty in strength."[10] When Luke accepts Yoda for what he is without the attached cultural bias, then the lessons are ready to commence between the student and a new space-father mentor.

The days ahead are quite demanding for Luke. The tiny alien (played endearingly by Frank Oz) reiterates that only a clear and patient mind is capable of employing the Force for the good of all life forms. Yoda's training, thus, consists of a number of meditative exercises involving progressive relaxation and self-hypnosis. Actually, these mental disciplines are crucial if Luke is ever going to attain the highest level of warriorship possible. Carol Pearson (1991) suggests that the warrior's most important battles do not lie outside the self, but rather within—where the "inner dragons" rage their fiercest. It is only when these demons are faced with wisdom and a controlled state of mind that the warrior can venture forth and accomplish the intended goals.[11] In this respect, Luke has a good deal to comprehend about himself: he has to admit that he has a number of weaknesses and deal with them before impulsively waging war on the Empire. Otherwise, the dark side of the Force will consume him, as it did Lord Vader.

One of the most symbolic parts of *The Empire Strikes Back* is Luke's psychic battle with his shadowy counterpart, Darth Vader, in the deep forests of Dagobah. Though the young one comes out the victor in this mental contest, he is haunted by the face of Darth behind the ripped mask. It is his own visage gazing back at him! Consistent with the Pearson explication, the deadliest enemy of all is one's own shadow for it contains negative aspects one cannot readily admit into consciousness. The Jungian "fear of the shadow,"[12] especially what it can do to the person's psyche if not properly handled, is the lesson to be learned here. The evil double of Skywalker is also representative of Luke's own biological father who was swayed at an early age by the wicked energies of greed and power. In fact, this scene provides the first clue that Darth is Luke's real space-father, a connection that our hero dare not make at this juncture if he wants to hold onto his sanity (as well as his apparent invulnerability to the Force's dark side).[13]

The pupil eventually abandons his mental exercises when he foresees the torture of his friends at the hands of Vader. Yoda and Ben's spirit advise him that it is more critical to complete the training and, hence, be prepared for any traps that the Empire might spring on him. But Luke gives in to his feelings and rather recklessly zooms out of the Dagobah System to confront the hated nemesis. While Luke's refusal to give up on those who need him is a mark of the true warrior,[14] he has not sufficiently advanced in his training to meet the enemy on *his* terms. Lack of a battle plan, combined with only rudimentary knowledge of the Force, will presumably decrease his chances of winning and might even imperil the entire galaxy. For any warrior, the cost of a battle can be very great, especially when someone else dictates the conditions of the fighting.[15] In Luke's case, the danger lies with his impetuous nature which might lead him forever down the dark path (as in his father's case). The old adage, "Like father, like son," seems to be particularly relevant at this point in the plot.

Not surprisingly, upon his arrival in the City Within the Clouds, Luke is too late to save Han from being carbon frozen and taken to Jabba the Hutt. Before he is able to catch his breath, the novice warrior is engaged in a deadly, light-saber combat with the more experienced Lord Vader and is soon cornered on a metal precipice. His right hand is not the only thing Luke loses when Darth proudly acknowledges that he is the real father of the boy. Luke finally has to deal with this half-suspected truth and it tears him apart inside. To have a father so evil and powerful, someone who mercilessly controls the destiny of others in his hands, is the archetypal dilemma with which many offspring are faced,[16] including Luke.

Vader at long last reveals his plans to the downed son: he wants to complete the boy's training and then, with Luke by his side, smash the forces of the Emperor and restore order throughout the universe under the new reign of the Skywalkers.[17] One clearly sees the negative characteristics of the warrior (and father) in Darth's statements. The Dark Knight is not really interested in developing a healthy relationship with his son; rather, he wants to reclaim the offspring so that more of the Force's evil side can be used against others. Vader is interested only in himself and his own personal aggrandizement. According to this egocentric view (as posited by so many shadow warriors), people are meant to be dominated so that the controller can ultimately grow in strength.[18] There is nothing noble in having Luke become part of Darth's administration since he will be treated in much the same way as the rest of the followers of the New Order. The injustices of the world will (sadly) continue to be maintained with such power-hungry, dictatorial space-fathers in charge.

Luke realizes he does not want to be included in his father's great scheme, and he takes his chances by plunging to his doom. Although this action is suicidal, it is much better than being victimized (perhaps even slain) by the evil Vader. But the psychic connection with the father cannot be broken, even after Luke is rescued by Leia and Chewbacca in their run-down vehicle, the *Millennium Falcon*, and returned to a safe spaceport. After he is healed and given a bionic replacement for his hand, the son senses the presence of the father and calls out to him by name. The contact is made with Vader, who recognizes that the offspring's destiny lies with him. For some strange reason, Luke does not want to abandon his father now that he has found him.

Perhaps the Jungian view can help explain the powerful, mental link that exists between the Skywalkers. The archetypal father can exert a strong, demonic hold on the children, even to the point of "possessing" them (in body and soul) for the rest of their existence on this planet.[19] No matter how sinful Lord Vader is, he is still part of Luke's flesh and blood and will remain so throughout eternity. The fact that the young warrior has a mechanical part attached to his body only strengthens the bond with the elder, who is more machine than human already.[20] *The Empire Strikes Back* leaves the audience with a good deal to comprehend, not the least of which is the establishment of this mysterious father-son connection. Will it be Luke's fate to follow in the tragic footsteps of his space-father, like other orphans who misguidedly put their trust in a pseudo-rescuer?[21] The answer can be found in the final chapter of the *Star Wars* trilogy, *Return of the Jedi* (1983).

RETURN OF THE JEDI: SPACE-FATHERS WHO ARE REUNITED WITH THEIR OFFSPRING

When Luke makes his entrance in *Return of the Jedi*, we notice that his character has changed immensely. No longer is he the lost orphan of *Star Wars* or the apprentice warrior of *The Empire Strikes Back*. Skywalker's bearing and attitude suggest that he has developed into a mature Jedi knight.[22] The priestly garments that he wears as well as the mind-controlling tricks he has mastered are indicative of his newly acquired vocation. Apparently, some time has elapsed between the second film and this one, explaining Luke's "miraculous" transformation into a younger version of his space mentor, Obi-Wan. (The pupil has indeed become the teacher!) Solo's cynical remarks that Luke is suffering from delusions of grandeur after he is freed from his carbonite tomb reflect a narrow sightedness on his part.[23] The temporary blindness Han experiences is representative of this tunnel vision; he still wants to be in charge of the situation and does not like to admit that he is dependent on others, least of all the resistance's junior member who has since grown into a capable leader.

The escape plan which Luke has carefully engineered in freeing Han from the repulsive Jabba the Hutt is in direct contrast to his earlier futile attempts. He has thought out every possibility of capture and is disciplined enough to control his emotions in the face of impossible odds. What the Jedi accomplishes is truly impressive: he is able to do somersaults around Jabba's troops and disable the enemy land cruiser with his handy lightsaber in short order. One might think the title, *Return of the Jedi*, sounds a bit strange; however, it simply reflects the ascendancy of the knighthood once more under the direction of the experienced Skywalker who can dis-

patch massive hordes of darkness like Jabba's rather effortlessly. Another
interpretation is that the skill and wit which Luke effectively exercises as a
Jedi can make it possible for communities to defend themselves against the
predatory primitives of the planet and eventually return to a simpler and
less oppressive way of life.[24]

But, not all the Jedi warrior's tasks are so easy to achieve, as Luke discovers upon his return to the Dagobah System. First, he learns from the
ailing Yoda that Darth Vader is indeed Anakin Skywalker, his real space-
father. Interestingly, Luke accepts this truth without resistance since it
merely confirms the gut-level feelings he had all along about the enigmatic
parent. Second, the Jedi experiences another death of a mentor, Yoda, leaving him (for the moment) isolated on the barren planet. Probably the most
significant event is that the ghostly form of Ben appears and relates the
half-truth he had told Luke originally: Vader did indeed "murder" his father when he turned to the Force's dark side. Ben's white lie clearly irritated
some, for example, Richard Meyers (1990) who pictured Kenobi's powers
as being totally pure and without deceit.[25] For this interpreter, the archetypal wise old man can use deception whenever necessary in order to sway
the hero to take a particular course of action. In many respects, there exists
an intimate connection between the old one and the mischievous trickster
of mythology.[26] That Ben lied was in keeping with the ambivalent nature
of all primordial images.

What really is perplexing about the plot of the *Return of the Jedi* is that
Ben wants Luke to kill his father so that the power of Jedi goodness can
be actualized. In other words, Luke has to stain his hands with the blood
of the parent in order to be a worthy successor to the knighthood. Obviously, our hero sees other options because he is not entirely convinced that
Vader should be destroyed. The psychic bonding with Darth in *The Empire
Strikes Back* might have allowed Luke to sense that there was something
still worth saving in the Dark One. After all, he cannot deny that a part
of the father's nature lives in him.[27] Therefore, Luke's opposition to the
position advocated by Ben should not be seen as a weakness; instead, it is
a strength which allows the Jungian hero to evolve to an even higher plane
of existence where good and evil coexist in everything and cannot be separated as easily as Obi-Wan suggests.

So that he does not have to deal immediately with the problem of Lord
Vader, Luke tries to involve himself in the mission to destroy the new Death
Star's shield generator located on Endor. He soon realizes, however, that
there is no escaping the impending confrontation with the space-father. In
fact, his mere presence (which radiates an enormous amount of the Force)
might actually jeopardize the resistance group's efforts. Before leaving Endor to rendezvous with Vader, he tells Leia the secret he recently learned
from Ben: she is his sister and, like any Skywalker, possesses the power of
the Force in abundance.

The Lucas script is excellent in making this association between the hero and princess, for it establishes the archetypal groundwork laid out by Jung decades ago. Leia can be likened to the "inner woman" in the hero (i.e., his anima), which can take the form of a daughter, sister, or beloved.[28] As Luke's feminine soul mate, she offers him the much-needed comfort and solace he requires before embarking on his journey. The bringing together of the royal pair, brother and sister, is a union of conscious and unconscious elements, heroic bravery with incredible sensitivity, respectively.[29] With his sister's encouragement and support, Luke surrenders to his father in the hopes that he can turn the parent back to the light of goodness. One might say that Leia works behind the scenes in *Return of the Jedi*, in a manner similar to the hidden female that drives all men on to achieve the greatness for which they were destined.

Luke does not give up trying to convert Vader back to his former self, even after he is escorted to the Emperor's chambers and watches the trap the enemy has sprung on his compatriots. It is too late to save the Emperor (played by Ian McDiarmid); there is just too much evil and hatred residing within the wrinkled, corpselike shell. Darth, on the other hand, does not proudly reveal his distorted features to anyone but himself. Maybe the father's perception that the dark side has brought about this deleterious change makes him a more rescuable villain. After all, antagonists might be victims too who need to be saved from further destruction,[30] especially if they are being manipulated by greater powers than their own (e.g., the Emperor). Thus, Luke undertakes the most heroic assignment of them all: to *transform* his sinning space-father into a person of nobility and grace.

By not giving in to his negative emotions, Luke is able to ward off the Emperor's spells and concentrate his resources on the parent. The warrior does not slay the space-father when attacked; instead, he cuts off the elder's hand and stops himself from inflicting more serious wounds. Coincidentally, Vader's injury is the same as Luke's which had happened in an earlier light-saber battle (see *The Empire Strikes Back*), reinforcing the link that still exists between father and son. After he spares Darth, Luke pledges that he will never be used as a pawn by the Emperor again. Like his father before him, he is a Jedi dedicated to upholding the truth and the light in the galaxy. These are powerful statements expressed by Luke, for they affirm a strong belief in the parent and what he represents. Simply put, even if the father does wrong, failing to recognize his children as key individuals, he is still protected by the offspring since there is nothing more important than the sanctity of the familial relationship.[31]

The final moments of the *Return of the Jedi* elevate the entire *Star Wars* trilogy to a great, archetypal work of art. Darth performs the bravest (and mightiest) action of his entire life. He rescues his son from being obliterated completely by throwing the enraged Emperor into a nuclear generator shaft, thereby sealing the latter's fate. However, the already weakened

Vader has taken the brunt of the death rays meant for Luke. The space-father's last request before he dies is to see his offspring without the mask. Luke obeys and is greeted by the kindest of faces (portrayed by Sebastian Shaw) which emits nothing but unconditional love and affection for the boy. Apparently, all the hate and evil left Vader's form when he accomplished his self-sacrificing deed, leaving in its place the man Anakin once was.[32]

Pearson notes that villains can be redefined as potential heroes if opportunities present themselves to create the new characters.[33] Luke gave his space-father that chance by believing in him, and his trust did not go unrewarded. As with any Jungian archetype, the father image has the capacity for good or evil, sacredness or sinfulness.[34] *Return of the Jedi* capitalized on Anakin's two-sided nature, with the result that the light overcame the darkness. The Skywalkers are finally reunited, and the elder can now expire having established the bond that proved to be so elusive in the past.

Everything else falls into place by the end of the movie: the energy shield protecting the second Death Star is blown up, and the mandala-like threat is removed from the universe by the Alliance forces. Amidst the celebration on Endor, Luke and Leia experience a comforting vision: Anakin, Ben, and Yoda are together again in the Force's spiritual dimension.[35] The three symbolize the archetypal trinity, the god-fathers who continue to oversee (as well as guide) the development of their race throughout eternity.

Three, a very mystical number, is associated with masculinity and the phases of thesis, antithesis, and synthesis.[36] In reference to *Star Wars*, the purity of the Force is the original stage, or thesis. Vader's breaking away from that purity and trying to overthrow it is the antithesis. The final step involves Vader's return to the fold, thereby resolving the conflict and creating a synthesis of the dark with the good. Jung would postulate that the fatherly triad can be complete only when the devil is rejoined with the godhead.[37] Anakin's acceptance by the other Jedi masters, regardless of his past crimes, makes it possible for the Force to be structurally whole once more. All seems definitely right with the universe and the space-father trinity by the time the credits roll in this last chapter of the Lucas trilogy.

With the recent theatrical release of the newly formatted *Star Wars: Special Edition* package, one can enjoy the tale from beginning to end once more on the big screen. Most important, the space-father archetype should not go unnoticed this time around; if anything, its presence should resonate throughout the hero's story thanks to the power of the "Jungian Force."

NOTES

1. Vincent Camby, "Review of *Star Wars*—A Trip to a Galaxy That's Fun and Funny," *New York Times*, 26 May 1977, Section C18: 1; Richard Meyers, *The*

Great Science Fiction Films (New York: Carol Publishing Group, 1990), 66; Maurice Phipps, "The Myth and Magic of *Star Wars*: A Jungian Interpretation," *Educational Resources Information Center*. 1983: 1–4 (ERIC Document Reproduction Service No. ED315–833).

2. Stuart M. Kaminsky and Jeffrey H. Mahan, *American Television Genres* (Chicago: Nelson-Hall, 1988), 121–22.

3. George Lucas, *Star Wars The Special Edition: A New Hope* (New York: Ballantine Books, 1997), 55–57; Carol S. Pearson, *The Hero Within: Six Archetypes We Live By* (San Francisco: HarperCollins, 1989), 27–29.

4. Lane Roth, "Vraisemblance and the Western Setting in Contemporary Science Fiction Film," *Educational Resources Information Center*. 1990: 4 (ERIC Document Reproduction Service No. ED312-708).

5. Carol S. Pearson, *Awakening the Heroes Within: Twelve Archetypes to Help Us Find Ourselves and Transform Our World* (San Francisco: HarperCollins, 1991), 89.

6. Meyers, *Great Science Fiction Films*, 79.

7. Lucas, *Star Wars: A New Hope*, 168–70; Pearson, *Hero Within*, 35–36.

8. Robert H. Hopcke, "Wise Old Man," in *A Guided Tour of the Collected Works of C. G. Jung* (Boston: Shambhala, 1992), 117–18; Carl G. Jung, "The Phenomenology of the Spirit in Fairytales," in *The Archetypes and the Collective Unconscious: The Collected Works*, trans. R.F.C. Hull (Princeton, NJ: Princeton University Press, 1990), 220–22.

9. Douglas Brode, *The Films of the Eighties* (New York: Carol Publishing Group, 1991), 37.

10. Jung, "The Phenomenology of the Spirit in Fairytales," in *The Archetypes and the Collective Unconscious*, 224.

11. Pearson, *Awakening the Heroes Within*, 103–4.

12. Robert Asahina, "Review of *The Empire Strikes Back*," *New Leader* 63 (2 June 1980): 20; Kath Filmer, *Scepticism and Hope in Twentieth Century Fantasy Literature* (Bowling Green, OH: Bowling Green State University Popular Press, 1992), 51; Carl G. Jung, "The Self," in *Aion: Researches into the Phenomenology of the Self: The Collected Works*, trans. R.F.C. Hull (Princeton, NJ: Princeton University Press, 1990), 33.

13. Donald F. Glut, *Star Wars: The Empire Strikes Back* (New York: Ballantine Books, 1997), 143–44.

14. Chogyam Trungpa, *The Sacred Path of the Warrior* (Boston: Shambhala, 1978), 33.

15. Pearson, *Awakening the Heroes Within*, 102–3.

16. Carl G. Jung, "The Significance of the Father in the Destiny of the Individual," in *Freud and Psychoanalysis: The Collected Works*, trans. R.F.C. Hull (Princeton, NJ: Princeton University Press, 1989), 314–15.

17. Glut, *Star Wars: The Empire Strikes Back*, 198.

18. Pearson, *Awakening the Heroes Within*, 96–97.

19. Jung, "The Significance of the Father in the Destiny of the Individual," in *Freud and Psychoanalysis*, 316–17.

20. Glut, *Star Wars: The Empire Strikes Back*, 45, 212–13.

21. Charles Champlin, "Review of *The Empire Strikes Back*," *Los Angeles Times*, 18 May 1980; Calendar, 1; Pearson, *Hero Within*, 35.

22. Gregory Solman, "Review of *Return of the Jedi*," *Films in Review* 34 (June–July 1983): 369.

23. James Kahn, *Star Wars: Return of the Jedi* (New York: Ballantine Books, 1997), 26–27.

24. Riane Eisler, *The Chalice and the Blade: Our History, Our Future* (San Francisco: Harper & Row, 1987), 186–87.

25. Meyers, *Great Science Fiction Films*, 255.

26. Hopcke, "Wise Old Man," in *A Guided Tour of Jung*, 119.

27. Carl G. Jung, "The Dual Mother," in *Symbols of Transformation: The Collected Works*, trans. R.F.C. Hull (Princeton, NJ: Princeton University Press, 1990), 333; Kahn, *Star Wars: Return of the Jedi*, 63–65.

28. Carl G. Jung, "The Syzygy: Anima and Animus," in *Aion*, 12–13; Phipps, "The Myth and Magic of *Star Wars*," 6.

29. Jung, "The Battle for Deliverance from the Mother," in *Symbols of Transformation*, 300–301.

30. Philip Strick, "Review of *Return of the Jedi*," *Monthly Film Bulletin* (July 1983): 181; Pearson, *Hero Within*, 77–78, 83.

31. Kaminsky and Mahan, *American Television Genres*, 122.

32. Robert Asahina, "Review of *Return of the Jedi*," *New Leader* 66 (30 May 1983): 19; Kahn, *Star Wars: Return of the Jedi*, 173–74.

33. Pearson, *Hero Within*, 85, 93.

34. Filmer, *Scepticism and Hope*, 51; Jung, "The Significance of the Father in the Destiny of the Individual," in *Freud and Psychoanalysis*, 323.

35. Kahn, *Star Wars: Return of the Jedi*, 181; Sloman, "Review of *Return of the Jedi*," 369.

36. Edward F. Edinger, "The Trinity Archetype and the Dialectic of Development," in *Ego and Archetype: Individuation and the Religious Function of the Psyche* (London: Penguin Books, 1972), 184–85.

37. Carl G. Jung, "Psychology and Religion. Dogma and Natural Symbols," in *The Basic Writings of C. G. Jung*, trans. R.F.C. Hull (Princeton, NJ: Princeton University Press, 1990), 541.

2

The *Star Trek* Movies: In Search of the Creator Archetype

When the original *Star Trek* series aired on NBC television, it barely captured the attention of most viewers during its three-year run from 1966 to 1969. Only after *Star Trek* was syndicated to international markets did it gain a respectable following.[1] The message the series transmitted, to seek out new races and civilizations under the banner of peace, proved to be a comforting one to a world engaged in continual warfare and strife. The success of the first *Star Wars* movie prompted *Star Trek*'s producer and creator, Gene Roddenberry, to continue the adventures of the *U.S.S. Enterprise* on the big screen beginning in 1979. The public's craving for more "treks" into the unknown seems to be insatiable, as evidenced by the number of movies and television spin-offs spawned by the series over the past two decades. *Star Trek* has indeed become a popular culture phenomenon of the 1990s as well as "a permanent part of our consciousness."[2]

A theme recurrent in almost all of the *Star Trek* films is that of the creator archetype. Though not necessarily referring to God per se, it shares many aspects of the divine entity, not the least of which is the ability to project its own life-giving essence onto those organisms not yet psychologically complete. An examination of all the various symbols for the Jungian creator will commence with the first movie in this science-fiction package, appropriately entitled *Star Trek—The Motion Picture* (1979).

STAR TREK—THE MOTION PICTURE: VEJUR'S SEARCH FOR THE MAKER

After several scripts were rejected for the first *Star Trek* picture, including Roddenberry's one about the starship *Enterprise* meeting God, Paramount Productions decided to go with a less controversial story involving an alien space cloud destroying everything in its path as it approaches our solar system.[3] Naturally, Admiral Kirk (played by series' star William Shatner) and his loyal team of followers have to stop the extraterrestrial threat. The premise for *The Motion Picture* was actually based on several *Star Trek* teleplays, including "The Doomsday Machine," "The Changeling," and "The Immunity Syndrome." While the idea was hardly an original one, Roddenberry was still able to insert his views on the relationship between humanity and its creator by focusing on the *Enterprise*'s contact with the powerful being throughout most of the movie. The result was a fairly interesting space adventure, tinged with elements of the mystical and supernatural.

En route to their destination, the *Enterprise* crew pick up the Vulcan science officer, Mr. Spock (series' veteran Leonard Nimoy), who demonstrates great curiosity about the alien intelligence. So strong is the link between Spock's mind and the space cloud that he fails to complete the ritual of *Kolinahr* (i.e., the total purging of all emotions) on his home planet, choosing instead to learn more about the mysterious object. Spock hopes that by communicating with the intruder, he will not have to abandon the feeling part of his nature, but rather integrate it more effectively with the Vulcan side.[4] The cloud offers Spock the opportunity to achieve psychic totality and wholeness, and as such can be likened to a mandelic "god image" that can fill the Vulcan's soul with more life than he has previously experienced.[5]

Not surprisingly, it is Spock who is able to decipher the alien code and divert the object from obliterating the *Enterprise*. Once the humans gain access to the cloud's inner chambers, a probe comes aboard the ship and matter transports Lieutenant Ilia (actress Persis Khambatta) to its domain where her body is reduced to data patterns out of which a perfect, mechanical replica of the Deltan woman is formed. The duplicate Ilia is then beamed aboard the *Enterprise* for the expressed purpose of making its intentions known to the crew. It should be noted that Spock would have been the logical one to undergo the assimilation process with the cloud had not Ilia intervened at a crucial moment.

Ilia's copy relates to Kirk, Spock, and Dr. McCoy (DeForest Kelley) that the entity known as Vejur is looking for its creator and will not hesitate to remove any carbon-based units (i.e., humans) in its search for the Maker. After some fairly extensive galactic traveling, Vejur has at last located its place of origin, the Earth, and is awaiting the joining with the creator on the third planet of Sol. Ilia discloses that the merging with the superior mind will allow Vejur to evolve to an even higher state of consciousness. Meanwhile, the female replica experiences strange feelings of love and affection which her prototype has obviously shared with William Decker (Stephen Collins), and this alone prevents the *Enterprise* from being absorbed into the Vejur being.

Spock confirms most of Ilia's story when he executes a space walk that eventually leads him to the center of the alien cloud. There the Vulcan begins what he desired all along, to mind meld with Vejur. But the energies radiating from the creature prove to be too much for Spock's frail body to contain. He passes out from the ordeal and is then sent back to the *Enterprise* to report his findings to Admiral Kirk. Although mentally exhausted, the science officer is able to describe what Vejur really is: a living machine with knowledge spanning the entire universe. It is "everything that Spock had ever dreamed of becoming . . . [its essence] so completely and magnificently logical."[6]

Yet, Vejur is lacking one fundamental component: the ability to feel. For all its accumulated wisdom, the machine remains barren since it cannot express simple needs or desires. The alien technology that provided Vejur with its advanced circuitry and self-repairing programs could not give it that life-sustaining element. Therefore, the entity reasons that by making physical contact with the creator, it can obtain the missing ingredient and complete itself. Ironically, Spock wanted to perfect himself through a mechanism that was itself imperfect. One might say that the Vulcan's goal was a very human one which was bound to fail. The mind meld, however, has shown Mr. Spock something of value: emotions should not be discarded or treated as irrelevant, for logic alone is not enough for meaningful existence.[7]

While incomplete, Vejur should still be regarded as an archetypal god image. Many representations of a powerful deity are deficient in something. For example, the Christ symbol is wanting because the dark side is separated from its nature and personified in the form of Lucifer.[8] Religious conceptions have portrayed evil (and its associated passions) as the lack of perfection, but it must be remembered that even the devil was at one point in time part of the perfect godhead.[9] Interestingly, Vejur needs those very passions to grow. Cut off from human emotions and desires, Vejur is like a terrible child, awesome in might but not yet fully developed. Perhaps all god images have elements of the child in them, so long as they possess an incomplete nature.

By the end of *The Motion Picture*, Kirk has bluffed Vejur into thinking that he knows something about the creator. The alien moves the starship into its very core in order to download the desired information. What greets the *Enterprise* crew is a startling sight. Vejur is actually one of the humankind's own constructions, the lost *Voyager 6* space probe. The machine race that modified its original programming was able to read only some of the letters on the hull surface ("VGER"), hence the designation Vejur. Since the desired contact now has to be made with one of the human creators, Decker volunteers to sacrifice himself so that Vejur may complete its primary objective. He embraces the Ilia replica, and together the feelings which both share are fed into the hungry circuitry. The merging of human being with machine produces the birth of a new, more transcendent life-form which the star-fleet team witnesses aboard the *Enterprise*.

The final scene is reminiscent of many of the *Star Trek* episodes in which the moral of the story is pointed out to the major characters and audience alike. Dr. McCoy hopes that the new "baby" which they have delivered has a healthy development, to which Kirk confidently replies it should, given its recently acquired human qualities. Spock adds that perhaps humanity will follow a similar course of evolution in the not too distant future. Roddenberry's novelization of the screenplay best sums up the sentiments expressed by these officers in the following statement: "The transcendence [of Vejur] became too lovely for them to comprehend, and so it was gone without ever really leaving."[10] The creator image remains a part of the human soul, and one need only look within to discover the beauty of becoming something better and more complete. The direction which the *Enterprise* takes as it heads out of Vejur's orbit is irrelevant, so long as the human occupants remind themselves that they are the ones carrying the "seeds of life" to other planets.

STAR TREK II: THE WRATH OF KHAN: THE GENESIS STORY REVISITED

As did *The Motion Picture*, *Star Trek II: The Wrath of Khan* (1982) relied on the television series for its story line. An archenemy from the episode "Space Seed" was brought back to plague the *Enterprise*, particularly Admiral James T. Kirk. Actor Ricardo Montalban reprised the role of Khan Singh, a genetically engineered mutant of the late twentieth century who was endowed with super intelligence, along with a propensity toward madness. When last seen in the *Star Trek* show, Khan and his group of fanatical disciples were exiled on the planet of Ceti Alpha Six to eke out an existence rather than spend their remaining days in confinement. *The Wrath of Khan* takes place fifteen years later, when the starship *Reliant* discovers their presence on the supposedly barren world. It would seem that the Federation of United Planets did not keep very accurate records on Khan's whereabouts (a sin most bureaucracies unfortunately share). While "Trekkies" were delighted to see the return of the larger-than-life villain, this author remains fascinated by the Vejur presence shown in the first film. An entity that does evil because it is ignorant of the sanctity of human life is a much more ambivalent enemy than one that commits atrocities out of sheer egotism, like Khan Singh.[11] The majority of viewers, however, preferred the archetypal struggle between the heroic Kirk and the malevolent Khan in *Wrath* instead of *The Motion Picture*'s more "cerebral" confrontation.[12]

What makes *Wrath* a truly great film is the inclusion of the Genesis device, which is another intriguing depiction of the creator archetype. Literally, the cylindrical instrument developed by Dr. Carol Marcus (played by Bibi Besch) and her son, David (the late Merritt Butrick), has the capacity to generate "life from lifelessness." Science-fiction writer Vonda McIntyre provides much more detail on the theoretical principle behind Project Genesis than the film contains, and so her explanation now follows. The procedure first involves the molecular structure of matter being broken down into subelementary particle waves.

> By manipulation of various nuclear forces, the sub-elementaries can then be restructured into anything else of similar mass. Precisely *what* they reform into depends upon the available mass. If sufficient matter is present, the programming permits an entire star system to be formed . . . capable of sustaining most known forms of carbon-based life.[13]

This is precisely what the alchemists wanted to achieve in their chemical experiments involving the transformation of base metals (lead) into more precious, life-radiating substances (gold). Both the alchemical opus and Genesis are designed to release the "spirit" from existing matter in order to bring a newer, more beautiful life into the universe—one that approaches ultimate perfection.[14]

As Kirk, Spock, and McCoy are briefed on Project Genesis, they are awestruck by the computer simulation showing how a living planet (complete with water, atmosphere, and a functioning ecosystem) can be miraculously formed out of barren rock. McCoy is astute enough to realize what the consequences would be if the device were aimed at an area where life already existed. In his matter-of-fact tone, Spock verifies McCoy's suspicions by indicating that Genesis would destroy such life in order to fulfill its original programming, the reshaping of matter into the new "creation matrix." Universal Armageddon would be one deleterious side effect if Genesis were ever placed in the wrong hands.[15] Possession of the mechanism would enable madmen like Khan to hold countless worlds hostage or construct new ones according to their own demented designs.

The *Enterprise* swiftly proceeds to the Regula One space station where Carol and David Marcus reside and encounters the missing *Reliant*, now under the command of Khan. Both ships are crippled in the ensuing battle, and during the respite, Kirk is able to locate Carol and David on the nearby planet of Regula. After beaming down a party to their precise position,

Kirk discovers that the very core of Regula has been converted to a wonderful paradise by the Genesis instrument.[16] Carol indicates that it took precisely one day to create the beauty before them, five days less than it took the Maker to create the earth.

Not only has the alchemical Dr. Marcus accomplished this godlike feat; she has also brought a human life into the world, Kirk's own offspring, David. The news surprises Kirk since it never occurred to him in all the years he served in Starfleet Academy that David might be his own flesh and blood. Of course, he never bothered to check with Carol because his attention was always directed toward encountering alien life forms. Curiously, the most fascinating life that Kirk could ever meet in all of his travels was that part of himself he had helped conceive. Responsibility for creating that life is something that Kirk must now bear, and it is a heavy load that he has to carry, maybe for the rest of his existence. Carol Pearson (1991) mentions that the most primitive stage in creation is when we unconsciously or unknowingly generate life. The more advanced level, which we should attain, is "to take control of our lives . . . and begin to feel real pride in our creative efforts."[17] Given all of his command experience, Admiral Kirk has yet to reach this point in his development.

Khan manages to steal the Genesis device out from under the very noses of the Federation officers, shaking Kirk out of his reveries. A contest of wills between the two commanders ends with the madman losing most of his crew and having his starship blasted apart. Before he dies, however, Khan activates Genesis so that the *Enterprise* will suffer the same fate he does. Spock performs the only logical action he can to save his shipmates from being eradicated by Genesis's energy matrix. He manually repairs some of the engine damage inflicted by Khan, making it possible for the *Enterprise* to warp speed out of danger. Spock's heroism has a deadly price: the Vulcan has exposed himself to lethal radiation and dies tragically within the sealed engine compartment with no living soul to comfort him in his final moments.[18]

The sacrifice made by Spock has archetypal significance for he has given Kirk and his team a reprieve from death. Like Genesis, the Vulcan has bestowed an extended life frame to those marked for termination by the ruthless Khan. It is not by accident that Spock's coffin is torpedoed out of the *Enterprise* vessel and sent to the new planet magically formed from the Genesis matrix. Spock is an integral part of the creation process; in fact, he becomes part of the "silvery-blue shimmer of the new world"[19] as his coffin melds with the steadily growing atmosphere around the mandelic planet.

And what about Kirk and his parental responsibilities? From Spock's death, the admiral has discovered the new life of parenthood and proudly accepts David as his son with no reservations. Kirk feels young, even reborn, because he now realizes that his existence goes beyond the limited confines of his Starfleet career. He can create and develop new skills without feeling "dried up and worn out" on the inside. Pearson's stage of creative liberation in which one's dreams are actualized characterizes the level that Kirk has finally reached.[20] His universe has expanded considerably by seeing Carol's brave, new world. To paraphrase Spock, the possibilities for developing one's inner potential are, indeed, endless.

STAR TREK III: THE SEARCH FOR SPOCK: REUNION WITH THE KATRA

Star Trek III: The Search for Spock (1984) is a continuation of the Genesis story, but with a new twist inserted into the plot. Spock's dead body has been given new life by the Genesis matrix. However, the physical shell is incomplete without the soul to sustain it. The Vulcan name for this essence, the *katra*, had been transferred to Dr. McCoy by Spock before the latter met his untimely fate in the *Enterprise*'s engine chamber. According to Spock's father, Sarek (played by Mark Lenard), the misplaced *katra* must be rejoined with his son's body so that harmony is restored to both Spock and the "schizophrenic" McCoy. Kirk is given the formidable task of traveling back to the Genesis planet in the decommissioned *Enterprise* to find Spock and then taking him to his home world where the soul and body can be united once again in the Vulcan refusion ritual, called *fal tor pan*.

By not being able to impart a divine spirit to Spock's resurrected body, the Genesis device possesses an obvious limitation. It cannot create something from nothing. Maybe the screenplay writer, Harve Bennett, intended to show his audience that any humankind invention (because it was humankind) had a definite restriction in its creative capacity. The study of alchemy also requires an essential prerequisite in order to be successful: a "base" substance which has a godlike life force already embedded within it. Only when that residing force is liberated from the *prima materia* can the transformation to perfection be achieved.[21] Since Spock has been denied the possibility of a unified existence, he remains a divided person throughout most of *Star Trek III*, with his corporeal half lingering on the Genesis planet and the remaining part fused with Dr. McCoy's collective unconscious.

One might address a relevant inquiry at this point of the treatment. Why did Spock ever mind meld with McCoy if he knew his *katra* would be separated from the body? A referral to Vulcan tradition seems to be in order here. (My thanks once again goes to *Star Trek* novelist Vonda McIntyre, who provides the necessary historical base in her adaptation of *The Search for Spock* screenplay). At the point of death, Vulcans wish to preserve their spirits in the Great Hall of Ancient Thought on the home planet. By making psychic contact with members of their own species, they can draw out the individual *katras* and channel them into designated vessels

where the mental powers of each will live on for all eternity.[22] Because
Spock did not have adequate time to prepare himself properly, he was
forced to choose a human host for the transfer of his soul, hoping that
Kirk would finish what he had started back on Vulcan. Naive about such
alien rites, the admiral instead gave Spock a hero's burial in space, little
realizing just what the effects of the Genesis matrix would have on his
friend's dead body.

Ignorance appears to be a sin shared by many of the characters in this
film, and it is ignorance that is responsible for so much of the chaos that
tragically unfolds. Kirk's son, David Marcus (reprised by Merritt Butrick),
is guilty of a most heinous crime. In his haste to make the Genesis device
operational, he used a highly unstable substance, protomatter, and failed
to inform his scientific team of this drastic modification. One of the Federation crew, Lieutenant Saavik (Robin Curtis), is surprised that David
would resort to such an unethical means. The scientist, however, attempts
to rationalize his action by stating that any instrument has the potential to
be destructive, but the risk must be taken if science is to progress.[23]

Clearly, David's mental attitude is not compatible with the alchemical
work in which he is engaged; only a pure mind can create a product that
transcends the body.[24] Genesis is really Armageddon: death—not life. The
incorporation of protomatter speeds up the growth cycle of matter to the
point where the physical universe cannot contain the unnatural explosion
of life. Therefore, the Genesis planet becomes a living hell where every
adverse climactic condition rages its fury at a birth that should have been
aborted in the laboratory.[25] The body of Spock, moreover, begins to age
before the eyes of Saavik and David who are investigating the strange effects. The danger to the Vulcan is very real: if Spock remains on the Genesis
world, his life force might wither just like the environment decaying all
around him.

Star Trek III is not without its villains. A Klingon commander by the
name of Kruge (played by actor Christopher Lloyd) illegally acquires information about the Genesis process and believes he can control the reaction by holding David and the others hostage. Although Kruge's thinking
is primitive at best, he resembles David in that he lets his passions (not
reason) dictate his behavior. This impulsivity leads to the death of Kirk's
son, the destruction of the Enterprise, and Kruge's own life. If anything of
value can come from these losses, it is that Kirk is able to recover Spock's
body before the entire planet breaks apart.

The ending of Star Trek III borders on the mystical as Spock's corporeal
form is brought to the top of Mount Seleya where the Vulcan high priestess
(Dame Judith Anderson) attempts to make Spock whole once more. In
sharp contrast to the Genesis process, the "refusion" ritual is successful.
This is primarily due to the inclusion of a divine presence within the Vulcan
alchemy. Praying to a god for help and guidance will make it possible for

humans and any other alien race to master the secrets of the unknown, especially those involving creation.[26] Conversely, technology will always fail to understand what life is all about if the supernatural agent that is responsible for that life source is not invoked.

A more innocent Spock is reborn, devoid of (and untainted by) memories of his previous existence. The *Enterprise* crew is given the difficult task of reeducating their science officer, but the challenge is gladly accepted by Admiral Kirk. Even though he might be stripped of his rank for having defied Federation regulations in going back to the quarantined Genesis planet, Kirk believes that "the needs of the one [namely Spock] far outweigh the needs of the many." Being reunited with Spock has restored the meaning to his life and has enabled Kirk to make some sense out of the death of his son. He can now create something wonderful by helping Spock discover his true potential. That "sense of great joy," which is an integral part of the creative process, permeates the final moments of *Star Trek III*.[27]

STAR TREK IV: THE VOYAGE HOME: GOING BACK TO ONE'S ROOTS

After several serious (yet very successful) stories about a machine seeking its creator, a device that could generate life, and a soul-less product of such a device trying to make himself whole again, it was time to introduce a bit of levity into the *Star Trek* universe. At least this was what actor Leonard Nimoy had in mind when he directed the next movie installment, *Star Trek IV: The Voyage Home* (1986). Nimoy felt that the series had reached a point where a lighthearted tale could be cinematically told, without detracting from the work's archetypal significance.[28] Humor can be used quite effectively to make Jungian images much more salient to the viewer.[29] Interestingly, both *Star Trek IV* and *Star Trek V* would employ comic relief in their story lines, contributing to fresher if not more entertaining plots.

Just like the Vejur object, *Voyage Home*'s alien probe enters Earth's atmosphere to determine whether there are any compatible life forms that will respond to its signal. Singing is the space traveler's primary mode of communication, and the songs it emits "connect many species of sentient creatures one with the other."[30] But, the "music of the intelligences" is strangely silent on our blue planet, causing great dismay in the probe. It would seem that sterilization is the only recourse left to the alien since it reasons anything of significant value would have registered its presence and communicated in the appropriate manner. Huge sections of the ocean are vaporized so that the Earth's surface temperature can be sufficiently lowered to the point where a future "reseeding of life" can take place, perhaps eons from the present century.[31]

This space creator commits one of the most egotistical mistakes attributed to any maker: it believes itself to be the "center of the universe" and that any other life form must conform to its pattern if it wishes to survive.[32] Sadly, the traveler is incapable of realizing that there are many types of existence, each containing the essence of the divinity within its nature. Even the primitive humans possess those godlike, creative elements, but they are barely acknowledged as the probe carries out its mission of destruction.

Mr. Spock's newly acquired memories are put to the test, and the Vulcan is finally able to deduce that the traveler's message is whale song, specifically of the humpback variety. He further infers that the ones piloting the probe are intimately related to the sea mammals. Perhaps they might even be a species of superwhale coming back to check on their own offspring.[33] The dilemma confronting the Federation is how the world can be saved when that very humanity has hunted "the children" of the traveler to the point of extinction. Kirk and crew must, therefore, embark on a time travel quest to an earlier century when whales were abundant and retrieve a few so that the angry space parent will be appeased and leave the Earth intact. The space voyage can be likened to a journey back to humankind's roots where aggression and barbarism are the norm. But it must be undertaken to "save the [more intelligent] whales"[34] and ourselves from an imminent extinction.

Their arrival in San Francisco in the twentieth century turns out to be quite a culture shock for the Federation officers.[35] Besides the antiquated modes of travel and bartering system, the futurists have to adjust to the language of the times which is often laced with colorful metaphors. As Kirk explains to Spock, swearing is the only means to get someone's attention. Only too happy to oblige, the science officer begins to copy these expressions—much to the chagrin of his commander (but to the joy of every science-fiction aficionado).

While the starship crew acclimates itself to the planet, Kirk happens to read a sign that discloses the whereabouts of the only two humpback whales ever to be held in captivity. The location is just a short distance away, at the Maritime Cetacean Institute in Sausalito. Jung would argue that any type of "magical coincidence" (like Kirk's accidental discovery of the whales) is meaningful because it connects the inner, psychological state of the person with events in the external reality.[36] The synchronism of Kirk's desire to find the sea mammals and the information magically being presented right before his eyes would suggest that some principle beyond the probabilistic is responsible for the correlation. A divine source which "penetrates and connects all things," both outer and inner, is Jung's explanation for these meaningful coincidences which operate even in the fictitious *Star Trek* universe.[37]

It is fortunate that Admiral Kirk finds a kindred spirit in Dr. Gillian Taylor (Catherine Hicks), the director of the Cetacean Institute. She is afraid that her humpbacks will be returned to the open sea in just a few days because the institute cannot afford to maintain their expensive diet.

Gillian's worst fears are confirmed when the whales are released ahead of schedule and are preyed upon by human hunters in the free waters. Armed with futuristic technology, Kirk prevents the creatures from being killed by his primitive ancestors and beams them to safety within the confines of his vessel. As he and Gillian gaze upon the majestic mammals in the holding tank, both realize that mankind was destroying its own future by eradicating species like this one from the planet. The antithesis of creation, which is destruction, can in the long run hurt ourselves just as much as others if we do not acknowledge the harm that we do.[38] It is good to be reminded of *Star Trek IV*'s message from time to time; otherwise, we may never stop our destructive behaviors from getting out of hand, thereby ruining our chances of ever achieving a more creative and fulfilling future.

After the whales are transported to the twenty-third century, they immediately begin their beautiful chanting. The music resonates throughout everything until it reaches the very core of the space probe and fills it with the message of life. The alien responds by terminating its sterilization program so that the songs of the young can continue to be transmitted for generations to come. The space creator leaves the planet knowing it is in safe hands, as long as a guiding intelligence is there to set things right.

Kirk is rewarded for his efforts in saving the Earth once again by being given command of the new and improved *Enterprise*, Model NCC 1701-A. But he has obtained an even more important prize: the knowledge that the human race must live in harmony with all worlds, including the natural world. Only by recognizing God in everything will contact with that divine presence be achieved.[39] Perhaps one day the probe might even return and appreciate the human species as an important life source not unlike itself in its creative capacity. At least Kirk hopes so, having foreseen what the course of human evolution might be like if the ecological order continues to be disrupted by our ever-expanding technological "gains."

STAR TREK V: THE FINAL FRONTIER: AN ENCOUNTER WITH THE GOD IMAGE

Following Nimoy's example, William Shatner decided to take the director's seat for *Star Trek V: The Final Frontier* (1989). Under his capable hands, the original *Motion Picture* premise of the *Enterprise*'s meeting God finally found expression, even if it was a decade later.[40] The insertion of Spock's half brother, Sybok (Laurence Luckinbill), into the screenplay gave a concrete dimension to the transcendental being since it was the Vulcan who had dedicated his entire life to pursuing this divinity actively, no matter what the cost.

Sybok's passionate mission is not the only thing that makes him distinctively different from others of his race. He also possesses a strange, mesmerizing power which can make those he encounters face their own hidden fears and "shadow anxieties." Most are rejuvenated by the therapeutic process and gladly take up Sybok's quest, feeling indebted to the one who freed them from their personal hells. As J. M. Dillard reveals in her *Star Trek V* novelization, the name Sybok means "seer," "prophet," and sometimes even "messiah."[41] Of all Vulcans, Sybok is the only one who can actually hear the voice of God speaking to him in his dreams, guiding him to the origin of all creation, the paradisiacal Sha Ka Ree. His empathic abilities are regarded as a gift from the Source, designed to lead others on the chosen path to salvation and immortal bliss. All that is required of potential converts is that they freely accept this beatific vision and claim it as their own (a not too difficult undertaking given each one's prior state of mind).

And so with a steadily growing band of followers, Sybok heads toward the Planet of Galactic Peace in the Neutral Zone and subsequently captures several important delegates in order to attract the attention of Starfleet. The response is immediate: the *Enterprise* arrives at warp speed in an attempt to rescue the hostages. However, many of the crew (including Chekhov, Sulu, and Uhura) fall under the spell of the charismatic Sybok. It is only a matter of time before the starship assumes a new heading, the legendary Sha Ka Ree situated at the exact center of the galaxy.

The positioning of the Promised Land has great archetypal importance. The Jungian "centre" is symbolic of the total personality, *both* conscious as well as unconscious elements.[42] More notably, it represents the transcendental nature of the supreme being, the godhead. The very core (or center) of the god state is whole, requiring nothing else to complete itself; all opposites are brought together to coexist in this unified form.[43] One of the human's major goals is to reach that perfect center, usually by undergoing a radical, psychological transformation which affects both body and soul. *Star Trek*'s Sybok is an individual who desires that transmutation so that the true purpose of his existence can at last be revealed. His journey to the center of the galaxy is really a voyage into the very self where, hopefully, any visions of the One (i.e., God) can be actualized and brought to conscious awareness.[44]

It would seem that Sybok's quest reaches fruition when the *Enterprise* miraculously penetrates the Great Barrier surrounding the fringes of Sha Ka Ree with hardly a scratch. At this point, some of the crew are convinced that an overseer might indeed be out there, protecting its offspring from harm. Yet Kirk remains steadfast in his convictions that there must be some explanation other than the obvious one. In fact, he is the only officer who is immune to Sybok's mind probes. In order to understand why this is so requires an analysis of Kirk's personality.

Like Sybok, the commander is a seeker of sorts who is searching for something beyond the physical reality. Kirk's "yearning to transcend" the limitations of the flesh is displayed at the very start of *Final Frontier* when he is seen scaling the mountainous El Capitan in Yosemite National Park. Though there is some risk involved in the attempt to reach the summit, Kirk believes it is all worthwhile. His ascent is a sacred journey for this is what he ultimately values in life.[45] Instead of taking a relaxing shore leave like everyone else, he would rather encounter the majestic wonder of God in nature by being an active participant in that unfolding. The fall of Kirk before arriving at El Capitan's peak merely confirms the heroic stature of the man; he realizes that death is an ever tangible presence, but this does not deter him from climbing higher and higher (or committing himself to future ascents) if it means attaining a "oneness" with the elements.[46]

Now Sybok poses a grave threat to Kirk's belief system. The Vulcan wants to remove the commander's hidden pain as well as his significant aspirations and then implant desires that are not his own. The probing might be comparable to a "psychological raping" of the mind, destroying whatever makes him most human. Moreover, Kirk considers the longing for an external paradise to be an unfulfilling journey. Only by realizing that what we seek is within ourselves, and not some imaginary Eden, can we go beyond the confines of this existence and meet our Maker.[47] In time, Kirk is able to convince Spock and McCoy to abandon the false dreams of Sybok and respond with their hearts to his position. Kirk's stubbornness, combined with his inner certainty, prove to be too much for Sybok to control. And so the Vulcan devotes his attention to setting up an expedition to explore Sha Ka Ree. He invites the disbelievers to join him, hoping that the presence of God will manifest itself and convert them to his cause.

The barren, desolate planet of Sha Ka Ree appears to be an unlikely place for God to dwell, but as Kirk's group approaches the center of a mountain circle (the symbolic import of which does not escape the notice of novelist Dillard), huge pillars of rock rear up from the ground to surround them. The "gigantic fingers of stone [eventually] interlace to form a shrine . . . [out of which] a brilliant beam of pure force explodes, blinding the onlookers with its raw beauty."[48] Then, a voice issues from the light, welcoming the travelers for being the first to cross over into its domain. A face, weathered by age yet possessing great wisdom, accompanies the booming voice and provides great comfort to Sybok who always knew that God's image would resemble this one: paternalistic, gentle, and loving.

Kirk is not taken in by appearances, however, and questions the motives of the god-image who wants nothing more than to have the *Enterprise* carry its power back through the Great Barrier so that all creation can share in its divinity. Suddenly, the being reverts to the Book of Job's destroyer. It lashes out at Kirk and then Spock with deadly energy rays emanating from its eyes. Sybok cannot comprehend why "his god" would cause so much pain and suffering to these simply inquisitive humans. Clearly, this is not the One in which he has placed his faith and trust;

instead, it is some malignant form of life seeking escape from its centuries old imprisonment on the planet.

Jung suggests that any god has an unconscious, dark side which can "let loose all the terrors of Nature" if allowed expression.[49] The only way Sybok can confront the evil part of his god which demands release is by realizing his image has been a false and incomplete construction of the deity. After adjusting his conception, the Vulcan tries to engage in a dialogue with the creature. When the conversation fails, he resorts to physical force and comes face to face with a shadowy doppelganger of himself. The battle with the unconscious form of the godhead (or inner self) reaches cataclysmic proportions, to the point where Sha Ka Ree breaks apart. Luckily, the Federation officers manage to avoid being consumed in the conflagration at the last possible moment.

As the archetypal trinity of Kirk, Spock, and McCoy reflect on Sybok's death (along with the creature's), the cosmic question as to whether God exists is raised. Kirk answers that the true image of any god lies within the soul of every sentient being, waiting to be discovered. The "final frontier" is to cross the bridge into one's own unconscious rather than devote time to an aimless pursuit of something outside of oneself as Sybok had.[50] The "Row, Row, Row Your Boat" segment the three sing upon their next shore leave at Yosemite Park reinforces the theme that life can be a satisfying dream or a misleading one depending on one's representation of the deity. For better or for worse, the god-image that we carry is responsible for our creative urges as well as our destructive behavior.[51] To accept the good *and* bad in ourselves is to appreciate more fully that underlying god-image.

STAR TREK VI: THE UNDISCOVERED COUNTRY: THE HUMAN AS CREATOR AND SAVIOR

The story of the Klingons establishing peace with the Terrans in *Star Trek VI: The Undiscovered Country* (1991) was an outgrowth of an idea already established in the preceding *Final Frontier*. One of the cities on Nimbus III, the Planet of Galactic Peace which Sybok had visited, was designed to be an experiment where the three major powers of the universe (Klingon, Terran, and Romulan) would put aside their differences and work out cooperative solutions for the benefit of all races. Although the end result of this venture had been a breakdown in authority by the transplanted peoples who felt it was more profitable to fight among themselves than establish universal laws,[52] story developer and executive producer Leonard Nimoy believed the subplot had considerable merit, especially when the political climate across the world was changing to one involving successful negotiation instead of constant warfare.

The Undiscovered Country's way of presenting an intergalactic glasnost starts off with an unforeseen explosion of the Klingon moon, Praxis. Not only is a major energy center of the Klingon race completely decimated, but the alien homeworld also lies at risk of meeting a similar fate. Forecasts suggest that the stellar catastrophe will deplete all oxygen on the planet in approximately fifty years, causing the deaths of millions and, ultimately, the extermination of the species. Klingons like Chancellor Gorkon (played by David Warner) have taken the initiative to begin peace talks with the Federation, hoping the Terrans will help them through this crisis. In a gesture of good faith, they have disarmed a significant number of weapons and have abandoned many of their military outposts along the Neutral Zone. Accepting the sincerity of their intentions, Ambassador Spock is able to convince his superiors that now would be the most logical time to establish the bonds of friendship with a longtime hated foe.

One person objects vehemently to the peace treaty proposed by Spock and Gorkon: Commander James T. Kirk. He still blames the Klingons for the death of his son (which occurred in *Star Trek III*) and would like nothing better than to see the entire race of "animals" die for their crimes.[53] The surprise which Spock shows Kirk confirms the differences between the two. The Vulcan responds to the Gorkon initiative in a rational, collected manner while his captain operates purely within the reactive mode, unwilling to assimilate the information into his biased scheme of things. Critics have suggested that the Spock and Kirk characters are two facets of the same identity,[54] and if this is so, both remain at odds with each other for a good portion of the movie.

Kirk's unresolved hatred is so strong that he allows his fellow officers, by his strained silence, to express openly their feelings of distrust toward Gorkon at what was supposed to be a pleasant communal meal aboard the *Enterprise*. After an attempt is made to assassinate the Klingon chancellor, Kirk helplessly watches McCoy try to save Gorkon's life, but it is in vain. The tragic death of Gorkon and the subsequent arrest of Kirk and McCoy for the crime demonstrate how prejudices can blind people (even starship captains) to the point where they can fuel already existing racial tensions and violence by their inability to keep their own "shadow impulses" in check.[55]

Because the god-image is a part of human nature, we have the capacity to be gods. This means that our importance and power can grow to exponential proportions, giving us the ability to create new societies and environments with our newfound divinity.[56] Gorkon's dying words reflect an insight into our "inner creator" when he advises Kirk not to let the treaty end in such a destructive fashion. The force Gorkon exerts to pull Kirk's head down next to his own before he expires is a powerful sign that the creative potential can be transferred from one species to another, so long as one believes in the worth of *all* life forms. If Kirk does not want Gorkon's dreams to perish, he must commit himself to making a trek through the "undiscovered country" of the Klingons in order to confront his bigotry and begin to develop new and lasting relationships with these people.

The journey begins on the penal asteroid of Rura Penthe to which Kirk and McCoy are sentenced to spend the remainder of their lives for the Gorkon assassination. Referred to as "the alien's graveyard," Rura Penthe has the most inhospitable of climates. The frigid air and continuous blizzards make it impossible to survive on Penthe's surface for long. The mines below are no better: the Klingon guards mercilessly work their prisoners to the point of exhaustion while the articles of clothing provided each felon (along with the meager quarters) offer little protection from the cold that penetrates even the most extreme depths. Yet, these conditions only strengthen James Kirk's resolve to escape and fulfill what Gorkon had conceived.[57] It could be said that the loneliness and unpleasantness created by Rura Penthe's alienating environment is the motivating force behind Kirk's call to the creative quest, as it is with so many wanderers who need to experience the negative aspects of life before they commit themselves to more productive and fruitful endeavors.[58]

The "road of trials" continues for Kirk and McCoy after they release themselves from their underground prison and brave the freezing temperatures above. Both become seriously frostbitten by the killing cold and are near the point of death when they confront a mysterious, shape-changing alien. The creature selects Kirk's form because his physique pleases it, and so the commander has no choice but to battle a psychic double of himself. That the Klingon guards intervene at just the right moment and kill the alien/Kirk instead of the real one indicates that they have been misled by physical appearances. If the Klingons had performed a more thorough investigation, they would have perceived a recently discovered humanity radiating from Kirk's very core and would have shot the correct target. Luckily for the commander, their mistake results in his salvation as it has given the *Enterprise* the precious time it needs to locate his position and liberate both himself and McCoy from Rura Penthe.

Kirk's travels do not stop once he comes aboard the starship. There are still factions which remain opposed to the Gorkon treaty and will stop at nothing to prevent its implementation, even if it means murdering another chancellor, in this case Gorkon's daughter, Azetbur (actress Rosana De-Soto). Kirk uncovers the identities of the conspirators who have infiltrated the highest levels of Starfleet and obtains enough evidence to implicate members of the Vulcan, Romulan, and Klingon governments as well. Racing to the new location of the peace talks, Camp Khitomer situated near the Romulan border, the commander is forced to kill a number of the spies before a repeat assassination occurs. The remaining members are arrested, with a few displaying genuine surprise at Kirk for bothering to save the life of Azetbur. After all, they regard the female Klingon as a lower life form not worthy of continued existence. Obviously these "people" believe they are better than other races, and it is their sinful pride that leads them on the path of self-destruction, in contrast to the route of self-regeneration which Kirk has freely chosen to follow.[59]

The Undiscovered Country's epilogue involving Kirk and Madam Chancellor Azetbur is a historic one for both species. All hatreds and prejudices are let go as human and Klingon finally communicate with each other as equals. Kirk confesses that it took Gorkon's death to make him see the error of his ways and that he is ready to grieve with Azetbur over the tragic loss. The Chancellor reacts with deep understanding and incredible sensitivity, stating that her father's faith in the unity of the two species has been restored. At the moment she expresses these words, her face brightens with an incredible radiance. "Jim Kirk had never seen a face more beautiful— be it Klingon, Vulcan, Romulan, human. He was not sure who reached out first. . . . In the end it did not matter."[60] When all is said and done, *Star Trek VI* makes us realize that everyone has the same spiritual core, the potential to save one's race from extinction and create lasting bonds of friendship. As Kirk expressed to Spock in an earlier scene, we are *all* human. This is hardly a racist comment; instead, it conveys the view that there are more similarities than differences in people throughout the galaxy. Whatever term one uses to relate those commonalities, the point is that all of us are connected. Therefore, it is our responsibility to draw out the "inner creator" in each other to make the world (and universe) a better place in which to live.

Through the *Star Trek* movies, we have observed an evolution of the Jungian creator archetype. Starting with the alien space probes like *Voyager 6* and then progressing to more Terran constructions such as the Genesis device, the life-giving essence has moved closer and closer to the sphere of human influence and manipulation. The later installments, *Final Frontier* and *Undiscovered Country*, show that the creative agent is at its strongest when it resides within the human spirit and is allowed complete expression.

The Starship *Enterprise*'s travels are hardly over on the big screen as the long anticipated *Star Trek: Generations* movie (1994) has proven its success, both financially and archetypally. In this film, our hero (James T. Kirk) dies a noble death defeating the evil Dr. Soran (Malcolm McDowell) so that another crew can be given new life to continue the starship voyages into the next century and beyond. Again, author J. M. Dillard does a splendid job of translating *Generations*'s final moments to the printed word: "Kirk stared sightlessly up at the sky, a pane of sunlight illuminating his features. All suffering seemed to leave him; his reflection grew reflective, peaceful. . . .And he died, releasing a slow, satisfied breath, in Picard's arms."[61] This description is very reminiscent of Jung's sun-god image in which the "young and comely" hero with the radiating countenance is able to provide light to future generations with his "rejuvenated splendour."[62] The creative energies released by Commander Kirk's phoenix-style death certainly pave the way for a new batch of *Star Trek* features to come—for example, *Star Trek: First Contact* (1996)—and, just as important, serve to remind each viewer that the greatest "trek" of all truly lies within the person, where contact with the inner creator is necessary if one ever hopes to understand the human condition and, hopefully, improve it.

NOTES

1. Richard Meyers, *The Great Science Fiction Films* (New York: Carol Publishing Group, 1990), 153.

2. Karen A. Romanko, "Where No Librarian Has Gone Before . . . The 10 Best *Star Trek* Episodes on Video," *Emergency Librarian* 21 (1993): 24.

3. William Shatner with Chris Kreski, *Star Trek Movie Memories* (New York: HarperCollins, 1994), 36–38, 51, 57.

4. Gene Roddenberry, *Star Trek The Motion Picture* (New York: Simon and Schuster, 1979), 5–9, 86–87.

5. Carl G. Jung, "The Self," in *Aion: Researches into the Phenomenology of the Self: The Collected Works*, trans. R.F.C. Hull (Princeton, NJ: Princeton University Press, 1990), 31–32; Jung, "Christ, A Symbol of the Self," in *Aion*, 40.

6. Roddenberry, *The Motion Picture*, 155.

7. Ibid., ix–x.

8. Jung, "Christ, A Symbol of the Self," in *Aion*, 41–42.

9. Carl G. Jung, "The Song of the Moth," in *Symbols of Transformation: The Collected Works*, trans. R.F.C. Hull (Princeton, NJ: Princeton University Press, 1990), 112–13.

10. Roddenberry, *The Motion Picture*, 179.

11. Carl G. Jung, "The Phenomenology of the Spirit in Fairytales," in *The Archetypes and the Collective Unconscious: The Collected Works*, trans. R.F.C. Hull (Princeton, NJ: Princeton University Press, 1990), 227.

12. Meyers, *Great Science Fiction Films*, 161, 229–31.

13. Vonda N. McIntyre, *Star Trek The Wrath of Khan* (New York: Pocket Books, 1982), 102–3.

14. Carl G. Jung, "Religious Ideas in Alchemy: The Work," in *Psychology and Alchemy: The Collected Works*, trans. R.F.C. Hull (Princeton, NJ: Princeton University Press, 1991), 295–97; Lane Roth, "Death and Rebirth in *Star Trek II: The Wrath of Khan*," in *Educational Resources Information Center*. 1990: 8–9, 11 (ERIC Document Reproduction Service No. ED311–515).

15. McIntyre, *The Wrath of Khan*, 105.

16. Carrie Rickey, "Review of *Star Trek II: The Wrath of Khan*," *Village Voice* 27 (22 June 1982): 54; Kevin Thomas, "Review of *Star Trek II: The Wrath of Khan*," *Los Angeles Times*, 3 June 1982; Calendar, 1.

17. Carol S. Pearson, *Awakening the Heroes Within: Twelve Archetypes to Help Us Find Ourselves and Transform Our World* (San Francisco: HarperCollins, 1991), 168.

18. Shatner with Kreski, *Star Trek Movie Memories*, 128.

19. McIntyre, *The Wrath of Khan*, 216; Roth, "Death and Rebirth in *Star Trek II*," 7.

20. Pearson, *Awakening the Heroes Within*, 169, 173–74.

21. Jung, "Religious Ideas in Alchemy: The Work," in *Psychology and Alchemy*, 312–13; Robert H. Hopcke, "Jung and Alchemy," in *A Guided Tour of the Collected Works of C. G. Jung* (Boston: Shambhala, 1992), 163–64.

22. Vonda N. McIntyre, *Star Trek III The Search for Spock* (New York: Pocket Books, 1984), 143–47, 291.

23. Ibid., 182–84.

24. Jung, "Religious Ideas in Alchemy: The Psychic Nature of the Alchemical Work," in *Psychology and Alchemy*, 270–72.

25. David Denby, "Review of *Star Trek III: The Search for Spock*," *New York* 17 (11 June 1984): 67; David Edelstein, "Review of *Star Trek III: The Search for Spock*," *Village Voice* 29 (5 June 1984): 65.

26. Jung, "Religious Ideas in Alchemy: The Work," in *Psychology and Alchemy*, 314–15.

27. Kevin Thomas, "Review of *Star Trek III: The Search for Spock*," *Los Angeles Times*, 1 June 1984; Calendar, 1; Pearson, *Awakening the Heroes Within*, 175.

28. Michael Wilmington, "Review of *Star Trek IV: The Voyage Home*," *Los Angeles Times*, 26 November 1986: Calendar, 1; Shatner with Kreski, *Star Trek Movie Memories*, 189.

29. James F. Iaccino, *Psychological Reflections on Cinematic Terror: Jungian Archetypes in Horror Films* (Westport, CT: Praeger Publishers, 1994), 167–79.

30. Vonda N. McIntyre, *Star Trek IV The Voyage Home* (New York: Pocket Books, 1986), 1.

31. Ibid., 61–62, 80.

32. Carol S. Pearson, *The Hero Within: Six Archetypes We Live By* (San Francisco: HarperCollins, 1989), 118–20.

33. Margaret W. Bonanno, *Star Trek Probe* (New York: Pocket Books, 1992), 18.

34. Steven H. Scheuer, *Movies on TV and Videocassette* (New York: Bantam Books, 1991), 1000.

35. Wilmington, "Review of *Star Trek IV: The Voyage Home*," 1.

36. Carl G. Jung, "Exposition," in *Synchronicity: An Acausal Connecting Principle*, trans. R.F.C. Hull (Princeton, NJ: Princeton University Press, 1991), 9–12, 21–22, 25.

37. Jung, "Forerunners of the Idea of Synchronicity," in *Synchronicity*, 76–78.

38. Pearson, *Awakening the Heroes Within*, 145–46.

39. Pearson, *Hero Within*, 119, 145–46.

40. Kim Newman, "Review of *Star Trek V: The Final Frontier*," *Monthly Film Bulletin* (November 1989): 346; Shatner with Kreski, *Star Trek Movie Memories*, 225–26.

41. J. M. Dillard, *Star Trek V The Final Frontier* (New York: Pocket Books, 1989), 4–5.

42. Jung, "Individual Dream Symbolism in Relation to Alchemy: The Symbolism of the Mandala," in *Psychology and Alchemy*, 106–7.

43. Jung, "The Alchemical Interpretation of the Fish," in *Aion*, 170–71.

44. Kevin Thomas, "Review of *Star Trek V: The Final Frontier*," *Los Angeles Times*, 9 June 1989; Calendar, 1.

45. Pearson, *Awakening the Heroes Within*, 130.

46. Jung, "The Song of the Moth," in *Symbols of Transformation*, 110–11.

47. Mario A. Jacoby, *Longing for Paradise: Psychological Perspectives on an Archetype*, trans. Myron B. Gubitz (Boston: Sigo Press, 1980), 207; Shatner with Kreski, *Star Trek Movie Memories*, 223.

48. Dillard, *The Final Frontier*, 265–66.

49. Jung, "The Hymn of Creation," in *Symbols of Transformation*, 55–56.

50. Suzanne Moore, "Review of *Star Trek V: The Final Frontier*," *New Statesman & Society*, 27 October 1989, 40.

51. Jung, "The Hymn of Creation," in *Symbols of Transformation*, 78.

52. Dillard, *The Final Frontier*, 40.

53. J. M. Dillard, *Star Trek VI The Undiscovered Country* (New York: Pocket Books, 1992), 38–39.

54. Romanko, "Where No Librarian Has Gone Before," 24; Roth, "Death and Rebirth in *Star Trek II*," 2–3.

55. David Sterritt, "Review of *Star Trek VI: The Undiscovered Country*," *Christian Science Monitor* 83 (12 December 1991): 14.

56. Jung, "The Song of the Moth," in *Symbols of Transformation*, 86–88.

57. Dillard, *The Undiscovered Country*, 214.

58. Pearson, *Hero Within*, 59–60.

59. Pearson, *Awakening the Heroes Within*, 131–32.

60. Dillard, *The Undiscovered Country*, 294.

61. J. M. Dillard, *Star Trek Generations* (New York: Pocket Books, 1994), 227–28.

62. Jung, "The Song of the Moth," in *Symbols of Transformation*, 109.

3

Planet of the Apes: The Evolution of an Archetypal Shadow Species

The Jungian shadow can best be described as the person's "dark, inferior side" which is more animalistic than human, more bestial than civilized.[1] At times the shadow can assume an outward identity so that it can display its primitive, demonic urges for all the world to see. The trickster figure is one such shadow projection. This character delights in playing malicious jokes on people and shows no remorse in whatever dangers he has inflicted upon humanity. One of the more common representations of the shadow trickster is that he is *simia dei*, or "the ape of God," to highlight his negative, subhuman nature.[2]

The science-fiction series *The Planet of the Apes* is an excellent extension of the shadow trickster. Here the apes of God are actual simians who acquire mankind's intelligence in the course of their continuing evolution, making them quite formidable adversaries. The plot of Pierre Boulle's original *Planet of the Apes* story (correctly translated as Monkey Planet), written in France in 1963, was novel enough to generate five movies and a television spin-off in this country during the late 1960s and early 1970s.[3] Plans are currently under way to revive the series in a new movie format, tentatively titled *Return to the Planet of the Apes*, which is supposed to be a more faithful retelling of the Boulle tale. One of the reasons why the interest in *Planet of the Apes* has not died down over the years is because these cinematic creatures do, in fact, possess the very part of ourselves we would like to keep repressed in our collective unconscious—but cannot. In watching the apes, we are looking at our own hidden nature reflected back at us. Let us now examine the "monkey politics" of this shadow species in further detail, starting with the first film in the five-part series.

PLANET OF THE APES: A SHOCKING CONFRONTATION WITH THE UNCONSCIOUS

Planet of the Apes (1968) kicks off with Colonel George Taylor (Charlton Heston) encountering some turbulence when his spaceship travels dangerously close to the speed of light. The craft eventually crashes in an ocean on a supposedly uncharted planet. Along with Taylor, two of the crew survive the catastrophe and make their way to the nearest landmass. As they explore the desolate landscape, Taylor explains that they have been catapulted into some future dimension. Before the ship sank, the computers had registered the actual year as being 2978, Earth time. The astronauts understand that the world they knew is long gone, and so they begin to adapt to their surroundings, hoping to make a new home in a solar system far removed from their own.

After several days of fruitless investigation for any signs of life, the travelers chance upon a tribe of humanoids apparently grazing in some fields. What stuns Taylor and the others is that the natives do not use a discernible type of language, which is surprising given their proximity to each other. What is even more baffling is that the group's facial expressions do not reflect any level of intelligence or conscious awareness whatsoever. Boulle's text relates the astronauts' encounter with these creatures in the following way: "We always imagined the presence of a mind in any living being. On this planet reality was quite the reverse: we had to deal with inhabitants resembling us in every way from the physical point of view, but who appeared to be completely devoid of the power of reason."[4] The mute life forms are a rather nice depiction of Carl Jung's archaic man. This primitive type of being possesses a "pre-logical" state of mind where concentrated, mental activity is impossible; instead, there is a strong reliance on emotions and a "belief" that everything is governed by external, magical forces.[5] The primitives in *Planet of the Apes* share these Jungian qualities, making them quite vulnerable to attack by superior forces.

In this case, the "superior forces" are apes on horseback. But these are not ordinary simians from our twentieth century. They are an evolved species of gorilla who exhibit some very human mannerisms. They appear comfortable wearing military uniforms, shoot guns with excellent precision, and, above all else, voice their intentions in a rational fashion to respective comrades in arms. Perhaps the most human attribute of all is the way in which the apes take perverse pleasure in hunting down their victims, killing some and herding the rest in holding pens to be transported back to Central City. John Chambers' creative makeup design in this film and the other

Planet features is remarkable; he is able to give each ape a distinctively human look enabling the viewer to relate to the beast's shadow nature.[6] In fact, it becomes fairly easy to recognize the actor behind the mounds of technical appliance since the unique face masks do not permit the concealment of the star's identity. As one Jungian interpreter notes, the shadow can be likened to a "looking glass" into Dr. Jekyll's soul where the sadistic Mr. Hyde resides.[7] The special-effects wizardry of John Chambers is able to draw out the bestial Hyde and merge it with the civilized traits of the Jekyll alter ego, resulting in a successful (as well as interesting) assimilation of simian and human personalities in these futuristic creatures.

Once inside Central City, Colonel Taylor finds that he cannot speak because his throat was injured by one of the trooper's bullets during the hunt. The others in his party are either presumed to be dead or held in confinement with the other savages. During his incarceration, Taylor befriends a fellow inmate (Linda Harrison) whom he calls Nova because her appearance is as striking as the most brilliant star. He also gets an opportunity to observe the ape society up close and notices a functional stratification in the members (which Boulle had originally posited).

Taylor sees that the ape world parallels his own in many respects—from the highest to the lowest levels. The orangutans mainly occupy positions of power on the High Council and preserve the traditional heritage of the species by overseeing the various religious systems. The most intellectual apes on the planet are the chimpanzees. Since they "are animated by a powerful spirit of research,"[8] the chimps frequently become physiologists and archaeologists so that they can acquire more knowledge about their roots. Finally, the gorillas might be considered the brawn of the ape order. They maintain law and order by being placed in charge of the police force. In addition, the hunting of wild animals (including humanoids) is a task reserved for this group which has developed keen sensory organs. Chimpanzees usually benefit from the gorilla raids since they are supplied living materials for their continual experiments, which is why Taylor finds himself in this precarious situation.

One female chimp, Dr. Zira (played by Kim Hunter), takes a liking to Taylor and senses there is something different about this human. She convinces her archaeologist fiance, Cornelius (Roddy McDowall), that "Bright Eyes" should not be sacrificed but studied further to determine what makes his nature so unique from the other lower life forms. However, head orangutan Zaius (Maurice Evans) is not impressed by Bright Eyes' handwriting skills or mouth mimicry of their language. As minister of science, Zaius uses his influence to convince the ape leaders that the beast should be lobotomized at once. Sensing the danger to himself, Taylor manages to escape from his cell, and it is at this point in the film that the confrontation with Jung's collective unconscious is shockingly displayed.

When Taylor races outside, he is attacked by a number of apes—young as well as old, male and female, civilian and official alike. He is shunned, beaten, stoned, and even whipped by the outraged simians. The fact that Taylor is crushed by this shadow species indicates just how powerful the Jungian unconscious is. Once it is freed from its restraints, the result can be a total destruction of one's ego.[9] Archetypal images of Prometheus's being eternally tortured or Christ's being crucified show just how much "godlike suffering" can come about when the forces of the unconscious fail to be integrated with more conscious contents.[10] This theme is further elaborated upon by Franklin J. Schaffner's superb direction. In several key chase sequences, the camera is inverted so it looks as though actor Heston is moving through the skies instead of on the ground. The significance behind these shots is that the unconscious can turn one's entire conscious world topsy-turvy so that one can no longer feel psychically supported. In Taylor's case, he is literally lifted off his feet by the apes who have caught him in their nets. The only thing the astronaut can do is throw curses at his oppressors, now that he has miraculously regained the power of his voice. Of course, this startles the gorilla troops and the onlookers—but only temporarily. After recovering from their initial shock, the apes feel more than ever a need to liquidate Taylor before his presence destroys their collective society which is based on the clear separation of man and beast (or conscious from unconscious self).

Luckily, Cornelius and Zira spirit Taylor and Nova away before the extermination sentence can be carried out. They take him and his female companion to Cornelius's archaeological site in the Forbidden Zone where they piece together the origins of the ape species. It seems that a more advanced civilization preceded the simian one based on the implements they uncover. Taylor conjectures it was probably humanoid because he recognizes many of the artifacts as belonging to his own kind, including a human-shaped doll that can talk (much to the amazement of the inquisitive chimps). That the astronaut finds clues to the ascent of the ape culture at the dig is extremely important because Jung indicates one has to go down a deep well or dark hole in order to come face to face with one's shadow side.[11] Taylor's sifting through the many layers of dirt represents his probing of the collective unconscious; buried at the deepest level lies the "hidden wellspring" of knowledge that men very similar to Taylor himself once reigned supreme on this planet before the apes assumed control. Why the human civilization de-evolved so that another could replace it is the paramount question on Taylor's mind, and one which has great archetypal relevance.

The answer is swift in coming when he and Nova ride off toward the coastline. They find an immense boulder blocking their path. Upon further inspection, Taylor is able to identify the object as part of a famous structure: the upper half of the Statue of Liberty. The astronaut becomes angry at the revelation that he never left Earth, but was transported one thousand years into its future. He pounds his fists into the sand, swearing at the human ancestors who, no doubt, used nuclear weapons to destroy their own society. Nova can only watch, powerless to intervene or comprehend the import of what Taylor has discovered. She and others like her are the product of that terrible war: a species robbed of both intelligence and language by the deadly radiation. *Planet*'s finale is a grim reminder that there exists in the human race an "irresistible urge to catastrophe" if the shadow instincts get out of hand and overpower humanity with their brute force.[12] One can only hope that the "neo-apes" have learned the lesson and do not disturb the natural order of things with their propensity toward violence and hatred.

BENEATH THE PLANET OF THE APES: WHEN SHADOW BEAST COLLIDES WITH TECHNOLOGICAL MAN

The first sequel to *Planet of the Apes*, *Beneath the Planet of the Apes* (1970), is basically a retread of the original film. Another space expedition follows Taylor's flight path and is sent through the same time warp into Earth's future. The only survivor of the interdimensional trip is astronaut Brent (Heston look-alike James Franciscus) who soon meets the apes but avoids their evil clutches, thanks to the assistance of Cornelius and Zira. The now married chimp pair direct him toward the Forbidden Zone where Taylor was last seen. Along the way, Brent finds a disoriented Nova who is wearing Taylor's military tags. She cannot tell him what happened, but she is more than happy to accompany the talkative Brent into the strange territory. The discovery of a derelict New York City subway station verifies Brent's hunch that he has indeed returned to his place of origin. As did Taylor, the man experiences a minor breakdown, fearing he is the only intelligent human left alive on the entire planet.

The second half of *Beneath the Planet of the Apes* is, by far, the better portion because it introduces a new race of mutant humans who are dwelling in secret, underground chambers.[13] Evidently, the bowels of the earth have provided some protection against the deadly inferno mankind inflicted upon his brothers topside. The effects of that war cannot be entirely escaped: radiation still lingers below and has eroded the physical features of the people. Just like their quarters, the humans are "crumbling, peeling, scarred and burned."[14] They attempt to cover their distorted flesh with beautiful, unblemished face masks and pure white robes in order to give the impression that they remain whole, complete, and otherwise unchanged. One important difference in their nature is the ability to communicate telepathically to each other as well as outsiders. This mental talent also allows the mutants to implant terrifying images in the minds of intruders, thereby keeping their society safe from detection. Probably the most interesting aspect of the subterranean culture is its belief system. All mutants worship the most destructive of humanity's weapons, the Alpha-Omega nuclear device. They pray to the bomb continually in their main cathedral. It is considered the source of life, a symbol of the human's rebirth into this new (albeit radiated) form.[15] Therefore, it is their primary responsibility to venerate the fully functional bomb in order to be reminded that beauty and goodness come from such human-made objects.

If the mute humanoids living on the planet's surface represent Jung's archaic man, the mutants below ground typify modern (or technological) man. Science has enabled modern man to "progress" to a higher level of material security where he is not wanting in any comforts or pleasures. Yet, for all these external developments, there still exists a void within the modern man's psyche. He requires something to believe in, to hold onto so that he can be spiritually sustained as well as materially sated.[16] This "psychic renewal" involves an abandonment of traditional creeds which do not offer much substance; instead, a deep and profound respect for the divine in one's own life is required to bring about the necessary internal transformation. This comes about with modern man's personally experiencing a new set of truths relevant to his own period.[17] Because the mutants have endured a terrible catastrophe, they have developed an "experiential" religion which has taught them the value and sanctity of human life. They will never detonate the bomb for doing so will make their existence utterly meaningless. Its presence will not only ensure the mutants' continuance as a species, but also their possible development into a higher form of being. A fascinating theme of *Beneath the Planet of the Apes* is that even technological weapons of mass destruction can be converted to ones of creative beauty when modern man truly "finds his soul."

The mutant leader, Mendez (Paul Richards), is finally able to extract from the unwilling mind of Brent the apes' objective: to wage war on anything not simian. Even as the mental interrogation proceeds, gorilla troops under the command of General Ursus (James Gregory) are conducting a military reconnaissance in the Forbidden Zone to find those responsible for the "mass hysteria" inflicted on several of the scouts. Ursus is a warmongering ape who cares little for the fate of his race. All that interests him is the glory of victory and the elimination of any life form not in the image of his own. One might almost liken the crazed Ursus to the archetypal Wotan, the god of storm and frenzy who unleashes those dark passions of the unconscious in full force.[18] Zaius and several chimp pacifists (including Cornelius and Zira) cannot convince Ursus to exercise some prudence should he meet up with a superior adversary. This sole ape is so "possessed" and driven by the shadow that he has infected most of the ape civilization with his dangerous views to the point where everything is heading toward total perdition. Jung explains that throughout our history, similar Wotan-like characters (for example, Adolf Hitler and Benito Mussolini) have plunged the world into chaos and destruction,[19] and so it should come as no surprise that the apes are bound to repeat the mistakes made by their human counterparts.

When the simians approach the underground city, the mutants try to stop them with frightening visions of martyrs being crucified on wooden beams, including the monkeys' very own Great Lawgiver. However, the shadow nature of the apes is so powerful that the mental images cannot be maintained for long. Mendez is left with no other recourse than to call his people to sanctuary and pray to the Divine Bomb for guidance. The scene is a very striking one for a number of reasons. First, this is the only time that the mutants have ever used their voices in unison, to sing praise to the awesome wonders of technology. Second, the cathedral has been designated as the blessed place where the subterraneans can reveal their "inmost selves unto the Bomb." The ritual basically involves the members of the congregation removing their face masks in one collective gesture so that the radiated flesh can be exposed in all its shocking and ghastly brilliance.

Jung might have compared this religious ceremony to the release of the normally inhibited unconscious. Horrifying shapes from "the land of the dead" want to find conscious expression, and so their voice grows stronger and stronger in an effort to be recognized[20]—similar to the hideous faces of the mutants which need to be shown on occasion. But, a more appropriate interpretation might be that Mendez and his followers have learned to develop an appreciation for their bodies, in whatever form, through spiritual communion. The futuristic humans might have actually discovered that most mysterious of Jungian truths: "the spirit is the living body seen from within, and the body is the outer manifestation of the living spirit—with the two [parts] being really one [nature]."[21] Thus, an integral part of the worship service is its focus on those physical aspects. Without that strong belief in the body to supplement the already existing spiritual conviction, the mutants will never be able to transcend their present condition and reach a more advanced level of psychological development.

Sadly, that opportunity never gets to be presented to these people. The apes brutally make their entrance, charging into the stunned humans with guns blasting and swords slashing. Brent and Nova, caught in the cross fire, become two more casualties in the rapidly escalating ape war. The Wotan-like force of these beasts is terrible to behold: it blows away the entire mutant order, leaving nothing to survive in its "cyclonic wake."[22] Even the most sacred of chambers, the cathedral, is violated by General Ursus and his troops, and the bomb is just another object that needs to be torn apart. The shadow irrationality of the apes is quite apparent as they begin to disassemble the nuclear device. Their tampering activates the detonator, and they clumsily back away from the bomb, hoping the damage will rectify itself. Heston's reappearance as Taylor is a nice insertion in the final minutes of the film. He sets into motion what the apes have started by pushing one of the switches down on the bomb's control panel. The result is a fiery explosion that destroys not only the mutant and ape cities but the entire Earth as well. As A. H. Weiler (1970) so succinctly puts it, the film ends "with a bang" for all life forms.[23]

But why does Taylor blow up his world? The answer is a simple one: he no longer wants to live on this planet ruled by apes above and mutants below. Given a choice, he would rather have Earth destroyed than salvaged. Jung advises that mankind might be faced with difficult decisions like these in the generations to come. Having atomic and nuclear weaponry at our disposal only aggravates such highly volatile situations.[24] Unlike Taylor, we must responsibly reflect on the global outcomes of our actions and not let our shadow nature get the better of us; otherwise, our very existence will be jeopardized as so blatantly depicted in *Beneath the Planet of the Apes'* fatalistic screenplay.

ESCAPE FROM THE PLANET OF THE APES: A JOURNEY INTO THE SHADOW WORLD OF CONTEMPORARY MAN

One would think that the *Planet of the Apes* series would have concluded with *Beneath the Planets of the Apes*. After all, nothing could have survived the Alpha-Omega blast, right? Not necessarily so. Taking his cue from the Boulle text, writer Paul Dehn placed Cornelius and Zira as far away from the nuclear device as possible. The two lovable chimps were in outer space at the time of the explosion, aboard Colonel Taylor's spaceship which they had retrieved intact from the ocean. Although the bomb did not harm them, the bomb's discharge was great enough to send the ape pair through a time portal to present-day Earth. *Escape from the Planet of the Apes* (1971) is an absorbing sequel due to Dehn's transposing of the plot of the original story. Instead of Taylor, Nova, and child Sirius hurtling back to an Earth ruled by apes,[25] Cornelius and a pregnant Zira return to a world in which humans are the dominant life form, and they are the discriminated minority. The shadow side of contemporary man, *not* evolved ape, would be the focus of this film and would explain why the downfall of the human species would be an inevitable occurrence.[26]

The chimps' arrival evokes a number of feelings in the populace: amazement, surprise, even fear and dread. Their ability to articulate complex thought processes only intensifies these emotions. Dr. Lewis Dixon (actor Bradford Dillman) and his associate, Dr. Stephanie Branton (Natalie Trundy), are the two exceptions. In studying Cornelius and Zira, the doctors have developed a fondness and love for these creatures. More than anything else, Dixon and Branton wish to protect the apes from the bureaucrats of their planet who want to perform a series of grueling cross-examinations on the "monkeys" (a term intended to show disrespect) in order to obtain more information on the simian culture, Taylor's disappearance, and the events that led up to the destruction of the Earth.

Unfortunately, the doctors do not have the power to stop the president's scientific advisor, Dr. Otto Hasslein (played with maniacal restraint by Eric Braeden), from conducting the governmental investigations. In time, Hasslein learns that an ape war in the year 3950 (one millennium later than *Planet*'s original time period) was accountable for the planet's annihilation. As though this news is not shocking enough, he finds out the future status of mankind from the apes and it is not a pleasant revelation. Humans are regarded as dumb mutes; their major functions in life are to provide hunting practice for the gorillas and to have their brains dissected by the chimps. Hasslein is faced with a difficult choice: should he let Cornelius and Zira live, knowing the fate that will befall his species, or should he murder them and their unborn offspring so that this future can be aborted?

Otto Hasslein's ambivalence is a characteristic consistently expressed by many Jungian magicians. In numerous fairy tales, magicians are the ones who ask the most important questions, primarily because they have the wisdom and insight to go beyond the mundane issues. However, for all their intellectual superiority, they can still be possessed by the dark forces of the shadow. This animal side can create such a dangerous "tunnel vision" in magicians that they limit themselves to seeing only one viewpoint and endorsing it to the point where it becomes a fanatical obsession.[27] Hasslein's "loss of [in]sight" comes when the apes accidentally kill a hospital orderly while escaping. Suddenly, the scientific advisor becomes a madman and issues orders to kill the fugitive chimps. Since the simians have already taken a human life, Hasslein reasons that they will repeat the crime over and over again until his entire race has been subjugated. What this contemporary magician does not consider in his blind haste is that *his* retaliatory actions might be the real cause for humankind's waterloo.

Dixon and Branton are able to offer their assistance to runaways Cornelius and Zira by bringing them to Armando's Circus. This location provides the chimps with the perfect camouflage; they look just like all the other caged apes on public display. During the interim, Zira delivers her baby and the newly formed family begin preparations for a trip to the Florida Everglades where they can start their own colony and, hopefully, live happily ever after among their own kind. Hasslein's minions interrupt these plans, however, by searching the premises of any animal house in the immediate vicinity of the ape breakout. Before leaving the circus, Zira switches babies so that no harm will befall her infant son.

The Christ-like aspects of the story should not escape the attention of the viewer. The ape trio are archetypal substitutes for Mary, Joseph, and Jesus, who are fleeing from a crazed Herod (the notorious Otto Hasslein). The birth of Zira's baby is depicted as a miraculous emergence of a "child-god," who will display great, messianic powers when he comes of age.[28]

Even Boulle's description of his fictional child is religiously adhered to in the screenplay. Here was "a splendid baby . . . lying on the straw like a new Christ, nuzzling against his mother's breast."[29] Thanks to Zira's foresight, her race will not die out, but instead, be reborn in her divine son.

The ending of *Escape from the Planet of the Apes* is not entirely optimistic. Although the child survives, the chimp parents do not. They are brutally gunned down by Hasslein, along with the substitute baby. In his quest to restore the world to its proper order, Hasslein has resorted to violence and bloodshed (similar to the historic King Herod). In a certain sense, Hasslein can be considered a tragic hero who is fated to die. He views his actions as ultimately benefiting humanity; however, he does not realize just how much harm and destruction he has produced by fulfilling this "noble" goal. It is Hasslein's lack of vision that causes his downfall as well as humankind's.[30] The "shadow magician" has not anticipated that the fatally wounded Cornelius would be clever enough to carry a gun, let alone know how to use one against him. The demise of Hasslein is lamentable for it has failed to alter the course of events. The rise of the apes will still transpire, as evidenced by the unnamed son of Cornelius and Zira crying out for his parents in the final scene. Perhaps the moral of the film is that humans might sin the most when they wholeheartedly believe they have nothing but the best of intentions to do good.[31] That damnable shadow-pride in ourselves as a species worth saving might be the one factor responsible for our future extermination on the planet.

CONQUEST OF THE PLANET OF THE APES: THE ASCENSION OF THE SHADOW BEAST

When *Conquest of the Planet of the Apes* (1972) opens, we find that human society has drastically changed from the time of Caesar's birth to his attainment of adulthood. In the short interval of twenty years, apes had been taken out of their natural surroundings to replace all the dogs and cats which had been killed by a lethal space virus. Once humans realized how easy it was to train their pet simians, they gave them more complex chores to do (housecleaning, cooking, and grocery shopping). Naturally, the conditioning procedures became more aversive if apes did not follow their masters' commands. Shocks delivered to the apes' brains or other body parts via portable rods, in conjunction with strong verbal reprimands, soon were the standard procedures used by each city's police forces to instill the proper obedience in these creatures. In the case of an unruly beast, clubbing or mauling the animal in a public setting was not unusual. What had been a lovable relationship between man and ape was transformed to one involving a basic power inequality in which humans ordered and simians followed. Because it was so efficient for human functioning, the master-servant association became the typical pattern practiced across the seven continents of the globe.³²

Into this racially tense atmosphere come Señor Armando (Ricardo Montalban) and Caesar (ape-star Roddy McDowall) who are seeking out a new clientele for their almost defunct circus. At first Caesar does not understand why he needs to be chained up or ordered about so fiercely by his mentor, Armando. After observing his fellow apes in captivity, however, it dawns on Caesar just how low his position really is on the economic ladder. He cannot contain himself any longer when he witnesses the brutal treatment of a gorilla by several human officers, and he screams out, "Lousy bastards," so that the entire world can register his outrage. Armando attempts to cover up for Caesar's mistake by saying he was the one who voiced the critical comment. The lawmen have no choice but to bring the circus owner in for further questioning when they discover Caesar has fled the scene of the crime.

The addition of Governor Breck (Don Murray) in the *Conquest of the Planet of the Apes* story line makes the picture a memorable one. Breck is a racist, pure and simple, who has nothing but contempt for the simians. Statements like "Some of them couldn't be any worse," "They're not responsible for what they are," and "I'm going to crush them once and for all" are examples of the type of dangerous thinking being exercised by Breck. Jung explains that politically powerful individuals might display a "hysterical dissociation of the personality" in which they reject their own shadow nature and look for everything dark and inferior in others. Thus, "hysterical" leaders avoid feelings of inferiority and insecurity by ascribing them onto those who already occupy subordinate positions within the society. In so doing, hysterics inflate their own prestige and self-importance at the expense of denying others theirs.³³ Breck typifies the Jungian hysteric who believes that *all* apes are burning with resentment and hatred toward their human masters instead of admitting that he himself holds such emotions. Breck's hysterical view of the world allows him to govern with an iron fist; he needs to keep the apes in their place at all times to prevent an uprising of his own repressed shadow which would, no doubt, totally incapacitate the man upon its release.³⁴

When Señor Armando throws himself out a window to certain death rather than subject himself to intensive mind-probing techniques, Breck is convinced that the fugitive ape is, in actuality, the offspring of the two talking chimps, Cornelius and Zira. However, the governor is so obsessed with stamping out every beast on the planet that he is not aware his latest addition to the staff is the missing Caesar, until his sources inform him of the ape's identity. The number one priority on Breck's agenda then becomes to expose the animal for the threat it represents to humanity. He subjects Caesar to a series of painful, electroshock treatments until he forces the poor creature into saying a few words. The effect on Breck is immediately apparent. He is ecstatic over this new development for it confirms, in his own mind, just how deadly the simians can be if they acquire the mutant strain of intelligence. By ordering Caesar exterminated through electrocution, Breck hopes he will be able to contain the menace and suppress any future insurrections, thereby ensuring his continued "god-almighty" dominance over this species.[35]

As in *Escape from the Planet of the Apes*, this film portrays Caesar as a neo-Christ (or in this case, Ape Redeemer) who will lead his people out of slavery to a new life of freedom and happiness. He even undergoes a mock "crucifixion" thanks to the help of an African-American human, MacDonald (Hari Rhodes), who is so sympathetic to the ape movement that he turns off the voltage at the critical moment. (It seems that some humans are just as likely to become disciples of Caesar as the apes, paralleling the various sects who followed Jesus in his day.) One important difference is that Caesar does not die. Since the Christian idea of sacrifice reflects the death of physical man and a renunciation of all of his animal instincts, the crucifixion of Jesus clearly separates out the Savior's shadow nature from his immortal, spiritual side.[36] Caesar, however, survives the ordeal—with his bodily functions intact. In this respect, *Conquest*'s simian is more like the Jungian Christ, who has integrated the godlike nature with the bestial.[37] This "god-ape" can only bring the "light" of salvation to his kind by using the forces of darkness (i.e., riots and arms) against the enemy. Therefore, Caesar has to rise from the dead, complete and whole, if the overthrow of the human masters is to succeed. Truly, his "return to life" is as much an ascension of the shadow as it is of the spirit.

In just a few hours, Caesar is able to muster an effective resistance group consisting of hundreds of apes and enough ammunition to arm each of its members. The war with the humans turns out to be a bloody one for both sides, but the apes have the element of surprise. They soon invade the Central Command quarters and capture several high-ranking human officials, including Governor Breck, whom they put in chains. Though Breck experiences some discomfort over the way he is treated by the simians, he endures the humiliation silently and does not give Caesar the satisfaction of showing any sign of weakness. When Caesar asks Breck why the humans made apes their slaves, the governor demonstrates a moment of rare Jungian insight into his collective unconscious. He explains that each man has an ape curled up inside which can totally transform his nature into a despicable savage if allowed expression. Following this reasoning, the "putting down" of the beast, inwardly as well as outwardly, becomes a necessary action if humanity is to remain in its civilized state. Possibly, it is the mob atmosphere that allows the governor to express his bigotry openly toward Caesar. It has been found that when people crowd together en masse or, in this case, are herded along by riotous apes, normally dormant shadow impulses are let loose upon the world in full force.[38] Whatever the explanation for Breck's perceptive state, he realizes his harsh words will infuriate the ape messiah into taking his life. But the former leader anticipates the moment, for it will support his contention that there is nothing redeeming in these external manifestations of the dark side.

Interestingly, MacDonald stops Caesar from spilling more blood by appealing to the ape's tender mercies. As a descendant of slaves, MacDonald knows that violence will only beget more violence, destroying any opportunity for a lasting peace on the planet. Caesar heeds the wisdom of the African American, recognizing a kindred spirit under the human flesh, and tells his kind to lay down their weapons and release their persecutors (including a very stunned Breck). The ape is, at last, conscious of the evil he has generated this night and feels an enormous amount of guilt over the crimes he has committed against humanity. However, Jung argues it is only when we are made aware of the devil inside us that we are in a position to improve ourselves and change our shadow nature for the better.[39] By the end of the film, Caesar has definitely attained a deep, psychic maturation. The speech he delivers to his fellows would suggest that a new society built on kindness and compassion toward all living creatures will be the ideal order they should strive for in future generations. Recognition of the "ascending shadow" has given Caesar the knowledge to improve the world of apes *and* men. One can only hope he will be able to impart this knowledge successfully to the rest of his species who are on the fringes of collective awareness.

BATTLE FOR THE PLANET OF THE APES: A RETURN TO THE SHADOW KILLING

The end times have come for humanity by the onset of the final ape sequel, *Battle for the Planet of the Apes* (1973). The great nuclear war has occurred, flattening the great cities of the world and killing millions of humans. In the aftermath of this destruction, the apes are at the helm having at long last acquired the power of speech. Caesar is the leader of one ape community situated in North America. He rules with a benevolent hand and treats the resident humans with respect, although he still does not regard them as equals. MacDonald (now played by Austin Stoker) is quick to point this out to Caesar on more than one occasion, arguing that the apes prefer being the superior race on the planet. They might even enjoy their dominance over the humans who had once persecuted them. Because of MacDonald's interpretation of the situation, Caesar begins to question the way he commands, wondering whether his leadership will guide *both* humans and simians safely into the next century (and beyond).[40] The answer lies buried under radioactive rubble in the Archives Section of the Forbidden City. Stored there are videotape records of Cornelius and Zira which will supply Caesar with the knowledge he needs regarding Earth's future. Perhaps he can use this information to change the human condition so that everyone's needs are satisfactorily met.

Setting up an expedition with MacDonald and fellow orangutan Virgil (rock star Paul Williams) to accompany him, Caesar begins his heroic quest across the desert. After a day's journey, the trio come upon one of mankind's great cities, now a jumbled ruin consisting of "twisted and melted girders, shattered automobiles, fallen buildings, and ruined highways.... [It was] a monument to madness, a tribute to the game of war."[41] Having some familiarity with the city's underground tunnel system, MacDonald directs Caesar and Virgil to the Archives Section where they find the desired tape. The voices of Cornelius and Zira echo throughout the chambers, announcing that the militaristic gorillas were responsible for the death of their planet. Caesar hopes he can prevent this event from happening. Adopting a scientific viewpoint (which the orangutans have been trained to do), Virgil reflects that time has an infinite number of futures, any one of which can occur depending on circumstances within the present. If the future is to be redirected onto a new course, the shadow killing must stop so that warfare becomes a thing of the past. On Caesar's shoulders rests a terrible burden; he must make combat obsolete for all thinking creatures, ape and human. This can be accomplished only by taking MacDonald's words to heart and by transforming his ape nature to one that is more humane and tolerant to other species. Then, and only then, can Caesar change others of his kind to the point where violence and hatred are replaced by gentleness and compassion, a goal befitting any skilled warrior-turned-diplomat.[42]

Almost every story involving a hero, like Caesar in *Battle for the Planet of the Apes*, has an antagonist who must be confronted. Here we have two enemies. The first one dwells under the radioactive remains of the Forbidden City. It is a race of scarred humans who have barely managed to survive the war, subsisting on canned foods and other goods they can scavenge from below. Ultimately, these people will become the telepathic under-dwellers of *Beneath the Planet of the Apes*, and their residence will be renamed the Forbidden Zone. They are led by Breck's successor, Governor Kolp (Severn Darden), whose purpose in life takes on new meaning when surveillance cameras pick up the images of three intruders entering their domain. Although he does not recognize MacDonald or Virgil, Kolp is able to identify Caesar as the chimp who organized the rebellion against the humans. He barks out orders to his men to capture the trio—alive if possible. By sheer cunning and determination, Caesar is able to avoid the clutches (and gunfire) of the numerous mutants massed against him. As with any Jungian hero, Caesar must descend into the underworld and attempt to deal with the fiery dragon (in this case, the "burning" humans) standing guard over the desired treasure (the tapes of knowledge).[43] It should be noted that the ape and his companions do not resort to violence in their encounter with the fierce foe. Rather, they use their speed to move up the tunnels swiftly while their pursuers, affected by the radiation, can follow only at a snail's pace.

Upon arriving at the surface, Caesar, Virgil, and MacDonald head back to Ape City where another enemy lies in wait. This enemy, General Aldo (played by the late Claude Akins), is a demented gorilla who has dreams of conquest and power. Aldo wants to do more than simply prepare himself for the day when the mutants leave their city and attack his homeland. He desires plenty of weapons to ensure his protection, and so he plots to invade the armory with his troops. Once the outside menace is overthrown, he will then crush Caesar and set up his own kingdom where humans are nothing more than serfs answerable to their ape overlords. Caesar's son, Cornelius (Bobby Porter), accidentally overhears the "Hitlerian" speech delivered by Aldo to his corps one night when he is looking for his pet squirrel in the nearby trees. Not wanting Caesar to know of his plans, the gorilla commander hacks at the branch Cornelius is perched on, causing the limb to break and the boy chimp to plummet to his doom. The way in which General Aldo sneaks around Caesar, developing his nefarious schemes in the dead of night, reminds one of the slippery and very poisonous serpent (another type of Jungian dragon symbol) which is shadow-driven by animal impulses to destroy and usurp.[44]

Before Caesar can investigate the incident of his son's death, Kolp and his ragtag team of followers attack the simians with guns, grenades, and bazookas fired from every conceivable vehicle with wheels (motorcycles, jeeps, even a school bus). Kolp attains his victory all too easily, reinforcing his view that the apes will never attain the level of intelligence his species already possesses in abundance. He drums this into Caesar's head as he advances upon the cornered chimp, indicating that reconditioning will be necessary so that all simians will know who are the real masters of the planet. David Gerrold's novelization of the *Battle for the Planet of the Apes* screenplay is a bit more flamboyant since Kolp is armed with a flamethrower instead of a mere gun. In the text, the crazed human herds Caesar along by firing concentrated bursts either on the ape's right or left side until the defeated leader falls to the ground, limping on all fours like some ordinary animal.[45] Just when it looks completely hopeless, the hero rises up along with his fellows, and, together, they mount a surprise assault on the mutants. Evidently, many of the apes were feigning death in order to draw the human horde into their city where they could be effectively neutralized.

In fighting his battles, Caesar is not only a good warrior, but an intelligent one as well. He knows that when faced with insurmountable odds, a strategic retreat makes good sense until preparations can be made to face the enemy on one's own terms. Further, Caesar has been made aware of the repercussions future warfare will have on his people; therefore, he engages in a "battle of wits" with Kolp and comes out the winner, with little bloodshed on either side.[46] "No killing" is the command Caesar gives as the humans are rounded up and taken prisoner. Ape law will not deny these people their rights, so long as they maintain their civility. It is not unusual that Caesar lets some mutants escape, including Kolp. By allowing them to save face, the expectation is that potential reprisals can be avoided, and peace will be considered the only viable option for all parties concerned.

Unfortunately, General Aldo has a different vision of what this brave, new world should look like. There is no room for diseased mutations, especially of the human kind, in his ape order. And so Aldo ruthlessly slays all the fleeing mutants, changing the future presumably for the worse since any remaining underdwellers will begin to cultivate the seeds of hatred for the simian species. Having tasted the blood of the kill, Aldo and his troops return to Ape City and are about to execute the humans under their care when Caesar halts the proceedings. The chimp leader has just learned from Virgil and MacDonald that Aldo was responsible for the death of his boy. The fundamental commandment, "Ape shall not kill ape," let alone an innocent ape child, has been violated for the first time in their recorded history. Caesar must deal with the perpetrator who has sinned before the community which he has helped organize totally collapses.

One would think that Caesar would treat the situation in a rational, objective fashion. Instead, he impulsively reacts, letting his shadow emotions get the better of him. All he can see is the frail body of his son smashed by the maniacal Aldo, and his blood starts to boil with vengeance. Caesar approaches the ape killer, weaponless yet armed with deadly hatred. Realizing what the crazed chimp intends to do, Aldo climbs up a tree hoping this will provide an adequate haven. However, Caesar still advances upon Aldo even in the uppermost branches until the gorilla has nowhere else to go.

The old, gnarled tree is an excellent place for the battle between the two apes. Besides the obvious interpretation that the simian species has returned to its savage roots (i.e., monkeys swinging in the branches), the tree itself represents a "life and death" symbolism. Many myths have associated the tree with paradise (such as the Garden of Eden) and the genesis of the human race. One Nordic creation story has God creating man by breathing the life-giving essence into a substance referred to as *tre* (or wood). In another legend, a new breed of humans emerges from the ashes of the old, wooden world.[47] Death is also linked with the tree symbol. In the Judeo-Christian myth, Adam and Eve break away from God by stealing fruit from the Tree of Life, and destroy their immortality in the process. Christ himself died on the wooden beams of the Cross, or Tree of Death. Actually, in a number of ancient burial customs, the deceased was buried in the hollowed-out trunks of trees so that they could return to the earth from which they sprang.[48] In *Battle for the Planet of the Apes*, General Aldo is destined to die at the hands of Caesar. The tree becomes the gorilla's coffin as Caesar grips with tremendous force the arm that is holding the sword against him. Pushing it aside, the chimp causes Aldo to lose his footing and fall to his death. This significant fall signifies the end of simian purity on the planet. Caesar has killed one of his cast-out brothers, resulting in a new (although bloodstained) beginning for his people. As MacDonald remarks, the apes have now been inducted into the ranks of the human race, for better *and* for worse.

The closing portion of the film leaves the audience with some expectation that the world might become a better place for all its inhabitants. Caesar frees the humans from their bondage and places them on a level equal with the apes, hoping this will offset the kernels of violence he himself has planted this day. That the chimp questions whether it was right to avenge one murder with another suggests there is hope for the simian species; perhaps they will not follow the path of the humans toward self-destruction. One is left with the feeling that some change might occur on the planet. The alternative is that no one will survive if the shadow impulses are released without some type of collective restraint.[49] The *Planet of the Apes* movies are excellent parables of the end times because they relate the perpetual struggle faced by humankind: the battle between one's conscience and the shadow. If mankind is to endure, it must try to appease both sides in new and creative ways.

NOTES

1. Edward F. Edinger, "Encounter with the Self," in *Ego and Archetype: Individuation and the Religious Function of the Psyche* (London: Penguin Books, 1972), 87.

2. Robert H. Hopcke, "Trickster," in *A Guided Tour of the Collected Works of C. G. Jung* (Boston: Shambhala, 1992), 122; Carl G. Jung, "On the Psychology of the Trickster-Figure," in *The Archetypes and the Collective Unconscious: The Collected Works*, trans. R.F.C. Hull (Princeton, NJ: Princeton University Press, 1990), 255, 264.

3. Steven H. Scheuer, *Movies on TV and Videocassette* (New York: Bantam Books, 1991), 824.

4. Pierre Boulle, *Planet of the Apes* (New York: New American Library, 1963), 23.

5. Carl G. Jung, "Archaic Man," in *Modern Man in Search of a Soul*, trans. W. S. Dell and Cary F. Baynes (San Diego, CA: Harcourt Brace Jovanovich, 1990), 126–30, 140–42.

6. Renata Adler, "Review of *Planet of the Apes*," *New York Times*, 9 February 1968, 55: 2.

7. Frieda Fordham, *An Introduction to Jung's Psychology* (London: Penguin Books, 1966), 49.

8. Boulle, *Planet of the Apes*, 74.

9. Carl G. Jung, "The Fight with the Shadow," in *Civilization in Transition:*

The Collected Works, trans. R.F.C. Hull (Princeton, NJ: Princeton University Press, 1990), 219–20.

10. Carl G. Jung, "The Relations Between the Ego and the Unconscious. Part One: The Effects of the Unconscious upon Consciousness," in *The Basic Writings of C. G. Jung*, trans. R.F.C. Hull (Princeton, NJ: Princeton University Press, 1990), 123–25.

11. Jung, "Archetypes of the Collective Unconscious," in *The Archetypes and the Collective Unconscious*, 21.

12. Jung, "On the Nature of the Psyche," in *Basic Writings*, 93–95.

13. A. H. Weiler, "Review of *Beneath the Planet of the Apes*," *New York Times*, 29 May 1970, 16: 1.

14. David Gerrold, *Battle for the Planet of the Apes* (New York: Award Books, 1973), 53.

15. Ibid., 142–43.

16. Jung, "The Spiritual Problem of Modern Man," in *Modern Man in Search of a Soul*, 199–209.

17. Jung, "Psychotherapists or the Clergy," in *Modern Man in Search of a Soul*, 231–35, 238–39.

18. Jung, "Wotan," in *Civilization in Transition*, 181–84.

19. Ibid., 185–86, 189–90.

20. Carl G. Jung, "Confrontation with the Unconscious," in *Memories, Dreams, Reflections*, ed. Aniela Jaffe, trans. Richard Winston and Clara Winston (New York: Vintage, 1989), 190–92.

21. Jung, "The Spiritual Problem of Modern Man," in *Modern Man in Search of a Soul*, 220.

22. Jung, "Wotan," in *Civilization in Transition*, 186.

23. Weiler, "Review of *Beneath the Planet of the Apes*," 16: 1.

24. Jung, "Epilogue to 'Essays on Contemporary Events,' " in *Civilization in Transition*, 242–43.

25. Boulle, *Planet of the Apes*, 125–28.

26. Roger Greenspun, "Review of *Escape from the Planet of the Apes*," *New York Times*, 29 May 1971, 10: 1.

27. Jung, "The Phenomenology of the Spirit in Fairytales," in *The Archetypes and the Collective Unconscious*, 226–27.

28. Jung, "The Psychology of the Child Archetype," in *The Archetypes and the Collective Unconscious*, 158.

29. Boulle, *Planet of the Apes*, 119.

30. Greenspun, "Review of *Escape from the Planet of the Apes*," 10: 1.

31. Carol S. Pearson, *Awakening the Heroes Within: Twelve Archetypes to Help Us Find Ourselves and Transform Our World* (San Francisco: HarperCollins, 1991), 206–7.

32. Gerrold, *Battle for the Planet of the Apes*, 7.

33. Jung, "After the Catastrophe," in *Civilization in Transition*, 206–8.

34. Howard Thompson, "Review of *Conquest of the Planet of the Apes*," *New York Times*, 30 June 1972, 24: 1.

35. Jung, "After the Catastrophe," in *Civilization in Transition*, 215.

36. Carl G. Jung, "The Sacrifice," in *Symbols of Transformation: The Collected*

Works, trans. R.F.C. Hull (Princeton, NJ: Princeton University Press, 1990), 433–35.

37. Jung, "The Dual Mother," in *Symbols of Transformation*, 367–68.

38. Jung, "Epilogue to 'Essays on Contemporary Events,' " in *Civilization in Transition*, 78–79.

39. Jung, "After the Catastrophe," in *Civilization in Transition*, 215–17.

40. Vincent Canby, "Review of *Battle for the Planet of the Apes*," *New York Times*, 13 July 1973, 19: 1.

41. Gerrold, *Battle for the Planet of the Apes*, 50.

42. Carol S. Pearson, *The Hero Within: Six Archetypes We Live By* (San Francisco: HarperCollins, 1989), 83–84.

43. Jung, "The Dual Mother," in *Symbols of Transformation*, 346–47, 365–67.

44. Carl G. Jung, "The Structure and Dynamics of the Self," in *Aion: Researches into the Phenomenology of the Self: The Collected Works*, trans. R.F.C. Hull (Princeton, NJ: Princeton University Press, 1990), 234, 244–45.

45. Gerrold, *Battle for the Planet of the Apes*, 126–29.

46. Pearson, *Awakening the Heroes Within*, 102, 104.

47. Jung, "Symbols of the Mother and of Rebirth," in *Symbols of Transformation*, 246.

48. Ibid., 233; Carl G. Jung, "Religious Ideas in Alchemy: Alchemical Symbolism in the History of Religion," in *Psychology and Alchemy: The Collected Works*, trans. R.F.C. Hull (Princeton, NJ: Princeton University Press, 1991), 460.

49. Canby, "Review of *Battle for the Planet of the Apes*," 19: 1.

4

From *Logan's Run* to *Battlestar: Galactica*: Archetypal Rebellions Against Shadow Destroyers

One of the Jungian hero's greatest adversaries is the shadow devourer (or destroyer), a monstrous abomination that lives underground or underwater. It is such a powerful entity that it consumes the hero entirely in its massive jaws. The major deed which the hero must undertake is to kill the beast from within and then escape unscathed. This sometimes involves severing one of the destroyer's vital organs or, more likely, starting a blazing fire in the creature's belly. The end result is that the hero frees himself from the "maternal womb" of death and experiences a rebirth of life as he ascends into the light of a new day to resume his battles, refreshed and invigorated.[1]

Shadow destroyers need not be restricted to types of mutated animals. They can be powerful humans (see Wotan in chapter 3) or even collective organizations that rob the individual members of their humanness in the quest to achieve the "ultimate good for the many." Two science-fiction movies have presented fairly interesting depictions of the latter kind of shadow destroyer. Both *Logan's Run* (1976) and *Battlestar: Galactica* (1978) show the viewer what technology can unleash when it is supported by the very constituents it is designated to enslave in the long run. Some of the more notable moments from each television series that the movies spawned will be investigated in an attempt to further understand the struggles of the lone hero against seemingly impossible odds (i.e., a society or species mobilized in full force to crush any and all signs of resistance).

LOGAN'S RUN: THE MOVIE—A FLIGHT FROM CLAIMED RENEWAL TO AUTHENTIC REBIRTH

In A.D. 2274 the world has survived the Great War and has established great, domed cities which maintain the proper atmosphere for the survivors. Computers run each of the cities and provide for every human want, ranging from physical sustenance to carnal gratification. But, there is something immediately foreboding about this perfect future. Citizens who reach their "Lastday" must engage in a ritual called Carousel, in which their present bodies are supposedly transformed into younger ones so that the cycle of life can repeat itself. Based on the book, *Logan's Run*, written by William F. Nolan and George Clayton Johnson, the film maintains the general premise of a society dedicated to renewing itself as soon as the members reach the age of thirty. In actuality, however, there is no reincarnation. The people have been deluded into thinking that their lives go on when, in fact, they are killed so that the computers can preserve the city's ecological balance.[2] Death is the only certainty that awaits humanity, and most of the populace never realize that the shadow destroyer is their very own machines upon which they have become dependent.

The Carousel ritual requires some additional discussion at this point. Similar to many rebirth ceremonies, all the members are actively involved. Those at the terminal age are sent soaring into the air where they are bathed by the light of a giant, glowing crystal which destroys their old bodies. The remaining people not only watch the proceedings, but also yell out words of encouragement to the "transformees." Their participation in this religious event is extremely important for it provides hope that an immortality will be eventually achieved by the initiates.[3] Although it is a false hope, it is necessary to have all the members channeled into the same activity if the rite is to be considered a highly meaningful and sacred one. The spatial layout of the Carousel is also interesting to consider from an archetypal perspective. Those designated to be reborn stand in a circle facing each other. Their platform becomes a rotating merry-go-round (hence the name, "carousel") which moves them at steadily growing speeds sufficient enough finally to catapult them into space. The circular orientation continues to be followed as the initiates' bodies float in steadily contracting arcs above the congregation before the termination point arrives. Now the Jungian mandala (or "circle") is regarded as the center of one's personality, the innermost point within the psyche by which everything is arranged. The energy emitted by this central point compels the person to become what he or she is destined to be, complete and whole.[4] Carousel is assumed to offer a guarantee of mandelic fulfillment by employing the typical motifs associated with perfection and immortality. Is it any wonder, then, that the majority of people are duped into believing that reincarnation is a viable reality, given the thought and care that have gone into each part of the carnival-style ritual.

Returning to the plot of *Logan's Run*, there exists an organized resistance group of Runners who are opposed to these state executions. They would rather take their chances at living beyond the age of thirty than ending it when the crystals in their palms blink a deadly red. A police force of individuals named Sandmen (or to use an earlier label coined by Nolan and Johnson, Deep Sleep men[5]) have but one important function: to track the Runners down by using the crystals as a homing mechanism and then to terminate them. The Sandmen do not regard their actions as destructive (i.e., they do not kill Runners); instead, they are "putting to sleep" a dissident faction that threatens the natural order of things. Because they are able to rationalize their shadow impulses, Sandmen rarely experience pangs of guilt or regret over what they are doing. One might say they are perfect extensions of the computer destroyers—living robots who are following the orders of their mechanized masters.

Into this world comes Sandman Logan-5 (actor Michael York) who is not like the others. He openly expresses his doubts about Carousel as well as the murders he has committed in the name of justice. Sandman partner Francis-7 (Richard Jordan) cannot convince Logan that the route he is pursuing is a pointless one, especially when his friend makes the most difficult choice to confront his "terrible and [oh!] so dangerous" shadow side.[6] Everything comes to a head when Logan picks up an ankh-shaped key from a Runner he has just terminated. When he displays his possessions to the master computers at the end of his shift, Logan is detained and subsequently queried about the object. His lack of knowledge concerning the ankh's significance is swiftly corrected when the machines provide some secret information about the Runner organization. Evidently, Runners have been using these ankhs for some time to escape into the outside world. It is up to Logan-5 to find the place where the Runners have assembled and destroy their Sanctuary so that future flights can be prevented.

All this comes as a shock to Logan. He has always believed that no Runner could avoid the Sandmen, let alone survive in the radioactive wasteland beyond the protective atmosphere of the domes. Furthermore, Logan feels that he is not able to infiltrate the resistance group as his Sandman identity will surely expose him. The computers, however, have been programmed to think of every eventuality; they have advanced the date on Logan's crystal to Lastday status so that he will be regarded as a Runner by Sandman and rebel alike.[7] Unlike the movie, the original story has the terminal Logan gladly embracing the assignment of locating Sanctuary in order to justify his already fading existence. "What if he could find it [Sanctuary] and destroy it in the last twenty-four hours of his life? [Why,] he would be a world hero; his life would end in glory. It would be a risk worth taking."[8] The *Logan's Run* screenplay is definitely the superior version since it presents the Jungian hero as one continually struggling to discover his own emerging identity which is separate from the collective one imposed by the mechanical destroyers. All his life the movie-Logan has been taught to accept what the computers have told him. Now he has to give his assent to the new classification of Runner, and internally, he begins to rebel against the machines because they have taken away precious years of his life and have lied to him: about outside, Lastday, everything. A "dawning of conscious awareness" as to what reality truly is characterizes Logan-5 and initiates him into an authentic (and heroic) rebirth,[9] in contrast to the printed prototype who wishes to remain a part of the system as much as possible.

On his quest to the mythical Sanctuary, Logan meets the beautiful Jessica-6 (Jenny Agutter), a fellow Runner who at first questions the validity of the Sandman's story. But when Logan saves the life of a woman who has reached the age of thirty, Jessica is converted and becomes his traveling companion. Francis-7, on the other hand, wants more than anything else to save his former partner from following the path to self-destruction. In keeping with his Sandman profession, Francis terminates the woman who has escaped Logan's clutches and then follows the pair to the underground headquarters of the Runners which he intends to eradicate once and for all, thus freeing Logan from the terrible hold that the dissidents obviously have over him. Calling in a backup force of Sandmen, he waits for just the right opportunity to spring his trap. Needless to say, Francis's plan backfires, and Logan and Jessica escape through some interconnecting tunnels, using their ankhs as keys to gain access to these restricted areas.

Francis-7 is an interesting, albeit somewhat two-dimensional, character for he represents the negative type of Jungian ego. As the "gatekeeper" for the total field of consciousness, the ego decides what is (and is not) admitted to awareness.[10] Rather than exploring the reasons why Logan is running, Francis would prefer to maintain the status quo and do what he has always done well: putting Runners to sleep with no reservations. His ego is selective to the point of being injurious; Logan has provided him with a wealth of psychic material to ruminate upon, yet little reaches the point of full consciousness whereby Francis's perceptions can be potentially challenged. He remains the perfect soldier of the shadow destroyers, unthinking and obedient. In this contest of the egos, Francis clearly comes out the loser and Logan the winner.

While avoiding Francis at all costs, Logan and Jessica come to the city's major reservoir and swim through the waters until they reach a concealed chamber directly above them. The pair of Runners not only need to acclimatize themselves to the brutal, subzero temperatures contained therein, but also have to face the strange denizen of this environment, Box (Roscoe Lee Brown). The box-shaped creature is an advanced type of android that claims superiority to man as well as machine. It has been "living" for the expressed purpose of keeping a continual food supply handy for its masters (who have long since perished). As the fish and plankton from the waters became less plentiful, Box had to adopt a new programming routine. In this case, it began to freeze a fresh "meat source" which entered its domain: namely, any Runner who attempted to penetrate the city's seals. Row upon row of humans suspended in a cryogenic state is the horrifying spectacle which Box proudly displays to a stunned Logan and Jessica, who wonder whether Sanctuary exists at all. Could anything have survived this frozen fate orchestrated by the maniacal Box?

The question remains unanswered since the android immediately advances upon the two, with freeze-gun aimed and ready to process the new food sources. Logan has no choice but to use his Deep Sleep pistol on Box. After immobilizing the threat, he points his weapon at the ceiling and fires, bringing huge chunks of ice down everywhere. Feeling confident that Box will never rise again, Logan escorts Jessica out of the crumbling chamber to the perimeter of the domes. The Nolan and Johnson novel indicates that because Box was half machine, it was very much like the other computers running the city. The same circuits were present in Box, and so "it was an integral part of the great Thinker's brain . . . sharing its great wisdom via ten billion, billion [mechanical] neurons."[11] What a pity that such devices invented by human hands could turn on their creators and destroy them, once they acquired the power to rationalize away one of the most meaningful of life's experiences, death. The viewer is left to ponder whether the Sanctuary Logan-5 and Jessica-6 are looking for is nothing more than a common belief held by a group of people who are desperately fighting a losing war against a lethal machine order for the right of self-survival.

One of the most symbolic parts of *Logan's Run* is the scene in which the two Runners break through the domes and enter the outside world. They immediately feel the sun's rays upon their faces and are blinded by the brilliance of the fiery star. It is an exhilarating event for the pair; they have finally freed themselves from the ever vigilant gaze of the shadow destroyers and are able to bask in their newfound independence. According to Jung, heroes are part of a solar myth which basically involves a death-rebirth process, not unlike the setting and subsequent rising of the sun.[12] Logan and Jessica have come out of Box's underworld of death and destruction intact. Both have also exited their "hellish" society and have survived well past their Lastday. The crystals on the palms of their hands have turned a colorless hue, meaning that the old ways no longer operate in this more natural environment. In a mythical sense, the Runners have been born all over again; they must form a new identity and eke out an existence on their own, without the aid of computers or other mechanical life-support systems. Unfortunately, Francis-7 has also found his way to the outside and continues to track our heroes. So intent is he on terminating Logan and Jessica that he hardly notices his changed surroundings. The potential for

Francis to be reborn into a more cognizant state is there, but the Sandman chooses to remain an enforcer of the computer order and, for that reason, denies himself the possibility of growth and self-actualization.

As the days ensue, Logan and Jessica make their way through the shambles of Washington D.C., and, after a lengthy trek, decide to rest in the Old Capitol building. While searching their surroundings, they discover an eccentric old man (played by actor Peter Ustinov) who has been living there with his hundreds of cats. The ancient one shares a number of characteristics with the archetypal sage. First, he is a solitary figure like so many others, leading a hermit-type of existence.[13] Second, Ustinov's strange mannerisms and quirky behavior patterns reflect a high degree of wisdom and insight into mankind's past. He is able to provide the two Runners with a highly detailed picture as to just what life was like before the Great War transpired. People knew who their parents were, lived with them a number of years before developing their own monogamous relationships, and finally engaged in burial rituals when the relatives passed on to the great afterlife. Most of this information is incomprehensible to Logan and Jessica, although both do see an advantage in forming a primary bond with one significant other for the duration of their adult lives. By his very nature, the old man quickly becomes their friend. His nonattachment to material possessions, coupled with a strong trust that things will turn out all right, makes the Ustinov character an endearing one.[14] Here is someone who can show others what true joy and happiness are, having recognized that "letting go" is more important than "fitting in."[15]

Before Logan and Jessica can profit further from the wise one's teachings, Francis intrudes upon the tranquil scene and battles Logan to the death. It is a sad day for Logan when he has to kill (not "terminate") his longtime friend and bury his body in the ground, chiefly because he was unable to convince Francis that the rules within the domed city oppressed rather than enlightened, destroyed life instead of extended it. So convinced is Logan in his new beliefs that he invites the old man to accompany them back to the domes as living proof that a better world does exist for all his people. In a Jungian sense, the ancient one is a part of the hero's collective unconscious; as such, he "expresses no more than what the hero could have thought out for himself [given time and the necessary reflection]."[16] Ustinov is actually Logan's other side, the essential piece that Logan needs to give love freely, to create new generations, and to grow old without fear of death. Having the sage return with Logan and Jessica is a nice addition to the screenplay for it informs the audience that wisdom and heroics are inseparable once the proper stage of cognitive development has been successfully reached.

Upon his arrival at the city's gates, the former Sandman is captured for trying to incite an insurrection in the populace and is brought to the master computers for mind probe analysis. After Logan's memories are thoroughly scanned, the machines experience what might be likened to a massive, ep-ileptic seizure. They simply cannot accept the input they are reading, par-ticularly that a device akin to themselves (i.e., Box) is responsible for the lost number of Runners as well as the presence of unaccounted life forms outside the domes whose age extends well beyond that of Lastday. Rather than integrating this new knowledge into their circuitry for future reference, the mechanical destroyers exterminate themselves and all the various au-tomated components within the city, thus allowing the people to break free of their tyrannical hold and make a life for themselves outside the domes with Logan as the proclaimed leader.

Some critics suggest that the ending to *Logan's Run* makes little sense. Having the computers blow up just because Logan "dared to be disobe-dient" is regarded by the reviewers as completely illogical.[17] But when one considers the Jungian import of just how these shadow destroyers operate, everything falls into place. The machine order was too inflexible to ever assimilate the elements perceived by Logan into its memory banks, for it would have to admit that the entire society was structured around a false-hood that life could never survive in the outside world independent of its control. Thus, an incredibly strong resistance was built up by the destroyers to keep what was "conscious" and known out of the mechanical "uncon-scious." This inability to integrate the two spheres, no doubt, resulted in a massive release of energy from the computers' "fractured personality" core which, ultimately, proved self-damaging.[18] The moral of *Logan's Run* is that sometimes the shadow side, even of machines, has to function blindly and without conscious reflection if it wants to maintain the archetypal or-der within its realm.

LOGAN'S RUN: THE SERIES—THE REVEALED FORCE BEHIND THE SHADOW DESTROYERS

Some significant changes occurred when *Logan's Run* was adapted to the small screen as a weekly series (1977–1978), besides the fairly obvious one of having new actors playing the principal roles of Logan-5 (Gregory Harrison), Jessica-6 (Heather Menzies), and Francis-7 (Randy Powell). Per-haps the most striking modification in the television pilot was the insertion of the Council of Elders, a senior-level group of human officials who were responsible for the programming of the machines that ran the City of Domes. Francis encounters the council right before he follows Logan and Jessica to the perimeter of the domes. The spokesperson for the elders, the enigmatic Morgan (played by actor Morgan Woodward), informs the Sand-man that Carousel is a clever ploy developed by the council to control the population growth within the city. Further, Logan and Jessica need to be captured and brought back so that they can be reprogrammed and, hence, speak out in favor of renewal for the benefit of the entire community. As an inducement to Francis, Morgan offers him a seat on the council and all the power that goes with the position. Seeing this as his golden opportunity for advancement, Francis accepts the assignment and, in so doing, sells his soul to the devilish elders.

"Exactly who is the doer" behind the unspeakable actions of the shadow is the all-important question humans need to answer if they want to be honest with themselves. The *Logan's Run* series addresses the Jungian inquiry by showing that people similar to us are behind the destructive deeds. Even if the Council of Elders had the noblest of intentions in organizing a self-sufficient society, the way they accomplished the goal was at fault (i.e., by sacrificing human lives). "The right deed in the hands of the wrong man (or men) will still have a disastrous effect [for all concerned parties]."[19] By making the populace dependent on them, the council removed all responsibility from their shoulders and, as a result, became too prideful. This "collective pride" without the associated guilt inevitably transformed the elders into animals so demoralized and degenerate that nothing short of a major catastrophe could ever bring them back on the road to salvation.[20] Francis's willingness to join the group reveals how far the Sandman will go for the sake of preserving the illusion of societal perfection.

If the *Logan's Run* series depicted humans at their worst, it also presented them at some of their best moments. The hope that Sanctuary exists is what drives Logan and Jessica throughout the pilot movie and the subsequent episodes. Because they have resided in the "land of shadows" most of their lives, they have achieved an insight into what their idyllic paradise should be like. Above all else, Sanctuary should be a place where freedom to make responsible choices is encouraged, not repressed. In Jungian terms, individuation of one's ego apart from the collective organization of the state (or in this case, the City of Domes) is the greatest aspiration which any type of Sanctuary should fulfill.[21]

Since there is no Box in the television series to detain Runners, it seems likely that some have escaped to the outside and have found the mythical refuge. Although Logan and Jessica encounter pockets of human communities throughout their travels, they recognize an incompleteness to the groups and, therefore, resume the journey to the Promised Land. Having survived on their own for so long without the city's computers has fortified them, giving them some immunity to deceptive visions involving Sanctuary. For instance, in "The Collectors" episode, written by James Schmerer, aliens from outer space capture Logan and Jessica as specimens for their intergalactic zoo. To make them placid and content during the lengthy confinement, the creatures pluck out images from their brains in order to fashion the "reality" that the two have arrived at Sanctuary. Initially, both are fooled into believing their run is over; however, this world is just "too perfect to be true" and, in time, the illusion falls apart. Already conned once in the City of Domes, Logan and Jessica are not so willing to fall victim to the same subterfuge again. If anything good has come out of those shadow destructive experiences, it is that the two Runners will not be a part of any social order that satisfies their every desire at the expense of taking away their identities.

The inclusion of the android Rem (portrayed in typical *Star Trek* Commander Data style by Donald Moffat), was a definite strength of the series. Here was a cyborg that functioned more like a human than a machine. The very name Rem, which in physiological terms denotes the rapid eye movements correlated with the dream state, is an appropriate appellation for the android who continually yearns to express his inner creative processes in new ways. More than anything else, Rem wishes to leave the robot colony he has been assigned to take care of for all these decades. The only "fun" he has ever experienced has been altering the machines' facial features so that he is not bored with their looks. When Logan and Jessica make their appearance, he realizes this is his chance for freedom from a life of perpetual servitude to automatons. The two Runners are delighted to have Rem accompany them on their journey to Sanctuary, recognizing a kindred spirit behind the human mask.

In comparing the mechanical life forms, Rem is the complete antithesis of the Box android and the city's computer systems which cannot function independently of their programming. For this reason, Rem is a shadow creator, not a shadow destroyer; he values such characteristics as spontaneity, strong emotions, deep insight, vitality, and vigor. These are the ingredients that give any human personality a "full-bodied, three-dimensional quality."[22] Sadly, the elders have not attained the level that Rem has already reached because they continue to operate like the machines in their custody, mechanistically and without feeling.

Besides the pilot movie, two other episodes of the *Logan's Run* series deserve mention since they reveal some additional aspects to the shadow destroyer image. "The Judas Goat" installment, written by science-fiction veteran John Meredyth Lucas, succeeds in presenting the archetype under a very human layer of skin. Sandman Joseph-8 (Nicholas Hammond) is transformed by the city's computers into an exact look-alike of a Runner he has just recently terminated, one Hal-14. The elders explain to Joseph-8 that his new identity, combined with the cover story that the people are ready to rebel against the machines, should be sufficient enough to sway Logan and Jessica to return to the City of Domes so that they can be at the vanguard of the long-awaited revolt. Logan is taken in by Joseph's persuasive charms up until the point where two Sandmen patrolling the perimeter of the city spot the man and give chase, believing Joseph-8 to be the Runner he so much resembles. They eventually catch up with the fugitive and terminate him, not realizing they have killed one of their own unit. By hiding their programmed destroyer under an unchanging persona of innocence, the computers had inadvertently created an inflexible dichotomy of light and darkness (i.e., an identity crisis) which could not be resolved except by the destruction of Joseph's entire personality. Logan, Jessica, and Rem ponder the tragic turn of events as they leave the city, wondering about the awful consequences of never being able to integrate the shadow into one's conscious (and physical) self.[23] The inability to establish a sense of individuality would seem to be a high cost to pay for continued allegiance to the mechanical overlords.

The "Carousel" episode, composed by noted author D. C. Fontana (with the assistance of Richard L. Breen Jr.), presents an interesting twist on the Sandman-turned-Runner tale. The fugitive trio, Logan, Jessica, and Rem, encroach upon the territory of an advanced race of beings. The humanoids protect themselves against the armed Sandman by wiping away his memories of the past year with a warp drug. The confused Logan goes back to the City of Domes with Francis, hoping that he can be reinstated as a Sandman in good standing. Though skeptical of his story, the Council of Elders decides to give Logan an opportunity to redeem himself; he must testify before the assembled people at the Carousel ritual and denounce the act of running to a place which apparently does not exist (and never has existed). Only then can Logan be accepted back into the fold. However, Elder Morgan has other plans for Logan. After the Sandman's testimony is given, the computers will exterminate him to ensure that no further insurrections will occur. Once again, it would seem the elders are chiefly responsible for the injuries inflicted upon their own species, hiding behind the mechanical devices they control so that their shadow impulses need never be directly confronted.

As his memories slowly return, Logan feels compelled to embrace the martyr archetype. In typical hero mode, the former Sandman is willing to sacrifice himself in order to save others from the certain death awaiting them in Carousel. He contacts Jessica and Rem via a prerecorded video transmission left in his chambers, relating to them he will publicly speak out against the "rebirth" ceremony that very night. Though he knows the dangers that await him, Logan is willing to take the risk. Like any other warrior-converted-to-martyr, Logan does not want to pass on the suffering to future generations of his people. Instead, he wants to absorb it into himself and declare "the pain stops here, with me."[24] One never knows whether Logan's "transformative sacrifice" would have succeeded because Jessica and Rem extricate him from the city before that given moment transpires. Possibly the series would have benefited if the Sandman had been given a noble martyr's death; certainly the community would have been in a better position to seek out the real enemy (i.e., the Council of Elders) and overthrow it, if for no other reason than to make Logan's sacrifice a meaningful one. As fate would have it, Logan's Run was canceled before this archetypal issue could be effectively resolved.

BATTLESTAR: GALACTICA: AN INTERGALACTIC FLIGHT AWAY FROM THE CYLON DESTROYERS

Although overt comparisons have been made between *Battlestar: Galactica* and *Star Wars*, [25] both of which came out at approximately the same time, the former movie has more elements in common with *Logan's Run* than the George Lucas space adventure. The Galactican heroes have to do battle with another type of mechanical destroyer, the Cylons, if they want to survive. Flight appears to be the only logical alternative for the resisters as the Cylons' power proves too great to endure. This time the run is across the stars to a brave new Sanctuary, the planet Earth, where it is hoped the people there can help the Galacticans fend off the menace. The dream of a perfect world in which humans can exist harmoniously and actualize their potential to the fullest without impediment is as much a part of the *Galactica* vision as it is of *Logan's Run*. Let us now examine the pilot film and some *Galactica* television episodes in more archetypal depth.

The original *Battlestar: Galactica* 1978 feature aired as a made-for-television movie, and it was later released theatrically to international audiences after the series was put on a one-year hiatus (to return eventually as the renamed *Galactica 1980*). The premiere episode starts the interstellar journey off at a pleasing pace, accompanied by an abundance of eye-catching special effects. The story premise is a simple one, but laden with Jungian symbolism. After a thousand yarns (which is the equivalent of Earth years), the warmongering Cylons have offered the hand of peace to the twelve colonies of mankind. An armistice has been arranged in space where the Quorum of the Twelve Colonies awaits the presence of the alien creatures aboard their giant fighting ships, the battlestars. Most of the quorum, including President Adar (Lew Ayres), have placed their faith in the Cylons' human liaison, Count Baltar (John Colicos), who has seen that the conditions of the peace treaty are favorable to both sides. But Commander Adama (played by series regular Lorne Greene) has grave misgivings, believing the Cylons still hate the humans "with every fiber of their existence" and will never embrace such human concepts as freedom and independence, even if they agree to the cease-fire.[26] He especially does not trust Count Baltar who seems *too* willing to have all the colonies' representatives at one particular (and very vulnerable) location out in space.

Adama's fears are confirmed when his two sons, Apollo (Richard Hatch) and Zac (Rick Springfield), report from their Viper craft that a mass of Cylon fighters are grouping along the fringes of their solar system. Not expecting enemy retaliation, all the battlestars save the *Galactica* are destroyed by the Cylon craft, along with their homeworlds. Adama himself suffers two personal losses, the death of Zac and his wife who resided on the planet of Caprica. Amidst the grief, the commander tells the few survivors "to set sail in every assorted vehicle that will carry them" into space where, hopefully, the *Galactica* will protect them from future attacks by the Cylons.

At this point in the story, it seems appropriate to delve into the Cylon psyche to understand better the intentions of this shadow destroyer. Once a reptile race, the Cylons advanced considerably until their technology made it possible to integrate mechanical parts with living flesh. Eventually, the Cylons rid themselves of their reptilian nature and became unthinking automatons, controlled by their governing head, the Imperious Leader (with the British actor Patrick Macnee supplying the menacing voice). Unlike the Cylon warriors (or Centurions) under him, the Imperious Leader possesses an additional brain which allows him access to a vast storehouse of knowledge extending back to the very beginnings of the Cylon culture. The organ also enables the Imperious Leader to monitor all of his troop's movements and implant commands directly into each of the Centurion's helmets so that language is unnecessary. The most important directive embedded in the leader's second brain is to preserve the natural order in the universe. Humans threaten that very balance: "their adventuresome ways, their tendency toward independent thought and action . . . could disturb the inhabitants of countless worlds whom the Cylons visit."[27] Based on this "machine logic," the surviving humans have to be eliminated so that the Cylons can remain the sole guardians of universal order.

Although the Imperious Leader does not regard his actions as strictly evil or good, just essential to the maintenance of the Cylon empire, Jung confesses any "collective psyche" has the power to crush its members to the point where all freedom and morality are removed from their individual natures. The Cylons can be likened to a herd of sheep, waiting for a shepherd (in this case, an Imperious Leader) to drive them into greener pastures. What oftentimes happens is that the shepherd seizes too much power and becomes a wolf, ironically preying on his own herd and destroying the very group he was assigned to protect.[28] The Imperious Leader would not hesitate to send Cylon warriors on kamikaze missions if it meant the eradication of all humans or the preservation of his own life. One must remember that in the War with the Colonies, many Cylon fighters did not have enough fuel to return to their base ships, and so they were sacrificed for the greater glory of the Cylon empire. Even the treasonous Count Baltar, who led his race to ruin, is beheaded once his usefulness to the Imperious leader is over (though John Colicos is revived by a new leader in the hour-long series). As long as one dominion prevails in the Cylon order, there is the inherent risk that all the subjects will be dispatched swiftly when they have outlived their service. This is the Jungian danger of any society that emphasizes reliance on the one instead of the many which compose it.

At first, Commander Adama does not want to take on the responsibility of nurturing a ragtag fleet of 220 ships out in deep space. He has seen far too many deaths and has experienced instances of man's inhumanity to his fellow man. He tells his daughter Athena (Maren Jensen) how he had to leave behind some survivors who could not fit into the cramped confines of the escape vessels, and how they clawed at him (and each other) in an effort to get on board. The troubles hardly end for Adama once the ships are assembled. Those with political power have hoarded huge stores of food for themselves and need to be forced at gunpoint to give up their most prized possessions. Based on these incidents, the commander does not think he is capable of assuming the awesome burden of leadership. Unlike Logan-5, Adama wants to curl up into a ball and suffer his own losses without having to worry about someone else's, let alone an entire community's. Continually giving to others without receiving anything back is more of a curse for Adama than a blessing. It is only the steadfast convictions of his son and daughter in his command abilities that finally make it possible for Adama to move out of Carol Pearson's (1991) suffering martyr role into the healthier ruler mode.[29] With his children's support, the commander is able to develop a vision of what he wants for his people, and he seeks a way in which to make this vision a reality.

The plan Adama has in mind is to search for a sister colony of humanity in a galaxy far, far away. The historical records refer to a thirteenth tribe from which the other twelve sprang. Adama intends to find that original colony on a planet called Earth and enlist the support of the people there against the Cylon foe. While most of the Galacticans embrace the commander's decision, some believe it to be a pointless religious quest. Nevertheless, after hearing from both sides, Adama remains committed to pursuing this goal. He realizes that if the Cylons should attack them now, they would be completely powerless against the superior force. Searching for the thirteenth world will at least give the Galacticans some hope that their condition could improve someday. By his actions, Adama is no longer afraid to claim the power of leadership. He wants to take charge of his life and dedicate himself to the greater social good,[30] instead of foolishly giving away his power to the newly elected Council of the Twelve who will not only seal his fate, but that of his people as well with its talk of peace and love toward the spurned Cylons.

Commander Adama's democratic style of leadership is in striking contrast to the Cylon leader's. The Cylon leader does not consult his troops on any command decision nor does he provide a sound rationale about why he must pursue this already weakened race (of humans) to the ends of the known universe, only that he must. Possibly the machine leader has been dealing with humans for so long that he has accepted into his programming many of their negative characteristics, such as the desire to hate anything different from oneself as well as the lust of battling an enemy to the death. Whatever the reason for the relentless hunting of the humans, this destroyer is entirely tyrannical in the exercising of his authority over the Centurions. His troops must locate and obliterate the *Battlestar Gal-actica* above all else, or answer directly to him. By giving in to his "Wo-tanish" obsessions, the Imperious Leader is allowing his shadow power to control him to the point where the force of the dark side will possess his "machine soul" and inevitably shatter it,[31] unlike Commander Adama who dispenses his power in a more healthy and constructive fashion (i.e., for the benefit of the entire society).

Before embarking on their long journey to Earth, the majority of the Galacticans decide to refuel their ships and obtain sufficient supplies at the planet Carillon. Adama is not very pleased at the prospect of being so dangerously close to Cylon territory, but he concedes to the will of the people as any effective ruler would. The Galacticans soon encounter the Ovions, an insectoid species which has resided under the surface of Carillon for hundreds of yarns. The mysterious life forms extend an invitation to the entire fleet to come visit their casino and partake of the amusements therein (though why the Ovions would have need of such a facility poses an interesting question to the most discerning viewers). When reports come back to the *Galactica* that people have missed their shifts or have never returned from their shore leaves, Adama suspects a Cylon trap and prepares himself for another encounter with the dreaded opponent. The wait is not long in coming.

Adama's son, Apollo, and his Viper pilot sidekick, Starbuck (Dirk Ben-edict), discover that the Ovions have been using the missing humans as a source of food for their recently hatched young. What's more, the Cylons have already landed on Carillon and are lingering in the Ovions' under-ground chambers until enough Galactican officers attend the festivities; they will then emerge from their hiding place and cripple the unmanned bat-tlestar with remarkable ease. By the time the Cylons expose themselves, Adama has put together a strike force of his most experienced officers which is able to terminate the machines, both on the planet and out in space. The Imperious Leader has not calculated the probability that Adama could be just as cunning and deceitful as himself. Having experienced the trickery of the Cylons at the supposed peace conference has given the Gal-actican leader the "street smarts" to perceive the true intentions of the machine race. He has kept the Viper pilots on board the *Galactica* and has sent in their place as many civilians as possible attired in the appropriate (though ill-fitting) warrior's garb. By counting the numerous costumes, the Cylons are fooled into thinking that the battlestar is defenseless, and this mistake costs them their lives as well as the Imperious Leader's.

Commander Adama has found an advantage to integrating archetypal elements of the trickster-fool and hero into his nature. It takes more than bravery and strong convictions to defeat a superior menace. It also requires a particular type of cleverness and unconventional behavior which only the Jungian trickster mentality can provide in order to overcome obstacles such as those the Cylons will continue to erect.[32] As the pilot movie closes, we are left with the feeling that the Galacticans will survive and perhaps even find Earth, so long as Adama cultivates in the people the belief *and* hope that "his little ragtag fleet can do the seemingly impossible as they flee from the Cylon tyranny."[33]

The critically acclaimed "War of the Gods" television episode, written by *Galactica* series creator Glen A. Larson, shows viewers that there are even worse (and more terrible to behold) shadow destroyers than the Cylons. After receiving a distress signal from an unchartered solar system, the Galacticans discover the wreckage of an immense spaceship on a supposedly lifeless world. The sole survivor is Count Iblis (portrayed this time in the flesh by Patrick Macnee), a humanoid who possesses a regal bearing, "all the more accentuated by his [flowing] robes of velvety white and high collar."[34] While Iblis admits he does not know how he came through the crash unscathed, he is very evasive about "the great powers" that destroyed his people's vessel. All Iblis is looking for is a place to rest; he hopes the battlestar can provide him sanctuary and, once recuperated, he would like to accompany the Galacticans on their quest to Earth. The mysterious stranger is immediately accepted by many in the fleet, including Viper pilot Sheba (Anne Lockhart), who finds his charms and winning smile irresistible.

But there is a dark side to this gentlemanly figure. Not long after he boards the battlestar, Iblis makes his intentions known to Commander Adama and his crew. Having been to Earth himself, he promises to lead the people to that treasured thirteenth colony. All he simply asks in return is their undying allegiance to him. Though Adama is wary about blindly accepting the promises of the count, the Council of Twelve requires little convincing, especially when Iblis delivers the human agent responsible for the holocaust (i.e., Baltar) into its hands for a fitting trial and sentencing. The council will even go so far as to elect Iblis to the presidency of its body so that the journey to Earth can proceed without delay.

The character of the count correlates very strongly with the magician archetype. Here we have a "kindly old man" who exercises his telekinetic powers and superior wisdom for the benefit of the community. Yet, there is a wicked aspect to this creature; he is a "death dealer" who wants to absorb the very souls of the Galacticans in exchange for fulfilling their most important desire of finding Earth.[35] A good way of describing the magical Iblis is that he is a "negative [though still powerful] father-figure" who will lead the space family which has adopted him to its doom.[36] Consistent with this interpretation, Sheba becomes his most obedient servant because she has recently lost her own parent in a Cylon battle and so comes to rely upon Count Iblis as the much needed substitute father. Only the perceptive Adama can see what beats under the magician's flowing robes of pure white: an evil-infested organ more alien to the human species than any

Cylon mechanical part. At least the commander is able to stop the council from transferring its power to Iblis until the origins of the "man" are more fully disclosed.

Perhaps the most interesting piece of dialogue occurs between the count and the imprisoned Baltar. Baltar immediately recognizes Iblis's voice, having heard it many times before. It belongs to the one he has allied himself with and from whom he takes his orders, namely the Imperious Leader. Iblis is delighted his "old friend" has identified him, indicating that he has existed for at least one thousand yarns, which approximates the point in time when the Cylons evolved from a reptile species to machine race. His most salient characteristics were transcribed into the first leader's programming, and one can infer that Iblis might have been responsible for the emergence of the Cylon "collective intelligence." Baltar is convinced the count represents a higher life form than man and so pledges his allegiance to Iblis, partly in fear that the alien who stands before him will take out his wrath on any dissenter.

With this episode, writer Glen Larson finally gave his audience an explanation for why the Cylons advanced the way they did. More important, the archetypal implications of their development should not be ignored. An agent more sophisticated than the mechanical destroyers was their "prime mover." But like any god-image, this creative force has an ambivalent nature: a satanic, destructive side to complement the life-sustaining essence.[37] Iblis, who possesses that dual personality, has implanted part of himself in the Cylon machines. Thanks to the count's influence, the mechanisms have attained the power of *creating* an orderly universe at the expense of *destroying* any other civilizations that desire the freedom to develop the way they choose.

Unlike Baltar and the Council of Twelve, not everyone is convinced that their destiny lies with Iblis. Upon his father's advice, Apollo returns to the planet on which the count was found, along with warrior companions Starbuck and Sheba. There they sift through the wreckage of the downed spaceship and remove a body which resembles the mythical version of the devil: "the fingers ended in talons and there were horns upon its head, sprouting from just above the eyes. . . . The thing [also] had hooves and a long, prehensile tail."[38] Apollo is at last able to piece together the missing elements to Iblis's story. The beasts aboard the craft were not only followers of the mysterious stranger but also members of his own race who had met their demise at his hands. Count Iblis represents the archetypal Mephistopheles (or the ancient name which Apollo uses: Diabolis), that malevolent aspect which at one time was united with the psychical powers of light and goodness, but has since broken away from the mandelic whole in search of new disciples to control and use for personal gain.[39]

Because of his egotistical nature, the count has not anticipated just how clever the humans are in discovering his identity or the ability of the superior, glowing entities he shares kinsmanship with to track him down and demand retribution for his crimes. Although Iblis manages to escape the encounter intact, the "angelic beings" inform the Viper pilots that they will continue to monitor his movements. These universal guardians, however, are not in a position to destroy the count. He is (or was) one of them, and he must be allowed to choose freely his own destiny as the Galacticans are encouraged to do. Perhaps one day the humans will evolve into a species like themselves, after they have seeded new worlds and grown in wisdom. As Apollo, Starbuck, and Sheba head back to the battlestar, they realize that the "war of the gods" will always be waged within their souls. And while the shadow side cannot be eliminated, as the devil cannot be removed from the Jungian version of the Trinity,[40] it can at least be turned toward more creative endeavors and pursuits. This is the message of universal hope that *Battlestar: Galactica* offers, which can effectively counter any destructive force in the galaxy (including that of the Cylons).

The guardians of light return in another episode, "Experiment in Terra," to inform the Galacticans that their journey will not be over for quite some time.[41] It takes at least another generation before the humans arrive at their destination point, except it is an Earth far different from the one they had expected. The Terran time period is 1980, and although the planet has technologically shown some progress, it is hardly sufficient to combat the forces of the Cylon empire. Thus, the Galacticans have to make contact with the scientists and other learned people in the various communities to help them develop to a point where they can defend themselves against the alien menace and provide the required sanctuary for the war-weary, space travelers.[42]

Two of the *Galactica 1980* entries are worth noting as they shed further light on the Cylons' destructive disposition. In "The Night the Cylons Landed," the robots have to make a forced descent to Earth after one of their ships is disabled in a space battle with the humans. The surviving Centurions attempt to signal the Cylon fleet, using one of the primitive Terran radio stations to transmit their distress call. Although their plans are thwarted by two rather spunky Viper pilots, Captain Troy (Kent McCord) and Lieutenant Dillon (Barry Van Dyke), this episode is a significant one because it shows that the Cylons are able to create androids that cannot be differentiated from Earth's inhabitants. The dangers are all too clear for the Galactican people. If the enemy cannot be discriminated from the potential ally, then any number of subterfuges can be sprung upon them. The result could be the annihilation of the entire space fleet at the hands of the human-like deceivers. In a Jungian sense, by taking on our appearance, the Cylon machines have transformed themselves into carbon copies of ourselves—both in body and soul. What this signifies is that their shadow side has become more like our own, with all the inherent capacities for every conceivable criminal behavior (i.e., murder, rape, child molestation, robbery, and even self-mutilation).[43] It would seem that the Cylons have advanced, or regressed depending on one's point of view, to the human level of destruction where they can become so totally dominated by this evil force that they may not want to ever stop their harmful actions, even when order is restored to the cosmos.

Likewise, in "The Return of Starbuck," Dirk Benedict reprises his character and finds that he too is powerless to prevent the destructive urge from taking over when he is marooned on a planet devoid of all life forms. Upon his discovery of a damaged Cylon craft, he immediately formulates a plan to bring one of the Centurions back to artificial life, realizing that in so doing he might be dooming himself to extinction. Perhaps Lieutenant Starbuck understands that, without an enemy to combat, his role as a warrior becomes unnecessary. Waging war on evil and all its manifestations is the method of problem solving in which all warriors (including Starbuck) have been trained; it becomes their religion, their way of life, their very identity, and they will risk anything to maintain this type of existence.[44] It is hardly surprising, then, that the Galactican warrior pours the shadow part of his soul into the task of reviving the Cylon. As soon as the robot is reactivated by the fuel cells in Starbuck's Viper, it advances upon the human and tries to fulfill its programming by exterminating him. But the lieutenant is ready and shuts off the Cylon's life-sustaining power with a special control unit he has made. By conditioning the Centurion to respond nonthreateningly when the unit's "power on" button is depressed, Starbuck is able to curb the violent tendencies of the mechanism, at least in his presence.

The two rapidly form a "friendship" of sorts, now that they are removed from their respective cultures. Working together, the warriors use parts of their ships to fashion makeshift quarters for themselves, allowing their bond to be further strengthened by such imposed proximity. With the passage of time, Starbuck develops feelings of affection for Cy, the nickname he has given the inquisitive Centurion, who wants to learn all it can about the former "enemy." Apparently, the destroyer archetype has been rechanneled into a more positive outlet for both human and Cylon. As Pearson (1991) reminds us, cleaning out one's closet can be an invigorating experience. We can let go of the outmoded ways of thinking and behavior patterns that are no longer appropriate to our "transformed" self.[45] Being exiled on the planet has really been a godsend for Starbuck and Cy for it has enabled them to appreciate their cultural differences as well as recognize their underlying similarities after the soldier role has been removed from their makeup.

Sadly, the uniting of the two enemy forces cannot be sustained. A group of Cylons has been dispatched by the empire to respond to Cy's distress beacon which had been automatically activated upon the ship's crash. Seeing Starbuck, they open fire. Cy intervenes at just the right moment and helps Starbuck eliminate his "brothers"; however, Cy is seriously wounded in the attack and expires in the lieutenant's arms. The human is too moved by the loss of his friend to do anything but hold vigil over the silent, mechanical life form.

This episode marked the end of *Battlestar: Galactica*'s all too short television run. Similar to the *Logan's Run* series, *Galactica* was transmitting the archetypal message that not all destroyers exist "out there" in dehumanizing organizations. Each of the individual members of that organization also harbors a Sandman- or Centurion-like shadow waiting to be freed. The possibility exists, as it did for Logan-5 and Commander Adama, to convert the inner destroyer to the more worthwhile creator that can fashion new worlds and societies out of devastation. All it takes is the realization that a shadow "full of sin" lies within each of us. By acknowledging our evilness, we are one step closer to discovering that "wellspring of grace" which also emanates from the shadow and to which we can devote the rest of our lives actualizing.[46] For Jung, creation (birth) and destruction (death) are intimately linked; one could not exist without the other.[47] If we want to participate in the heroic quest, we must face both the positive and negative forces in ourselves and accomplish an effective reconciliation, without losing our identity in the process. This is one of the most powerful themes underlying any successful science-fiction series to which we should attend.

NOTES

1. Carl G. Jung, "The Dual Mother," in *Symbols of Transformation: The Collected Works*, trans. R.F.C. Hull (Princeton, NJ: Princeton University Press, 1990), 346–49; Jung, "Symbols of the Mother and of Rebirth," in *Symbols of Transformation*, 248–49, 251–52.

2. Vincent Canby, "Review of *Logan's Run*," *New York Times*, 24 June 1976, 25: 1; Bruce Eder, "Videodisc Review: *Logan's Run*," *Video Magazine* 16 (August 1992), 44; Richard Meyers, *The Great Science Fiction Films* (New York: Carol Publishing Group, 1990), 23–24.

3. Carl G. Jung, "Concerning Rebirth," in *The Archetypes and the Collective Unconscious: The Collected Works*, trans. R.F.C. Hull (Princeton, NJ: Princeton University Press, 1990), 117–18.

4. Jung, "Concerning Mandala Symbolism," in *The Archetypes and the Collective Unconscious*, 357; Jung, "Mandalas," in *The Archetypes and the Collective Unconscious*, 387–90.

5. William F. Nolan and George Clayton Johnson, *Logan's Run* (New York: Bantam Books, 1976), 4–7.

6. Jung, "Archetypes of the Collective Unconscious," in *The Archetypes and the Collective Unconscious*, 20–23.

7. Canby, "Review of *Logan's Run*," 25: 1.

8. Nolan and Johnson, *Logan's Run*, 22.

9. Robert H. Hopcke, "Hero," in *A Guided Tour of the Collected Works of C. G. Jung* (Boston: Shambhala, 1992), 113–14; Jung, "The Origin of the Hero," in *Symbols of Transformation*, 205.

10. Calvin S. Hall and Vernon J. Nordby, *A Primer of Jungian Psychology* (New York: New American Library, 1973), 34–35; Carl G. Jung, "The Ego," in *Aion: Researches into the Phenomenology of the Self: The Collected Works*, trans. R.F.C. Hull (Princeton, NJ: Princeton University Press, 1990), 4–5.

11. Nolan and Johnson, *Logan's Run*, 62–63.

12. Jung, "Concerning Rebirth," in *The Archetypes and the Collective Unconscious*, 145; Jung, "The Origin of the Hero," in *Symbols of Transformation*, 201–2, 205.

13. Robert H. Hopcke, "Wise Old Man," in *A Guided Tour of Jung*, 117; Jung, "The Phenomenology of the Spirit in Fairytales," in *The Archetypes and the Collective Unconscious*, 222–23.

14. Canby, "Review of *Logan's Run*," 25: 1.

15. Shirley G. Luthman, *Energy and Personal Power* (San Rafael, Calif.: Mehetabel, 1982), 62; Carol S. Pearson, *Awakening the Heroes Within: Twelve Archetypes to Help Us Find Ourselves and Transform Our World* (San Francisco: HarperCollins, 1991), 217–18.

16. Jung, "The Phenomenology of the Spirit in Fairytales," in *The Archetypes and the Collective Unconscious*, 218.

17. Meyers, *Great Science Fiction Films*, 25–27.

18. Carl G. Jung, "The Fight with the Shadow," in *Civilization in Transition: The Collected Works*, trans. R.F.C. Hull (Princeton, NJ: Princeton University Press, 1990), 221; Jung, "The Shadow," in *Aion*, 9–10.

19. Carl G. Jung, "Introduction to the Religious and Psychological Problems of Alchemy," in *Psychology and Alchemy: The Collected Works*, trans. R.F.C. Hull (Princeton, NJ: Princeton University Press, 1991), 31.

20. Jung, "After the Catastrophe," in *Civilization in Transition*, 200–201.

21. Ibid.; Carl G. Jung, "The Relations Between the Ego and the Unconscious. Part One: The Effects of the Unconscious upon Consciousness," in *The Basic Writings of C. G. Jung*, trans. R.F.C. Hull (Princeton, NJ: Princeton University Press, 1990), 137–38.

22. Hall and Nordby, *Jungian Psychology*, 49, 51.

23. Robert H. Hopcke, "Shadow," in *A Guided Tour of Jung*, 81–82.

24. Jung, "The Sacrifice," in *Symbols of Transformation*, 431; Carol S. Pearson, *The Hero Within: Six Archetypes We Live By* (San Francisco: HarperCollins, 1989), 103.

25. Janet Maslin, "Space Operetta: Review of *Battlestar Galactica*," *New York Times*, 18 May 1979, Section C12: 1; Meyers, *Great Science Fiction Films*, 134.

26. Glen A. Larson and Robert Thurston, *Battlestar Galactica* (New York: Berkley, 1978), 10–11.

27. Ibid., 34–38.

28. Jung, "After the Catastrophe," in *Civilization in Transition*, 201.

29. Pearson, *Awakening the Heroes Within*, 113, 185.

30. Ibid., 184.

31. Jung, "Wotan," in *Civilization in Transition*, 184–86.

32. Pearson, *Awakening the Heroes Within*, 66.

33. Larson and Thurston, *Battlestar Galactica*, 241.

34. Glen A. Larson and Nicholas Yermakov, *Battlestar Galactica 7: War of the Gods* (New York: Berkley, 1982), 25.

35. Jung, "The Phenomenology of the Spirit in Fairytales," in *The Archetypes and the Collective Unconscious*, 227.

36. Jung, "The Dual Mother," in *Symbols of Transformation*, 351.

37. Jung, "Psychology and Religion: Dogma and Natural Symbols," in *Basic Writings*, 541–43.

38. Larson and Yermakov, *War of the Gods*, 138.

39. Jung, "Individual Dream Symbolism in Relation to Alchemy: The Initial Dreams," in *Psychology and Alchemy*, 69.

40. Hopcke, "Shadow," in *A Guided Tour of Jung*, 83.

41. Glen A. Larson and Ron Goulart, *Battlestar Galactica 9: Experiment in Terra* (New York: Berkley, 1984), 151.

42. Meyers, *Great Science Fiction Films*, 135.

43. Pearson, *Awakening the Heroes Within*, 145.

44. Pearson, *Hero Within*, 77.

45. Pearson, *Awakening the Heroes Within*, 145.

46. Jung, "After the Catastrophe," in *Civilization in Transition*, 216.

47. Jung, "Epilogue to 'Essays on Contemporary Events,' " in *Civilization in Transition*, 229.

Part Two

A Jungian Analysis of Fantasy Films

5
_____

Back to the Future Again and Again: Archetypal Exploits of Alchemic Travelers

As we have observed in Part One of this volume, archetypes within the science-fiction film genre have concentrated on life in the future. Some have portrayed that upcoming reality as a deadly struggle between humans and shadow destroyers (*Battlestar: Galactica* and *Planet of the Apes*), while others have presented a more hopeful world in which humans have tapped into the creative potential of the shadow in order to coexist with alien races (*Star Trek: The Motion Picture* and *Star Trek VI: The Undiscovered Country*). The focus will now change to images within the fantasy film category. Elements of science fiction can be contained in this genre, but they are more likely to be expressed as a "personal, dreamlike, childhood exploration of our less-than-conscious thoughts."[1] Out-of-body experiences, wish fulfillments, interdimensional travel, and coexisting and changeable realities are just a few of the science-fiction features incorporated in the fantasy. Because the normal laws of time and space do not apply to this genre, our dream world need not be limited to just one context; it can extend from a historical point in time (e.g., the *Indiana Jones* chronicles) to a very altered present (the *Superman* and *Batman* series) as well as the unknown future (the *Highlander* trilogy), with imaginative leaps occurring back and forth across these periods. It should be noted that the dream world is not always cast in an optimistic light. Sometimes it can take on a frightening, oftentimes oppressive, reality when horror components are inserted directly into the story lines (see chapter 8 on the *Omen* films).

The *Back to the Future* trilogy is a nice place to begin our investigation of the fantasy film genre, as seen through the eyes of adolescent Marty McFly. The Marty character has a Jungian base in the archetypal (and often youthful) wanderer who is trying to establish his own sense of identity and position within society. He accomplishes this through an alchemical process of time traveling: in this case, a nuclear-powered car which has the ability to cross the lanes of one dimension into another. As do many fantasy characters, Marty discovers the real world is a less interesting and far less dangerous place to be, compared to these other intriguing time frames through which he journeys.[2]

BACK TO THE FUTURE: THE JOURNEY BEGINS IN THE SHADOW PAST

The personality of Marty McFly (played by television celebrity Michael J. Fox) is revealed in the opening of the first *Back to the Future* (1985) movie. Here is a teenager who loves to race around town recklessly on his skateboard, rather than use a more conventional means of travel (i.e., bicycle). Marty also shows a stubborn defiance toward authority figures, like any wanderer who attempts to define himself (or herself) in direct opposition to the conformist norm.[3] He consistently misses his classes and is reprimanded by principal Strickland for being a "slacker," yet he does nothing to correct his irresponsible behavior. The most important activity to which Marty devotes his full attention is playing rock n' roll music on his guitar. For the most part, his parents serve as inadequate role models: George (Crispin Glover) is a meek and timid father bullied by his supervisor, and Lorraine (Lea Thompson) is a tired alcoholic who is almost drained of her maternal energy. Marty is, therefore, able to do pretty much what he desires without being held accountable for his actions.[4]

The only two friends McFly has are Jennifer Parker (Claudia Wells), a sweet girl who loves him in spite of his faults, and an eccentric scientist, Dr. Emmett Brown (performed with maniacal abandon by Christopher Lloyd). "Doc" Brown and Marty are really two of a kind: both have removed themselves from society to pursue their own dreams. Marty wants to be a great rock musician, and Doc Brown wants to develop an invention that actually works. By combining their talents, the two can fulfill each other's needs. Brown can supply Marty with the most advanced stereo equipment as well as the isolated quarters to perform his noisy guitar playing. In return, Marty can provide the scientist with the necessary aid and manpower so that the doctor's "temporal displacement" experiments will succeed.

While alchemists like Emmett Brown can be classified as "decided solitaries" who prefer working in the laboratory by themselves,[5] these magicians still have the desire to teach others their craft or, at the very least, give their pupils the opportunity to reflect on the knowledge they are transmitting.[6] Marty McFly has that student potential in him. Doc Brown is able to perceive that behind Marty's rough exterior exists a mind eager to learn new concepts and acquire the type of wisdom not found in schoolbooks. And so the unorthodox scientist takes Marty under his wing, hoping that one day the boy will come of age and continue his endeavors when he becomes too old and feeble.

Apparently, the partnership is an effective one since Dr. Brown is able to complete the work on his time machine. One night he proudly displays his device to Marty. It is a refurbished DeLorean with some extra features, including a dash crammed with every conceivable time control mechanism and a gasoline tank which now accepts pure plutonium as its fuel source. As the doctor relates to Marty, if one is planning to do some "heavy traveling," one better go in style.[7] This remark is a clear indication of just how much of the child is still in the scientist. He is like some bright-eyed boy on Christmas Day who cannot wait to open his presents and start playing with them. For Doc Brown, the wanderer's journeys are hardly over; they are just beginning, and he welcomes the opportunity to start off on his new adventures.

But something unforseen happens which puts a halt to the doctor's plans. Emmett has stolen the plutonium which powers his interdimensional car from some Libyan terrorists who want to see him dead. They "kill," or believe they have killed, Dr. Brown and then force Marty into the DeLorean. By recalling how his mentor operated the machine, Marty is able to reach the desired speed and is instantaneously transported back in time to November 5, 1955. The "new world" that greets the adolescent is so strange and overpowering that he becomes temporarily lost in it. Even the language that Marty uses cannot adequately convey the ideas he wishes to express. For instance, no one has ever heard of a Pepsi-free soda; if Marty desires a Pepsi, he has to pay ten cents just like everyone else. Acclimating himself to this period and its interesting colloquialisms is the task that confronts Marty if he is ever going to rid himself of the wanderer's feelings of alienation and loneliness.[8]

While he is exploring his new surroundings, McFly encounters his mother-to-be, Lorraine Baines, who is so enamored by the "weird" teen that she never notices Marty's father, George. Seeking the counsel of the 1955 Doc Brown, he learns that his presence is altering the normal flow of events. Because Lorraine has a crush on Marty, he will never be born, thus condemning him to spend the remaining years of his life in the past. Although this "temporal paradox" is hard to grasp, the teenager realizes he has to correct the imbalance and have his parents develop the fateful relationship that will ensure his own survival in the future.

Douglas Brode (1990) and others suggest that *Back to the Future* possesses a "bizarre Oedipal theme" since the family film flirts with incest in a heartwarming, not tasteless, way.[9] However, this seemingly innocent mother-son encounter has a deeper archetypal base. Before heroes start on their journeys, they have to free themselves from the seductive and terrible power of their mothers. It is the mother who can keep a potential hero in a perpetually dependent, clinging childlike state just by her presence in his life.[10] Therefore, one of the first "dragons" faced by heroes is the maternal demon; they must battle this paralyzing force and vanquish it in order to assume their awesome, almost superhuman responsibilities on the planet.[11] The heroes' subsequent wanderings will then be filled with a conviction and purpose that they can indeed emerge victorious in any upcoming challenge. Breaking all incestuous ties with the parent is something Marty McFly must do to exist and give his life meaning in the other time continuum. Marty simply cannot yield to Lorraine's advances; otherwise, his future world (and self) will be destroyed forever. The heroic "life and death" struggle with the Jungian mother should not go unnoticed by the viewer, even when it is presented in such a playful fashion by *Back to the Future*'s director, Robert Zemeckis.

By the film's conclusion, Marty is able to bring both of his parents-to-be together at the annual school dance. He is able to get a little help from the town's bully, Biff Tannen (Thomas F. Wilson), who attempts to rape Lorraine in the school parking lot right in front of the eyes of mild-mannered George. This unfortunate set of circumstances instills in George the necessary confidence to clobber Biff with all the strength he can muster, thereby proving his manhood to an eternally grateful Lorraine. The two immediately fall in love, ensuring that Marty's past is back on track once more.

The time-traveling adolescent leaves the "lovebirds" with the comment that his experiences have been quite educational. He has learned something not so readily apparent about his future parents: they were just like him at one point in time, trying to cope with the pressures of young adulthood as well as the associated identity crises.[12] Marty also comes to realize that he can look up to Lorraine and George. Both are good people who have a decent set of standards which he hopes he can emulate upon his return to the future. Marty has changed for the better since journeying down the wanderer's "road of trials."[13] He has become a much more mature individual who is able to recognize the positives in life as well as the negatives.

Back to the Future closes with Marty and the professor tapping into the energy of a lightning storm which gives the DeLorean the much needed push to move it forward into the mid-1980s. The scene that greets Marty does not resemble the one which he left. Doc Brown is alive and well, having taken the precaution of wearing a bulletproof vest in case of an anticipated terrorist attack. More changes await Marty after he returns home. His father is no longer a wimp, but a celebrated science-fiction author. And his mother is no longer a problem drinker, but resembles the endearing version of herself back in 1955. Even Marty has his very own dream truck parked in the garage, with girlfriend Jennifer alongside it waiting to be taken for her much promised ride.[14] It would seem that the heroic teenager has made a better world for everyone in it (including himself) by his "past" actions.[15] The awareness that what one chooses to do can have far-reaching effects on the environment is the all important lesson communicated to the not so young McFly at the end of *Back to the Future*.

BACK TO THE FUTURE PART II: MOVING FORWARD AND BACKWARD AT DANGEROUSLY HIGH SPEEDS

If one thought Marty's travels were over, the advertisements for the first *Back to the Future* sequel, *Back to the Future Part II* (1989), announced that "getting back was only the beginning." A distinguishing feature of the archetypal wanderer is that his entire life might be devoted to answering the soul's call to adventure. The wanderer's journeys might have their start in late adolescence and early adulthood when the time to explore new lands and new ideas is at its strongest, but this does not mean that the travels necessarily end at this developmental period. Even in old age there is still the need to undertake these trips, so long as the hunger is present in the wanderer to participate in "the grandeur of the universe."[16] Although Marty might have reached a level of contentment, Doc Brown has not and is quite eager to find out what the future will be like for the residents of the Hill Valley community. *Future II* centers on the time travels of Doc Brown in his flying DeLorean which begin in the future and then continue in the present and past periods. Marty goes along for the ride, not so much committed to undertaking these journeys as to provide companionship for the bright-eyed mentor. What entails is a somewhat confusing time tale into which the viewer and Marty are pulled at breakneck speeds, with the doctor providing the only stable point of reference in this constantly fluctuating universe. Because of the intricate plot twists, much criticism has been leveled at the second *Future*;[17] however, the film more than satisfactorily presents a wide assortment of temporal leaps extending from 2015 back to 1955, fulfilling the needs of any aspiring wanderer in the audience who wants to fantasize about reality on a more global time plane.

Future II kicks off with a fantastic jump into the not too distant future where Marty's son, Martin Jr. (also portrayed by Michael J. Fox), will be sentenced to the state penitentiary for a robbery into which he was coerced by Biff's grandson, Griff. Dr. Brown (again played by Christopher Lloyd) believes he can change history by having the strong-willed Marty assume his son's identity, thereby ensuring that the unholy alliance with Griff will never transpire. The plan does work, and it looks as though the McFly household will not be tainted with a criminal record. But, Doc has not foreseen how the personality changes in Martin Sr., the Marty of the future, will still lead his family to almost certain doom, regardless of the scientist's kindly intervention. Like many alchemists who foster social change by their radical views, Dr. Brown has yet to recognize that there are forces out there that can retard people's development and "keep them stuck" in their own personal hells.[18]

The "hell" for Martin Sr. is the course his life took almost thirty years ago. At that time, someone had called Martin "chicken." He reacted rather impulsively to the remark and he hit the name-caller with such force that he did permanent injury to his hands. McFly could no longer play his music and soon gave up on his aspirations, spending the remainder of his life feeling sorry for himself and becoming (of all things) an unfulfilled corporate businessman. Given this parental history, it makes perfect sense that Marty Jr. turned out the way his father did: a drifter without a purpose, wandering aimlessly down the streets of Hill Valley and scoping out women. When we last gaze upon the older McFly, it is a depressing sight. The man has just lost his job for embezzling funds from the company. He cannot convince his boss, Mr. Fujitsu, that another coworker put him up to the awful deed. All Martin can do is sit alone in the family room, plucking at his guitar strings with little feeling behind the movements. Even the alchemic powers of Emmett Brown cannot alter this preordained future.[19] One wonders whether Marty Jr. will follow the tragic footsteps laid by his father when the time travelers leave the McFlys of 2015 and head back to their own, uncomplicated period.

The present, however, has radically changed since the time of Marty and Doc's departure. The contemporary Hill Valley community has turned into a nightmarish ghetto, with gangs taking over the streets and residents taking up arms in fear that they will be plundered of their meager belongings.[20] High school dropout Biff Tannen (reprised with notable gruffness by Thomas F. Wilson), is the only one who has made something of himself in this topsy-turvy reality. He is a multimillionaire, whose palatial home and gambling casino occupy a prominent position in the otherwise obscure town. In addition to amassing great wealth, Biff has married the widow Lorraine McFly, who has compromised everything (even herself) for the sake of attaining material security for the rest of her days. Marty cannot believe he is now related to the despicable Tannen, especially after learning that Biff murdered his real father so that he could possess the vulnerable Lorraine.

It is hardly accidental that the time stream has taken this new, and more dangerous, path. Doc has discovered that while they were correcting things in the future, the Biff Tannen of that period was using their time vehicle for his own purposes. Going back to the year 1955, Biff has given his younger self a copy of *The Sport's Almanac* which lists the outcome of every competitive event up until the year 2000. With that knowledge, Tannen is able to gain his huge fortune. His older version returns to the future before the DeLorean is missed, assured that his life will take the direction he always hoped it would.[21]

Jung's concept of synchronicity is especially relevant to the *Future II* plot. As defined by the famous psychoanalyst, synchronicity involves the simultaneous occurrence of a person's psychic state with one or more external events.[22] Biff wants to make something of himself, but he is much too old to follow a new career path. Instead, he wishes he can go back into the past and alter things for his betterment. As if by magic, events unfold which make Biff's dreams a living reality. First, the flying DeLorean is left unattended for a fairly lengthy period; next, the almanac which Marty has purchased is discarded in a trash bin by the more prudent Doc Brown, only to be noticed by passerby Biff Tannen; and finally, the DeLorean automatically transports Biff back to that fateful year 1955, without his even having to set the complex controls. These "magical" happenings might be regarded as sheer coincidences by many viewers. However, Jung notes that certain "magnetic and electrical" powers lie within each of us which can have a direct effect on our surroundings.[23] Biff's self-interests are so strong that seemingly unrelated incidents (e.g., the unlocked DeLorean and the visible almanac) become meaningfully connected in his plan to change the past. It is almost as if Tannen is the psychic attractant, taking advantage of all the opportunities provided by the unsuspecting time wanderers.

Marty and Doc, in the meantime, do not appear to be aware of just how much their presence in 2015 has disturbed the natural order of the universe, until it is too late. Although the duo's efforts have helped Marty Jr., they have unleashed a far greater evil in the time stream (i.e., Biff) due to their never considering the possibility of being detected by any future inhabitants, including their own selves. In this respect, Marty and Doc possess all the qualities of the archetypal wanderer—both good and bad. In their blind haste toward self-fulfillment, they have undertaken some actions that are "crude and clumsy ones [at best]."[24] As Jung reflects, intelligence and understanding are required if any alchemic works are to succeed.[25] Because Marty and Doc have not mentally prepared themselves to consider all the destructive repercussions of interfering with a predestined reality, they have actually made things worse for the Hill Valley community, not better. Both must now take responsibility for their mistakes and try to correct the temporal imbalance which they have created. Only by continuing the wandering process in the past can their universe be set right in the present. It seems a shame that wanderers do not learn all the lessons they need to at the outset. Sometimes they have to circle back and begin their travels all over again in order to achieve the necessary insight into their flawed characters.[26] For Marty and Doc, this means going back to the year 1955 once more and undoing everything the future Biff has altered.

The assignment is not an easy one for the pair since the younger Biff has already acquired the almanac and is in the process of poring over its mysterious contents. After several unsuccessful attempts to remove the book from Biff's grasp, Marty is able to use his expertise on a hoverboard (the futuristic equivalent of a skateboard) to obtain the object before any serious harm is done by the dull-witted Tannen. He follows the doctor's advice and burns the text; almost immediately, the 1985 time stream is returned to its normal track. However, one casualty does result from this temporal tampering: Doc Brown is catapulted back to the Old West of 1895 and remains stranded in that period. Marty commits himself to finding his lost mentor as the *Future II* credits roll. This cliff-hanger ending might have detracted from the overall enjoyment of the film for those viewers who desired some closure to the series.[27] On an archetypal level, however, it proved to be a nice depiction of the insatiable urge of the wanderer to continue his heroic travels into a new time and place in order to derive additional meaning to his rapidly developing identity.[28]

BACK TO THE FUTURE PART III: THE WANDERER COMES OF AGE IN THE PAST

In the concluding chapter of the fantasy trilogy, *Back to the Future Part III* (1990), Marty receives a message from Doc Brown which advises him to go back to 1985 without the scientist. Emmett is perfectly happy living the remainder of his existence in the Old West as the town's blacksmith; as proof of his new life, he has buried the DeLorean in a mine shaft so that he is never troubled by the wanderer's desires again. He has provided Marty with a detailed map of the car's exact location so that it can transport the adolescent back to his respective time. Brown specifically instructs his student to cease pursuing him as any "unnecessary time travel only risks further disruption of the space-time continuum."[29] He further advises Marty to destroy the time machine after it returns him home. Clearly Doc Brown is aware of the dangers he has introduced by his unexpected appearance in other temporal periods and does not want to expose Marty and other people to these perils. After reading the communication, McFly reacts with a certain amount of disbelief. He cannot accept the fact that his mentor is gone forever, trapped in a past that is not his own. He partly blames himself for the set of circumstances and wants to set things right, even if it means removing the now settled Doc from the "world of his dreams."

For the still unfulfilled Marty, excavating the DeLorean and restoring it to its original working order are just the first tasks in his quest to find Doc Brown. What really motivates the boy is his accidental discovery of Doc's tombstone in the Hill Valley cemetery. Apparently the scientist has met a grisly fate back in 1885: he was shot in the back by one of Biff's ancestors, Buford (a.k.a. "Mad Dog") Tannen, over the matter of a mere eighty dollars. Since none of the Browns immigrated to the Americas until 1908,

Marty reasons that history has already been changed by Doc's unrecorded presence in the past.[30] Therefore, he infers he can do no harm by bringing his mentor home; if anything, he hopes that the space-time continuum will be returned to normal by his intervention.

Again, the process of synchronicity is used by *Future* screenplay writer Bob Gale to provide the foundation of Marty McFly's time travels to the turn of the century. Gale establishes a "meaningful cross-connection" between the adolescent's need to retrieve Doc Brown and his subsequent stumbling upon the scientist's remains in the cemetery.[31] It is almost as if, by magic, the justification was presented to Marty to defy Doc's orders and use the DeLorean on another mission of salvation. But has the boy really learned anything from his previous wanderings, or does he blindly enter the temporal dimensions, unconcerned about what his meddlings will do to the present reality?

Adopting a synchronous viewpoint, Marty sees his fate intertwined with the doctor's. As a student of the alchemist, he perceives that both of their lives are interconnected, to the point where any personal powers of growth and self-actualization are grounded in the maintaining of this relationship (no matter how many decades separate the two). In a way, the roles of the mentor and protégé are reversed in *Future III*; Marty now plays the character of the all-wise guru who must come to the aid of the naive and powerless Brown. McFly shows a certain maturity in the last film, chiefly because he has been exposed to a good and caring role model whom he does not want to abandon. The adolescent-turned-adult is at last able to comprehend the more macrocosmic picture of human existence: each person can be the hero of his (or her) own drama and can simultaneously have an impact on another person's life story through that "great web" of dependence.[32] Only by acknowledging that connectedness with other people can Marty attain the alchemic powers that Doc Brown already possesses and be an equally effective magician in his own right. The future would appear to hold much promise for Marty as he takes off in the DeLorean to retrieve the lost scientist.

It is a very different, almost transformed Doc who greets Marty upon his arrival in 1885. The elder is hopelessly in love with a schoolteacher, Clara Clayton (actress Mary Steenburgen), so much so that he seems totally oblivious of the fact that he will be shot by Tannen by the end of the week. Marty needs to remind him from time to time just how important it is to prevent this unfortunate incident from happening. But everything becomes incidental to Doc's infatuation with Clara. He has never met a woman like her before—one who appreciates the works of Jules Verne or, for that matter, any writer who is willing to go beyond the confines of his (or her) life and dream of a better tomorrow.[33] Clara finds Emmett's aspirations just as appealing and soon displays equally strong feelings of affection toward the spellbound scientist.

Evidently, Doc Brown is no longer possessed by the wanderer's yearning to travel to new places and lands. His former "period of solitude" has moved him to a new archetypal level: an autonomy defined within the context of interdependence. Through his journeys, Emmett has developed a strong enough sense of self to know who he really is and, most especially, what he needs out of life. He is no longer afraid of forming a human connection with a significant other, even if it means abandoning his assorted time travels.[34] At one point in the film, Doc even tells Marty that he would rather settle down with Clara and raise a family than continue his risky temporal leaping. Carol Pearson (1989) suggests how truly ironic is the fate of the wanderer. The movement away from society into isolation and loneliness ultimately leads back to the very community one has rejected.[35] Emmett's "reward" for all of his soul-searching is his relationship with Clara, which is representative of his reentry back into a world that unconditionally accepts and respects his unique talents.

The confrontation with "Mad Dog" Tannen, however, still needs to be resolved so that the older wanderer can establish lasting ties with Clara and the younger one can start his own with Jennifer in the future. To save the Doc from his appointed death, Marty challenges Tannen to a duel, but then appeals to his opponent's sanity by throwing down his weapons at the critical moment (hoping that Tannen will do likewise). This is a significant action for Marty. All his life he has been intimidated by others and coerced into doing things against his better nature. Now he finally has enough courage to stand up to a bully like Tannen and be true to his hidden self, instead of acting out in an uncontrollable rage. Marty's wanderings have taught him something very important: to exercise the appropriate discipline so that heart and mind are one, working together every instant in every human interaction.[36] Since Tannen has not reached this stage in his development, he chooses the cowardly route of shooting the unarmed Marty directly in the chest. Fortunately, Marty is prepared for the attack. He has taken the cast-iron door off of Doc's stove to serve as the equivalent of a bulletproof vest. "Mad Dog" cannot believe his eyes when his downed foe miraculously recovers and kicks the pistol from his grasp. In a brief hand-to-hand skirmish, Marty uses his skills as a gymnast to overthrow Tannen. The young wanderer at last has integrated the shadow nature into his overall personality so that he can defeat a longtime enemy. Many searchers of the truth easily fall prey to their dark side as they begin their travels, but with age and experience comes a great wisdom. Similar to Ursula Le Guin's fictional character of Sparrowhawk, Marty McFly has learned to "soar" above his shadow so that it does not possess him and lead him down the path of ruin.[37]

Given his strong sense of self, Marty can accomplish any number of wonders including getting back to his own time period (with the Doc's help, of course). The two travelers calculate that the speed of an express train should be sufficient to propel the fuel-starved DeLorean forward into the future; however, if the plan fails, the vehicle will reach the end of the tracks and plummet into a nearby ravine. Marty believes the risk is worth taking and hopes that Doc shares his sentiments. The mentor is able to power up the train's engine while Marty sits in the DeLorean, which is hitched to the cowcatcher, waiting for his companion to arrive. At the last possible second, Doc decides to stay behind with Clara recognizing this period is his new home. Meanwhile, the time vehicle whisks Marty to 1985 and is then smashed to pieces by an oncoming diesel, eliminating the possibility of McFly's ever going back to search for his friend. Marty's words, "Well, Doc, it's destroyed . . . just like you wanted,"[38] confirm how synchronous the universe really is. Nothing ever happens by chance. In this instance, there is a reason why the DeLorean was totaled. It allows Marty the opportunity to make something of his life on his own, without the foreknowledge that the time machine could have provided. He can stop being an aimless wanderer and move on to a deeper archetypal plane, consisting of a stronger commitment to authenticity and more intense soul-searching.[39]

Doc does make an unexpected (and grandiose) appearance at the end of the *Future* trilogy. He arrives in a new time machine, which curiously resembles a souped-up version of an old-fashioned locomotive. The scientist introduces Marty and Jennifer to his family: his wife, Clara, and their two sons, Jules and Verne. Doc has returned to the future specifically to give certain words of advice to the wide-eyed teenagers. To paraphrase his statements, nobody's future has been preordained. For better or for worse, one's life is based on a continually evolving series of decisions. Therefore, Doc encourages Marty and Jennifer to take the time to make the best possible choices they can so that their future together is a bright one.[40] When Marty asks him if he plans to visit the future again, Doc answers that he has already been there and then sends himself (and his family) back into the past. Brown's reply to Marty is not a surprising one, in light of his previous remarks. The reformed wanderer does not feel obligated to find how his life turns out. He has already changed it by marrying Clara and having children. Seeing his destiny would rob him of the excitement associated with any impromptu decisions he would make from this point forward. For Doc the journeying has ended because he has found a significant other to make himself whole and complete. The hope is that Marty and Jennifer will also reach this point in their relationship so that they can abandon their solitary travels. *Back to the Future* concludes with our two alchemic wanderers ending their quest and reintegrating themselves back into the loving arms of an ever present society.

NOTES

1. Stuart M. Kaminsky, *American Film Genres* (Chicago: Nelson-Hall, 1988), 131–32.

2. Ibid.

3. Carol S. Pearson, *The Hero Within: Six Archetypes We Live By* (San Francisco: HarperCollins, 1989), 51–52.

4. Douglas Brode, *The Films of the Eighties* (New York: Carol Publishing Group, 1991), 137.

5. Carl G. Jung, "Religious Ideas in Alchemy: The Work," in *Psychology and Alchemy: The Collected Works*, trans. R.F.C. Hull (Princeton, NJ: Princeton University Press, 1991), 422.

6. Carl G. Jung, "Archetypes of the Collective Unconscious," in *The Archetypes and the Collective Unconscious: The Collected Works*, trans. R.F.C. Hull (Princeton, NJ: Princeton University Press, 1990), 35–37; Jung, "The Phenomenology of the Spirit in Fairytales," in *The Archetypes and the Collective Unconscious*, 216–18.

7. George Gipe, *Back to the Future* (New York: Berkley Books, 1985), 51.

8. Edward F. Edinger, *Ego and Archetype: Individuation and the Religious Function of the Psyche* (London: Penguin Books, 1972), 48–50.

9. Brode, *Films of the Eighties*, 137; David Denby, "Review of *Back to the Future*," *New York* 18 (15 July 1985): 64; J. Hoberman, "Review of *Back to the Future*," *Village Voice* 30 (2 July 1985): 49.

10. Robert H. Hopcke, "Puer/Divine Child," in *A Guided Tour of the Collected Works of C. G. Jung* (Boston: Shambhala, 1992), 108; Jung, "Psychological Aspects of the Mother Archetype," in *The Archetypes and the Collective Unconscious*, 82, 85–86.

11. Carl G. Jung, "The Battle for Deliverance from the Mother," in *Symbols of Transformation: The Collected Works*, trans. R.F.C. Hull (Princeton, NJ: Princeton University Press, 1990), 298–301; Jung, "Symbols of the Mother and of Rebirth," in *Symbols of Transformation*, 251–52, 259–60.

12. Denby, "Review of *Back to the Future*," 64.

13. Brode, *Films of the Eighties*, 138; Pearson, *Hero Within*, 67.

14. Gipe, *Back to the Future*, 246–47.

15. Chogyam Trungpa, *The Sacred Path of the Warrior* (Boston: Shambhala, 1978), 34.

16. Carol S. Pearson, *Awakening the Heroes Within: Twelve Archetypes to Help Us Find Ourselves and Transform Our World* (San Francisco: HarperCollins, 1991), 125–28.

17. Edmond Grant, "Review of *Back to the Future Part II*," *Films in Review* 41 (March 1990): 165; Suzanne Moore, "Review of *Back to the Future Part II*," *New Statesman & Society* 1 December 1989, 42; Steven H. Scheuer, *Movies on TV and Videocassette* (New York: Bantam Books, 1991), 58.

18. Pearson, *Hero Within*, 150.

19. Craig Shaw Gardner, *Back to the Future Part II* (New York: Berkley Books, 1989), 105–6.

20. J. Hoberman, "Review of *Back to the Future Part II*," *Village Voice* 34 (5 December 1989): 117.

21. Gardner, *Back to the Future Part II*, 146–48.

22. Carl G. Jung, "Exposition," in *Synchronicity: An Acausal Connecting Principle*, trans. R.F.C. Hull (Princeton, NJ: Princeton University Press, 1991), 25; Hopcke, "Synchronicity," in *A Guided Tour of Jung*, 71–72.

23. Jung, "Exposition," in *Synchronicity*, 32–33.

24. Pearson, *Hero Within*, 64.

25. Jung, "Religious Ideas in Alchemy: The Psychic Nature of the Alchemical Work," in *Psychology and Alchemy*, 260, 270–71.

26. Pearson, *Hero Within*, 63.

27. Sheila Benson, "Review of *Back to the Future Part II*," *Los Angeles Times*, 22 November 1989, Calendar, 1; Brode, *Films of the Eighties*, 139; Grant, "Review of *Back to the Future Part II*," 165.

28. Jung, "The Origin of the Hero," in *Symbols of Transformation*, 205.

29. Craig Shaw Gardner, *Back to the Future Part III* (New York: Berkley Books, 1990), 14–15.

30. Ibid., 34–35.

31. Jung, "Exposition," in *Synchronicity*, 10–11.

32. M. S. Mason, "Review of *Back to the Future Part III*," *Christian Science Monitor* 82 (22 June 1990): 10; Pearson, *Awakening the Heroes Within*, 201–2.

33. Gardner, *Back to the Future Part III*, 116–17, 157–58.

34. Peter Rainer, "Review of *Back to the Future Part III*," *Los Angeles Times*, 25 May 1990, Calendar, 1.

35. Pearson, *Hero Within*, 72–73.

36. Ibid., 64–65; Edinger, *Ego and Archetype*, 61.

37. Ursula Le Guin, *A Wizard of Earthsea* (New York: Bantam Books, 1968), 180.

38. Gardner, *Back to the Future Part III*, 235.

39. Pearson, *Awakening the Heroes Within*, 128.

40. Gardner, *Back to the Future Part III*, 247.

6

From *Superman* to *Batman*: Divided Superhero Archetypes

Another interesting character, besides the time traveler, has been seen in the fantasy film genre: the comic book superhero. The Jungian archetypes of the shadow and persona can be directly correlated with this fascinating figure. Outwardly, the superhero appears to be a normal, everyday individual who wears a "mask" that does not differentiate him from others in the crowd. But underneath this commonplace persona lies a shadow side that possesses all of the hero's superpowers and abilities. Usually, the superhero has to keep these strengths hidden from others in order to be an effective crime fighter. There is a price to pay for this anonymity, however. The superhero continually vacillates between the human persona and the shadow side, never living a full existence in either one. The end result is a fragmented person who feels ambivalent about his (or her) superpowers since they prevent the complete expression of the more human identity.[1]

A HISTORICAL INTRODUCTION TO THE SUPERHEROES

It seems wise to discuss briefly the origins of two very popular comic book superheroes, Superman and Batman, before an investigation into their movie incarnations proceeds. Jerry Siegel and Joe Shuster's Superman figure made its debut in *Action Comics* in 1938. As the tale unfolds, the extraterrestrial being from the planet Krypton discovers that he possesses mighty powers in Earth's atmosphere. He can leap forty feet into the air, lift automobiles, and deflect bullets from his invulnerable skin.[2] When his foster parents die, Superman decides to become the "champion of the oppressed" and selects a costume to reflect that patriotic goal: blue and red tights with the distinctive "S" insignia on the chest, a flowing cape, and matching boots.[3] So as not to frighten anyone with his titanic strength (and other abilities), he assumes the persona of shy, mild-mannered Clark Kent and obtains employment as a newspaper reporter in the great city of Metropolis. While fellow reporter Lois Lane regards Clark as a bespectacled and ineffectual milksop, Superman is able to use his alter ego effectively to prevent Lois and others from finding out about his super-shadow nature.

Over the decades, the Superman character became "the ultimate wish-fulfillment fantasy for every reader who ever dreamed of being someone greater and stronger than he or she was. [Anyone could be the mightiest person on the planet; all it took was an active imagination coupled with the proper heroic identification.]"[4] By 1948 the comic book hero was appearing in movie serials, and by 1953 Superman had his own syndicated television show, which introduced George Reeves as the Man of Steel. Of all the superheroes, Superman is still considered to be the most resilient, as evidenced by the number of financially successful motion pictures (starting with *Superman: The Movie*, 1978) and more recent television spinoffs (*Superboy*, 1987 to 1989 and *Lois and Clark: The New Adventures of Superman*, 1993 to 1997).

While Superman immersed himself in the daylight fighting criminals, Batman clung to the dark shadows like his mammalian namesake. The May 1939 issue of *Detective Comics* shows how Gil (a.k.a. "Bob") Kane's conceptualization of the "Bat-Man" was a radical change from Siegel and Shuster's caped superhero. Young Bruce Wayne witnesses the brutal slaying of his parents by a faceless thug who is attempting to rob them. Bruce vows to avenge their deaths by devoting the rest of his life to waging war on the criminal element in Gotham City. He chooses one of the most supernatural creatures of the night, the bat, as the shadow symbol to strike fear in the hearts of villains everywhere and attires himself in a mysterious hooded cowl with accompanying bat ears and a dramatic scalloped cape that gives the illusion of huge bat wings.[5] Unlike many other superheroes (including Superman), Batman does not have superpowers: "he cannot fly, read minds, or become invisible . . . he is one of the few who is *only* human."[6] Therefore, it takes years for Bruce Wayne to develop his athletic powers and mental capacities to the point where he is ready to start his crime-fighting career as the ominous superhero.

When Batman makes his first appearances, he is a masked vigilante who is no better than the evildoers he is pursuing. He even uses a gun to shoot and kill criminals rather than bringing them to the courts for trial. Such inappropriate behavior for a superhero prompted the comic book editors to "humanize" this too dark character. The police made Batman an honorary member of their force, which allowed him to work on the side of the law. The inclusion of a youthful sidekick, Robin the Boy Wonder, also provided Batman with a more noble role: that of mentor and protector to his ward.[7]

Producer William Dozier was so impressed by the tales of the Dynamic Duo, Batman and Robin, that he decided to do a television series. The *Batman* show gained immense popularity during its three-year run (from 1966 to 1968), mainly because it tried to emulate the comics in a campy style.[8] All sorts of fantastic gadgets were used by actors Adam West (Batman) and Burt Ward (Robin) in the teleplays, extending from every type of conceivable vehicle (Batmobile, Batplane, Batboat, Batcopter, and Batcycle) to a never-ending assortment of devices contained within the super-heroes' own utility belts (batropes, baterangs, batbombs, batpellets, and so on). One of the chief attractions of the series was the incredible fight sequences. Whenever Batman engaged in a brawl with the super-villain's henchmen, striking visual balloons (WHAM!, ZAP!, KAYO!) would immediately flash on the screen which blocked out the expected sights of hits and punches so that the viewer had to read the action instead of directly observing it. These visualized sound effects proved to be so popular that many superhero magazines assimilated them into their story lines, along with the familiar cliff-hangers which tied two or three teleplays together.[9]

By the late 1960s, the Batman craze was dying (like so many other popular culture phenomena), and a new incarnation of the Caped Crusader slowly rose from the ashes—one that was much more realistic and deadly serious in nature.[10] The image of the "Dark Knight" not only became the favored one by comic book fans, but also served to mold the *Batman* films throughout the last decade.

Given this brief history of our two superheroes, we are now in a better position to interpret the archetypal significance of their larger-than-life movie versions. One variation from past serials and television shows is that the films do concentrate on each superhero's split personality and the attempt to resolve the conflict between each one's inadequate persona and unexpressed shadow side. We will start the analysis with the *Superman* movie quartet and follow with the first three *Batman* films.

SUPERMAN: THE MOVIE—YOU'LL BELIEVE A MAN CAN FLY BECAUSE OF HIS PERSONA

It was not the exceptional special effects or the number of notable stars (Ned Beatty, Marlon Brando, Glenn Ford, and Gene Hackman) that made *Superman: The Movie* (1978) a critical success.[11] Rather, it was the original script written by Mario Puzo, author of *The Godfather* (1972), that developed the comic book character into a real, "wonderfully heroic" person on the screen. Although other writers were called in at the last minute by producer Ilya Salkind to insert some "*Batman* TV style" camp into the story, Puzo's influence can still be seen throughout the film, particularly in the opening scenes involving Superman's persona of Clark Kent.[12]

It is a joyous day for the childless couple of Martha and Jonathan Kent (played with marvelous charm by Phyllis Thaxter and Glenn Ford) when they discover that the occupant of a crashed spaceship happens to be an alien baby in need of their love. They raise the boy as their own and try to hide the fact that young Clark (Jeff East) is different from others. Clark, nevertheless, soon realizes that he possesses incredible powers and asks his foster father where he came from. Though Jonathan is ignorant of his son's origins, he does tell the boy that there is a reason why he has been sent to them (as well as to the human race).

Clark finds out that hidden purpose only by experiencing one of the most heart-wrenching losses in his life: the death of his human father. In frustration he relates to his mother that all his super abilities could not save Jonathan from dying from a massive heart attack. Clark's introspection into his shadow nature is hardly a pleasant experience. But "looking inward" is essential if some value to human existence is to be derived. As Jung notes, "It is just the most unexpected, the most terrifyingly chaotic things [in life] which reveal a deeper shadow meaning . . . for in all chaos there is cosmos, in all disorder a secret order."[13] Although Clark was unable to prevent his father's demise, he comes to realize that he was not meant to interfere with the natural harmony of the universe which includes death as much as life. The crystals from his home planet instruct him in this all important, archetypal truth. Clark, therefore, decides to leave home to discover just what his destiny is in the given scheme of things. Mother Kent has been expecting the departure for some time, and she wishes her son good luck and godspeed.

Guided by the Kryptonian stones, Clark journeys to the farthest northern region of the planet and establishes his Fortress of Solitude. Alienating environments like this one are often necessary to develop an awareness of the total self, which includes a recognition of one's masked, shadow side.[14] It is within the Fortress that Clark learns who he really is from holographic images of his biological father, Jor-El (Marlon Brando). He is named Kal-El, the sole survivor of a race of sophisticated beings who perished in a deadly, interstellar conflagration. Because of Kal-El's alien molecular structure, he is able to have such impressive abilities as great strength and speed, along with a penetrating X-ray vision and the power of flight. In the course of his twelve-year stay at the Fortress, Kal-El is schooled by Jor-El in the wonders of the galaxies, and he begins to develop an appreciation for the Terran culture. According to his father, the humans can be a great people; they only need a light to guide them onto that better path. By the end of his training, Kal-El believes that he can be that source of inspiration to the

Terrans, a "Superman" who will help them along but never directly interfere with their intended evolution.

Superman's two fathers, natural and foster, have had a profound effect on his developing psyche. They have enabled the adolescent to mature into a confident and wise man, ready to carry out his heroic mission on Earth. One wonders whether archetypal parents like Jonathan and Jor-El do not possess magical powers of their own, considering how their presence (in flesh or in spirit) shape the offspring into their very image.[15] The inclusion of Jor-El's Kryptonian seal (the big-lettered "S") into the superhero costume as well as the adoption of the mild-mannered, reporter persona so reminiscent of Jonathan Kent's are attempts made by Superman to integrate the two fathers' personalities into his own self. Thus, both the hero's outer mask and inner shadow can be viewed as complementary halves, based on a human and an alien paternal image, respectively.

The latter half of *Superman* is not as intense or thought provoking as the first part due to its heavy emphasis on the slapstick and absurd. The villainous roles of Lex Luthor (Gene Hackman) and Otis (Ned Beatty) are hardly menacing and their drawn-out, comic routines detract from the splendid performances of Christopher Reeve as the Man of Steel and Margot Kidder as the love interest, Lois Lane.[16] In spite of these flaws, some clips are worth noting.

When Reeve saves Kidder first in his persona as Kent and then as Superman, the audience detects a chemistry rapidly forming between the two characters. Lois worries (perhaps much more so than a friend) that Clark might have been injured by a thug who was attempting to rob them in broad daylight. The roles then become inverted in the darkness of the night: it is now Superman who is concerned about Lois's well-being after she plummets out of the cockpit of a malfunctioning helicopter to almost certain doom. Both scenes demonstrate how the split personality of the superhero can be further exaggerated by the opposite reactions our damsel in distress expresses at her two rescues. Lois is more brash and assertive in front of the bumbling Clark but instantly turns meek and introverted standing next to the "godly" Superman. Obviously, superheroes are not the only ones who have to deal with conflicting sides of their nature. Even the less powerful mortals like Ms. Lane have to come to terms with their own ambivalent attributes.[17]

Shortly after Superman begins his crime-fighting adventures, he grants Lois an exclusive interview and takes her on a romantic midnight flight above Metropolis. One might question at this point in the film whether Lois is really in love with the Man of Steel or simply feels dependent upon him for saving her life, similar to any eternally grateful (yet, oh so helpless) orphan.[18] Since Salkind intended to produce a traditional love fantasy updated for the 1970s, the viewer has to conclude that Lois has genuinely strong feelings of affection for Superman.[19] Any orphan-like support she requires from the superhero comes only in the unnatural medium of the air; on the ground she can still stand on her own without his assistance. Maybe this is one of the reasons Superman finds her so appealing. Lois is a woman who is not afraid to speak her mind, whether it be at the *Daily Planet* office or at home, where she questions him on his likes and dislikes.

Returning to Lois's penthouse from the sky immediately destroys the magical experience for the two lovebirds, especially when Superman resumes the drab alter ego of Clark Kent who plans to take Lois out on his first date. As she gets ready, Clark rather impulsively removes his glasses and announces (with puffed-up chest) that he has something important to tell her. This is a critical moment in the *Superman* movie because the split superhero no longer wants to keep his identity a secret from the woman he loves. However, the moment is a fleeting one. Clark puts his wide-framed lenses back on his face and reverts to his timid persona when Lois reenters the room. There are at least two reasons why he does this. First, superheroes have to maintain their mythic stature of anonymity to be effective crime fighters.[20] Second, and just as important, Superman feels Lois is not ready yet to handle his secret identity. Like his comic book prototype, he believes that people will be afraid of him and might even come to reject him if the truth ever be known that Clark Kent and Superman are one and the same.[21] Rather than risking the possibility of being spurned by Lois (and others), Superman decides it is best to keep his girlfriend in the dark regarding his super-shadow nature. In Jungian terms, our superhero does not want his identity brought to the light of conscious awareness but instead desires that it remain in the darkness of the human unconscious (and perhaps his own as well).[22]

By the end of the movie, Superman has thwarted Lex Luthor's plan to devastate the entire West Coast of North America by striking the San Andreas fault line with a nuclear missile. The aftershocks of the contained explosion still produce some rather horrendous effects, one of which is the death of Lois Lane whose car is crushed in an earthquake fissure. Superman is so busy resealing the fault that even his super speed cannot rescue Lois from this fate. After removing her body from the earth, the Man of Steel breaks down and cries, unable to restrain his human persona any longer. So overcome is he by his strong emotions that he deliberately disobeys the principal commandment handed down by Jor-El: Thou shalt not interfere with human history. Moving at faster than light speeds, Superman reverses the Earth's orbit and turns back time to before the disaster struck. A very much alive Lois does not realize what has transpired as our superhero flies away. She can only express relief that his superpowers have been able to save countless lives—including her own.

While some critics consider the last sequence to be totally illogical and "one of the biggest cop-out cheats in cinematic history,"[23] there is a purpose behind Superman's apparent madness. Like any other orphan who has been abandoned by his biological parents, Superman needs the hope that he will be cared for by someone on the planet. Lois Lane happens to be the one who has "rescued" him from his orphan state. She can help him embark on his heroic journeys and move him beyond this dependent mode he is experiencing. As Carol Pearson (1989) remarks, "Relying on someone outside of themselves . . . will allow them [orphans] to take charge of their lives. . . . the essential tool for helping all orphans is love—[given by] an individual or group who shows [genuine] care and concern."[24] Therefore, it becomes necessary to violate the prime commandment of noninterference if Superman is ever going to satisfy his human wants and desires. In a certain respect, by meeting the needs of his outward persona, Superman can more effectively use his super-shadow side to save others. And so returning Lois to life gives our superhero a renewed conviction that all human existence is sacred, especially Lois's who can eventually assist him in the integration of his divided personality in the next installment, *Superman II* (1981).

SUPERMAN II: AN ATTEMPT TO UNIFY THE COMPONENTS OF THE SUPERHERO SELF

Many reviewers, including the author of this book, regard *Superman II* as a better film than the original, chiefly because it attempts to treat the Lois Lane–Superman relationship with more seriousness and far less camp.[25] While the two characters are being developed to a greater extent, a crisis of almost global proportions threatens the world. Three criminals from Superman's home planet, Krypton, escape from their interdimensional prison located within the Phantom Zone and decide to come to Earth to rule over the primitive inhabitants with their combined superpowers. Lois and Superman find themselves so focused upon each other that they are totally oblivious to the danger for a good portion of the movie, bringing new meaning to the adage, "Love is blind [especially to everything else transpiring in the environment]."

What contributes to this narrow sightedness is the accidental discovery by Lois of Superman's secret identity. In his bumbling guise of Clark Kent, the superhero loses his footing and trips into a fireplace, yet he is able to recover quickly with no detectable flesh burns on his hands from the raging fire. Unable to provide a stunned Lois with a satisfactory explanation for the incident, Superman chooses to reveal his hidden shadow side, hoping she will accept his dual nature and not turn away. When Lois announces she is in love with him (*and* his Kent persona), Superman puts everything else on hold and flies the reporter to his Fortress of Solitude so that he can spend some significant time with her. The quarters are so far removed from civilization that nothing can interfere with the couple's intended romance, least of all the menace posed by the Kryptonian villains.

The creative genius of Mario Puzo can be seen at this point in the film. The writer had developed his first screenplay around the theme of Superman's becoming mortal so that he could form a deeper and more permanent bond with Lois.[26] Although the idea was rejected by the producers, Puzo was able to convince them to include it in *Superman II*, immediately following the scene where the two commit themselves to each other. The result was one of the most powerful cinematic sequences of all time, and we will now comment upon its archetypal impact.

While Lois is asleep, Superman decides to consult with a holographic image of his Kryptonian mother, Lara (reprised by Susannah York), in the hope that her wisdom will help him in his quest for mortality. She reveals that if he places himself in a crystalline chamber buried deep within the Fortress, all his superpowers will be removed. Before her son enters the enclosure, Lara asks him whether this is where his true destiny lies. Superman's reply is a simple one: his love for Lois has made everything brilliantly clear. As the chamber begins to rob the superhero of all his strength, Lara's image vanishes never to return. Along with many mythical heroes, Superman must "sacrifice his childhood," especially the dependence upon his parents.[27] This entails the death of his super-shadow side, which has linked him for so many years with his extraterrestrial family. Only by breaking away from his alien past can Superman ever attempt to develop lasting ties with the human race and, in particular, one very special woman. Thus, the ordeal our hero puts himself through represents a rite of passage from a clinging type of adolescence to a more responsible (and mature) adulthood.

The rays emitted from the chamber sear off the Superman part from the Kent persona to the point where all flesh is stripped away from the superhero's face, leaving a leering death's-head behind. Upon his emergence, Clark is in a more mortal attire; the cape and tights with which he entered the chamber are mysteriously gone. The significance here is that Superman has divorced himself from the fantasy world and all its inherent magical powers to be human and, thereby, more real. Even his reporter guise has been sacrificed for a more down-to-earth attractiveness. From a Jungian perspective, a heroic rebirth has occurred.[28] A whole new sphere has opened up for Clark. He can now be sexually intimate with Lois and procreate, ensuring that his line will continue for many generations. While some would argue that "*Superman II* is all about powerlessness,"[29] it is actually quite the reverse. Superman's abandonment of the superhero role for an ordinary mortality takes great strength and determination. By placing Lois before all the rest of humanity, he can finally fulfill his inmost need for human companionship. It seems a shame that the "more together" Clark must eventually return to his weaker, fragmented self by the film's conclusion.

The reversion back to Superman takes place in a series of stages. First, Clark quickly learns that he cannot protect Lois or himself from the bullies of the world while in the mortal frame. He is beaten up and thrown to the ground by one despicable character at a sleazy diner. Clark is astonished to find that he can bleed just like any other human, and this fact forces him to accept some of the more negative consequences of having such a vulnerable form. As though this incident does not present enough problems for the transformed hero, a television newscast relays to Clark and Lois that the world is being held hostage by three extraterrestrial renegades from Superman's home planet: the cunning General Zod (Terence Stamp), the vile Ursa (Sarah Douglas), and the brutish Non (Jack O'Halloran). They demand a confrontation with Superman; otherwise, they will kill an inestimable number of innocents until they achieve their objective. This is the second test Clark fails. Perhaps he might be able to stand up to ordinary human villains given enough training and endurance; however, superpowered ones are a different matter entirely. Clark realizes he is left with little choice but to go back to his Fortress of Solitude and hope he can reverse the process before a good portion of humanity suffers at the hands of the evil aliens.

Any hero (including Clark) has to accept one of the greatest paradoxes of human existence: the struggle with evil will never end, and any victory will be a short-lived one. It is the hero's misfortune to face new dangers and risks each and every day and hopefully rise above them; the alternative is "to go under" and die.[30] For Clark, returning to the Superman identity is one of these seemingly endless, life-and-death struggles which results in the termination of his mortality and a return to shadow invincibility (without the dependency on a Lois to sustain him).

Superman II's ending has an ironic twist to it. Our superhero is able to trick the villains into placing him within the strength-sapping chamber once more, thereby allowing them to think that the only obstacle in their path of global conquest has been permanently removed. In actuality, however, he has reversed the effects of the machine so that anyone outside (rather than inside) the enclosure will be robbed of their powers. Zod, Ursa, and Non are, thus, rendered impotent by the very device that temporarily gave Superman his more integrated type of existence. The trio become permanent residents in the Fortress of Solitude, forced to live out the rest of their mortality in isolation from those they had wished to subjugate.

While executive producer Salkind wanted *Superman II* to conclude on an upbeat note with the Man of Steel informing the president of the United States that he would not let the nation down again,[31] there remains a poignant scene between the superhero and Lois back at the *Daily Planet* office which should be further examined as it does color one's future perceptions toward this cinematic character. Lois relates to Clark/Superman that she is having difficulty dealing with his dual identity, especially when it comes to expressing her feelings of affection and love toward the "man" she wants to marry but cannot so long as crime fighting is the number one priority in his life. Because Lois is so emotionally torn over the situation, Clark decides to wipe her memory clean of the past few days by giving her a magical kiss. He is pleased to find the old Lois back, treating him in a platonic fashion once again.

The "fairy tale" spell which Superman places over Lois can be likened to the Jungian unconscious which possesses the reporter so completely that she forgets all the things she had intended to share with Clark.[32] By performing this action, our superhero has decided to return to his fragmented and unfulfilled self, which is regrettable. Unlike the *Superman* series of comic books, which did explore such incredible moments as a proposal and eventual marriage to Lois Lane,[33] the film sadly suffers by limiting the super potential of this figure in the area of human relationships. This is dismally manifested in the two remaining sequels, *Superman III* (1983) and *Superman IV: The Quest for Peace* (1987).

THE LESS THAN SUPER SEQUELS: THE SUPERHERO MAGIC IS FINALLY DISPELLED

In the second sequel, *Superman III*, Clark decides to return to his hometown of Smallville and while there rekindles a romance with his childhood sweetheart, Lana Lang (Annette O'Toole). Lana quickly becomes dependent on Clark, hoping that he might be the one to look after her mischievous son, Ricky, as well as rescue her from living out her remaining days in the small town—alone and unfulfilled. By the end of the film, Clark is able to convince his editor, Perry White, to hire Lana as a secretary so that the two of them (and, of course, Ricky) can be close to each other, much to the surprise of Lois Lane who has spent the last few weeks vacationing in Bermuda. It seems a shame that, apart from a cameo, Lois is written out of this screenplay since one yearns for the more passionate relationship between the fellow reporters.[34] An important question immediately comes to mind: why would the Man of Steel involve himself with a new woman and her familial burdens when he is still having problems dealing with his "fatal attraction" to Lois?

A Jungian interpretation might be that as middle age rapidly approaches, some humans have a difficult time coping with their perpetual singlehood and so retreat into their past looking for that special someone to give them comfort and security. Such individuals "can never have things as they would like them in the present . . . [and so] can only fan the flame of life by reminiscences of their youth [and all those lost loves]."[35] For Superman, it is his super-identity that prevents him from maintaining a normal existence with Lois.[36] And so like many adults dissatisfied with their current lifestyle, the superhero wants to turn back the clock to a simpler time before he became the invincible fighter of truth and justice, to a time when he was just an "ordinary" farm boy growing up with his adopted family in Smallville. By focusing on a childhood sweetheart, who has always accepted (and secretly loved) the Clark persona, Superman believes he can fully involve himself in a human type of relationship without any interference by his super-half.

Sadly, the Man of Steel cannot sustain the association with Lana much longer than what is depicted in *Superman III*. By not telling her who he really is, namely an extraterrestrial with superpowers who is committed to protecting the entire planet of humans, he is deceiving her and forcing himself to live a lie similar to those who impulsively want to change established careers and professions but cannot owing to obvious limitations.[37] Not so strangely, producers Alexander and Ilya Salkind decided to drop the Lana Lang character from the final *Superman* movie, acknowledging the inherent problems of continuing this already tenuous romance.

Despite this flaw, one major element did strengthen the *Superman III* plot. This had to do with the major battle between Superman's two sides: the upright, moralistic part and the repressed, yet intensely hedonistic, half.[38] The dangerous, "dark [super-] brother"[39] is released when the villains of the story, billionaire Ross Webster (Robert Vaughan) and computer hacker Gus Gorman (Richard Pryor), manufacture a piece of kryptonite to rid the world of the pesty superhero. Instead of robbing Superman of his powers and then killing him, the imperfect stone manages to bring out the hero's negative shadow qualities. The good part can barely contain the "restless, violent, stormy side" of Superman's character,[40] and so the Man of Steel engages in one destructive act after another (for example, sinking oil tankers and ruining the Olympic games), reveling in all the chaos he has created. He even starts to drink to highly addictive levels and womanize with some of the less desirable members of the opposite gender, transforming himself into one of the most despicable and amoral creatures on the planet—one whom children, as well as adults, can no longer look up to and respect.

The ultimate confrontation occurs in an auto graveyard when Superman's evil side manages to split off his outer shell, the Kent persona, from himself so that no force can ever restrain him again. The war between Superman's separated identities is an engaging one to watch because both opposites have superpowers: Clark has the energies of light and goodness on his side while Superman possesses (or is possessed by) the furies of hell and darkness. As the fight wages, the decaying setting reminds one of just how much the superhero's psyche can destroy itself if it has not attained the proper balance of gratification and denial of its own shadow impulses.[41] Ultimately, Kent gains the upper hand and strangles his doppelganger literally out of physical reality. The result is a reintegration of the dark side with its counterpart, which causes Superman to regain his psychic wholeness once again.[42] It is unfortunate that the film veered away from this intriguing subplot to the much campier super-villain finish, as it reminded one of all the comic book tales of shadowy doppelgangers (e.g., from the imperfectly formed Bizarro to an alternate earth double), who plagued Superman with their devilish, inverted powers.[43]

While *Superman III* might have had its redeeming moments, *Superman IV* was a monumental letdown.[44] Even Margot Kidder's return as Lois Lane and Christopher Reeve's coscreenplay of nuclear disarmament in humanity's "quest for peace" could not salvage the film from its obvious defects. Large chunks of past *Superman* story lines are presented in this installment but without the painstaking care and wonderful magic of the previous productions. Lex Luthor (reprised by Gene Hackman) is at it again, trying to find a way to destroy Superman once and for all; Lois recovers her repressed memory of Superman's secret identity only to find herself falling under the "amnesic kiss" a second time around; a gutsier and more liberated version of the Lang character, Lacy Warfield (played by Mariel Hemingway) sets her sights on Clark but fails to win him over with her womanly charms; and another malevolent super-double called Nuclear Man (Mark Pillow) is cloned from the genetic strands of Superman's hair and, naturally, causes all sorts of mischief in the city of Metropolis until he is put down by our hero. Though *Superman IV* had a team of new writers, including Lawrence Konner and Mark Rosenthal, it is apparent that the prior trilogy of films significantly shaped their work to the point where any original scenes were few and far between.

One of the picture's more creative sequences takes place when Nuclear Man slashes Superman's skin with his irradiated talons. The wounds run so deep that our superhero begins to lose all his powers and soon enters a feverish, near comatose state. He ages so rapidly that there is little hope of a cure from an almost certain death, until he recalls a "racial memory" implanted in one of the Kryptonian crystals. It speaks in his mother's voice, telling him that the energy residing within the stone can save him—but only once! Holding the crystal in his feeble hands, Superman regains his strength (and shadow side) and, thus, is able to conquer Nuclear Man in a final showdown. As represented in so many myths, the hero is able to regenerate himself by reestablishing ties with the one person he has fought so hard against, namely the mother.[45] By heeding her maternal advice, Superman establishes the much needed reunion that will ensure his continuation as a noble and valiant hero. It would appear that Kryptonians are no different than humans; both races must resolve parental conflicts if they are to survive and grow. And so the Superman saga ends on a happy note with our Man of Steel soaring upward to the sun, like a resurrected phoenix,[46] on the lookout for any new dangers that might pose a threat to humanity.

BATMAN: THE MOVIE—THE EMERGENCE OF THE "DARK SHADOW" HERO IN THE DEAD OF NIGHT

While Superman performed most of his crime-fighting exploits during daylight, the night was appropriately reserved for that darker, more mysterious superhero, Batman. Gotham City provides the perfect setting for Batman's war against the ever-expanding criminal element. Unlike the brightly colored, candy floss exteriors of the *Batman* television show, the movies (beginning with the 1989 feature) portray a harsher, more jagged skyline of the city with its gigantic, grey slabs shooting upward in an endless fashion. The barely recognizable (yet immense) constructions are intended to reflect the escalating fear of the populace who are being preyed upon by every assorted cutthroat.[47] Into this environment arrives a sinister Batman whose shadow side has to be just as mean and vicious as those predators he seeks to conquer. To make Gotham City a more habitable place for its citizens, the superhero has no choice but to strike fear and terror in the hearts of all criminals; to accomplish this, Batman must give the shadow full reign at the expense of abandoning his persona while in the hero's guise. Interestingly, this image of the Dark Knight shared a good many features with another popular, cloaked vigilante of the 1930s and 1940s, The Shadow. As a matter of fact, The Shadow inspired Bob Kane to create the archetypal character of the "Bat-Man" and was one of the pivotal forces in shaping the more recent movie incarnations.[48]

If the Batman shadow menaces, the Bruce Wayne persona (enacted by Michael Keaton) worries, sometimes too much. Though he is one of the richest men in Gotham City, Bruce is not comfortable with his inherited wealth, and he is, at times, awed by the expansiveness of his mansion. Bruce possesses some other eccentric qualities, which make the character appear very human, comparable to "any man off the street" who has a myriad range of troubles with which to deal.[49] An absentminded man, he forgets the names of several of his guests and requires Alfred's (Michael Gough) assistance in finding his socks. Like a typical voyeur, he monitors people within the confines of the Batcave to see what they are saying about him as well as to "call up" a reality he has missed out on because of the all-consuming crime-fighting priority.[50] The hidden cameras focus on one lovely photojournalist in particular, Vicki Vale (Kim Basinger), to whom he is sexually drawn yet intimidated by. Eventually, Bruce does seduce Vicki by getting her (and himself) drunk. When Vicki wants to develop a serious relationship with the man she has "bedded," Bruce invents some rather lame excuses not to see her again to maintain his secret identity.

As several critics have commented, Batman has a "neurotic" persona which cannot effectively function in the real world. Thus, the superhero retreats to a fantasy realm in which he battles bizarre criminals and confronts their even stranger machinations in order to cope and derive some meaning to his existence.[51] What causes the "split" for Bruce is the murder of his parents, which he witnessed as a child. He is so traumatized by the loss that he cannot share his pain with anyone—even Vicki. It makes psychological sense that, on the day right after he has sex with Vicki, Bruce buys two long-stemmed roses and lays them in the alleyway where his mother and father were gunned down. The Batman persona cannot find peace and happiness in that state so long as injustices are committed on the planet similar to the one to which he was so brutally exposed. Therefore, the shadowy alter ego is adopted as the hero's major identity. As an "obsessed (and essentially depressed) loner," Bruce-as-Batman can survive, but he can never let any humans come too close for fear that the fate that befell his parents might befall them.[52]

Into Batman's troubled universe comes the first film's principal adversary, the Joker (Jack Nicholson), who blames the caped figure for his "acidic" birth. In reality, the Joker's alter ego of gangster Jack Napier has caused his own persona's demise by attempting to gun Batman down in the Axis Chemical Factory. The bullets ricochet off of the superhero's armor and hit Napier directly in the face; blinded by the pain, the thug loses his balance and topples into a cauldron of toxic waste. Thus is born the Clown Prince of Crime who is crazed by the creature he has now become: a perpetually smiling jester with green hair, rouge-red lips, and a chalk-white face. The transformed Napier dedicates his very existence to bringing chaos into the world and opposes anyone (especially Batman) who strives to impose order and balance onto his demented universe.[53] To accomplish his mission, he shoots crime-lord Carl Grissom (Jack Palance) and takes over the organization. So that his employees do not cringe at his features while executing his insane commands, the Joker puts on a flesh-toned "mask," hoping to recapture some of his lost persona. However, the sickening smile cannot be covered up, and the makeup soon peels away, revealing the indelible shadow beneath. Inevitably, the Joker stops applying the facial masks as he recognizes the permanency to his new identity. This super villain is the very antithesis of the Batman figure who gives into his "dark humor shadow" completely, allowing it to twist his personality into everything foul and wicked.[54]

In a series of stages, the Joker changes Gotham City into a macrocosm of his twisted form. First, he laces hygienic products with a toxic chemical, appropriately named Smylex, which not only induces death in the unsuspecting Gothamites but also leaves rigor mortis grins on their faces.[55] Next, the Joker flings acid at his girlfriend Alicia (Jerry Hall), turning her into an exact carbon copy of himself. For the remainder of the movie, she is seen wearing a porcelain doll's mask to hide her "shadowed" disfigurement. Anything that represents beauty is subsequently corrupted by the Clown Prince of Crime. He "defaces" one artistic masterpiece after another at the Gotham City Museum, spray painting his name over each surface. Even technology is interfered with, as the Joker interrupts normal television broadcasting and inserts his own gruesome advertisements into the programming schedule.[56] Perhaps the crowning achievement comes when the villain includes his own garish procession of floats (with accompanying poison gas balloons) in Gotham City's 200th anniversary parade. The pedestrians are too busy to notice the deadly clouds of gas descending upon them because they are distracted by hordes of greenbacks the Joker has thrown out into the crowd. Again, an orderly procession of events is converted into complete chaos as the citizens fight each other for possession of the stray bills.

Batman manages to foil most of the Joker's schemes, finding an antidote to the Smylex compound and removing the lethal floats (with his trusty Batplane) before they can do permanent harm to the Gothamites. It is inevitable that the two opposing forces finally confront one another atop Gotham City's cathedral. Both "shadow" figures cannot escape their destiny (because there is nowhere to go but down), and it is here that the two learn about their mysterious, symbiotic relationship.

As Jenette Kahn (1989) indicates, Batman and the Joker have shared a "Yin/Yang duality" since the very beginning, with the superhero's obsession against crime complementing the madman's rage against anything normal.[57] This duality of the shadow natures is strikingly revealed in the film's dialogue: the Joker announces that Batman created his pathology when the crime fighter did not rescue him from that deadly plunge into the vat of acid; Batman responds that his parents were murdered by the Joker's persona of Jack Napier, making him an obsessed (and forever solitary) creature of the night. Credit should be extended to screenplay writers Sam Hamm and Warren Skaaren for effectively linking up the origins of both the hero and villain in such cruel twists of fate. Neither Batman nor the Joker "truly understands the bond" that is shared by the other until the final moments of the film, and by then it is too late.[58] Unlike the cinematic magic of a *Superman* movie, where time can reverse itself and destiny can be changed, there is an established permanency to the shadow identities. The only way Batman and the Joker can rid themselves of their "split-half" is through death.

In keeping with this argument, the Joker perishes by falling off the cathedral's belfry to his doom. Fortunately, Batman survives to fight another day. He cannot, however, resume a normal life as millionaire Bruce Wayne. There is too heavy an investment in the super-shadow side of his personality which cannot be removed, no matter how hard he tries. This is clearly seen at the film's conclusion when Vicki waits for Bruce in his limousine, and waits, and waits. Having discovered he is the Dark Knight, she realizes that Bruce's first order of business will be to vanquish crime and corruption in the streets of Gotham City, with little time left over for anything (or anyone) else. In her eyes, Bruce Wayne/Batman will always possess this fragmented self, until the day he meets a fate as tragic as the Joker's.

BATMAN RETURNS: MORE "SPLIT" VILLAINS INVADE GOTHAM CITY

The second *Batman* movie, appropriately titled *Batman Returns* (1992), lingers more on the personalities of the Penguin (Danny DeVito) and the Catwoman (Michelle Pfeiffer) than it does on the superhero of the tale. Similar to the comic book prototypes of the 1940s, these cinematic super villains prove to be more than just supporting characters; they become an integral part of Batman's universe and, consequently, share the same troubled nature as the Dark Knight.[59] Like Batman, both Penguin and Catwoman assume the form of a shadow animal (a vicious fowl and a slinky feline) to deal with a moral dilemma in their lives. Both become so comfortable in their new roles that there seems little hope of ever recovering their "lost" personae.

The prologue of *Batman Returns* centers exclusively on the pre-Penguin identity of Oswald Cobblepot. Oswald is born in a highly deformed state, with flipper-like appendages for hands, an aquiline nose, and a rotund frame which makes him waddle instead of walk. His wealthy parents cannot bear to look at him, let alone handle him with affection, and so Oswald is kept penned up during his brief stay with them. One night the Cobblepots decide to take the boy for an evening stroll and, without any remorse, throw him (and his baby carriage) into the sewers of Gotham City.[60] A nest of penguins that inhabit the underground quarters chance upon the child and rear him as one of their own. Upon reaching adulthood, Oswald proclaims himself to be the Penguin, relishing the idea that he is more animal than man, and he vows to bring down all the upper class of Gotham (as he considers them primarily responsible for his ostracism from human society). Though it is easy to see why the Penguin takes on the shadow guise that he does, in time this subterranean creature turns into the "pure embodiment of evil" who gives in to his bestial impulses freely and without reservation.[61]

Director Tim Burton deliberately takes more time explaining the birth of the Catwoman since her alter ego of Selina Kyle is just as complex (if not equally neurotic) as Batman's Bruce Wayne.[62] Selina is introduced as a drab, mousey type of individual who has little backbone when dealing with her oppressive boss, Max Shreck (Christopher Walken). She caters to Max's every want and desire, making him coffee, picking up his dry cleaning, and even tolerating his quite obvious sexual advances toward her. But, Selina is hardly a fulfilled woman. Outside of performing her menial jobs at work, she lives a life of complete loneliness in her bachelorette apartment with her only companion, a cat named Miss Kitty. Neo-Jungians Carol

Pearson and Katherine Pope (1981) note that many women like Selina are denied any heroic stature for it is the privileged males of our society (such as Max Shreck) who make them feel inadequate, inferior, and imperfect.[63]

Interestingly, it is Shreck who forces Selina to adopt a new identity when he catches her snooping around his office late one night. Selina's feline curiosity has led her to the discovery that Max intends to sap all of Gotham City's electric power with his fully automated power plant, and it is her curiosity that ultimately "kills" the Kyle persona. Shreck cannot allow Selina to live with this knowledge; subsequently, he throws her out of a window to solve a corporate problem. But fate intervenes: all of the stray cats congregate around Selina's body and magically restore her to new life as the Catwoman by breathing their very essence into her body. Selina's fall from the building of Shreck Industries is symbolic of the Jungian hero's descent into the shadowy depths of the underworld. Only by being defeated by an apparently invincible enemy can the hero (or in this case, anti-heroine) gain new strength as well as a renewal of convictions to win any upcoming battles against the same foe.[64] Selina does not die but becomes something larger than life: an unbeatable shadow feline possessing nine lives and a powerful vindictiveness against all males who had forced her to repress her animus cravings for so long.

One of the best scenes in *Batman Returns* occurs when the "transformed" Selina goes back to her apartment and trashes the place, spray painting the pink walls and eggshell furniture with a sickly black color. Intending to remove all aspects of her former identity forever, she even throws her stuffed animals into the garbage disposal.[65] Then, in honor of her awakened shadow, Selina sews the remaining scraps of her clothing into a slinky, vinyl costume complete with needle-sharp claws and accompanying hood. The Catwoman surveys her new home, satisfied that her neon sign now announces the message "HELL HERE" instead of the former "HELLO THERE." For the very first time, this woman is able to express herself with "a power and grace she never admitted to in her earlier [more juvenile] life."[66]

After making herself comfortable, the Catwoman sets her sights on the male species, targeting cutthroat and police officer alike. As she dispatches one mugger, the antiheroine proudly hisses to the dismayed female victim, "I am Catwoman . . . hear me roar," in a send-up of the 1970s Helen Reddy feminist lyric, before she slinks away into the night.[67] Later, when she confronts two security guards, the villainess is sickened by one of their sexist remarks, "I don't know whether to open fire or fall in love."[68] She responds rather haughtily that the pair cannot tell the difference between their guns and genitalia and then torches the store they were so impotently guarding. Clearly, Selina/Catwoman is avenging not only her wrongs, but also the injustices visited upon her entire gender. She uses her shadow side as a vehicle to combat her daylight persona of female inferiority and dependency, and so the Catwoman reflects the feminist equivalent of the more masculine-oriented, animus archetype.

Batman and the Penguin are not spared from this vengeful creature's wrath, and both are openly attacked with claw and whip when it suits her purpose. One wonders why the Catwoman allies herself, albeit briefly, with the Penguin in order to destroy Batman.[69] After all, like Shreck, the Penguin represents everything she hates about the world of male privilege, especially when the fowl felon plans to impose more masculine order and control by running for the position of Gotham City's mayor. Philip Orr (1994) attempts to give a rationale for Catwoman's actions. Quite simply, Batman "is a man" and represents the oppressive patriarchy just as much as the Penguin does.[70] Therefore, the Catwoman tries to play one foe against the other, using her feminine wiles to get what she ultimately wants: the total destruction of the male order. In time, the Penguin sees through her deceptive (albeit pleasing) exterior and attempts to hang her with one of his flying umbrellas when their fiendish union is not consummated in wedded bliss. Even Batman is repeatedly taken in by the Catwoman's charms and is punctured more than once by her "loving" claws, until he treats her as a suitable adversary and punches her with all his might. Although she falls to her death at the hands (or umbrellas) of each of these enigmatic males, the feline figure manages to come back from the grave—reanimated and whole each time. The Catwoman cannot (and will not) be killed, so long as the shadow female voice needs to be heard and asserted in this lopsided male-oriented culture of ours.[71]

Curiously, the "feminist avenger" is attracted to Batman's persona of Bruce Wayne and falls in love with him. She recognizes in Bruce a kindred spirit of the night and seeks the companionship that she was denied in her pre-Catwoman existence. The feelings are mutual, and before Bruce and Selina realize it, they are in each other's arms first at his mansion and later at the Masquerade Ball. But, their romance is destined to end in disaster for how can two split personalities establish a lasting bond when their shadow sides keep getting in the way?[72] For Selina, the problem is even more magnified: how can she give in to her more sensitive, womanly nature, or anima, when she has made a vow to crush all males?

After Bruce and Selina discover each other's dual identity, the "love-hate tension in the Bat-Cat relationship" quickly escalates.[73] The unmasked Bruce has high hopes that the split both have lived with can be mended by the other's presence. The still masked (and symbolically hidden) Selina responds that Bruce's fairy tale dream is so typical of his gender, adding, "I'm not a house cat . . . I just couldn't live with myself [like that]."[74] She then rakes his exposed face with her claws, showing him that the Catwoman side is just too powerful to ever control with love and affection. The scene is a tragic one for both Bruce and Selina: neither can function in the real world with their inadequate personae. So the "Romeo and Juliet" pair must retreat back into the fantasy existences of bat and cat, covering up their psychic wounds as best they can.[75]

By the end of *Batman Returns*, everyone is playing their shadow roles to the hilt. The Penguin schemes to lure all the first-born sons of Gotham City's wealthiest into the sewers to drown, in a reenactment of his own grisly childhood experience. However, Wayne puts on his cowl once more and prevents this from happening, defeating the nefarious bird in a round of good old-fashioned fisticuffs. Humiliated, the Penguin attaches missiles to each of his fowl-feathered friends and directs them via electronic signal to destroy all the borns (first to last) of the great metropolis. Being the sophisticated wizard that he is, Batman jams Penguin's signal and sends the birds back to their lair instead where the bombs go off, sending the "freak of nature" to his watery grave. While this is a fitting death for the Penguin, the final confrontation between Catwoman and Max Shreck is the more eagerly anticipated one. Upon seeing Shreck, Catwoman demands "a die for a die." Not even Max's bullets can stop her from grabbing a generator's open fuse box with her talons and electrocuting both of them. Because she has the immortal properties of a feline, Catwoman is able to survive the deadly jolt. Shreck, on the other hand, is not so lucky and is burned to a crisp.

This modern fairy tale would appear to end on a somewhat ambivalent note. On the positive side, by slaying her male captor (as well as rejecting her male lover), the Catwoman is finally able to control her own destiny and does not need to conform to the expectations of the repressive patriarchy ever again.[76] Conversely, by embracing the darkness of her new identity, our antiheroine is just as alone as Batman, lingering on the rooftops of the city like some stray kitten without an established residency to call her own.[77] The fate (or curse) of these super characters is that the division between their shadows and personae run so deep that nothing can ever make them complete or fulfilled. As Tim Burton so indelicately phrased it in a number of interviews, "They're all fucked up," and perhaps therein lies their archetypal appeal.

BATMAN FOREVER: THE "SPLIT" SIDES OF HEROES AND VILLAINS REMAIN FOREVER INDELIBLE

Batman and *Batman Returns* set the mold for this third Dark Knight outing, entitled *Batman Forever* (1995). Once more there are two super villains who possess "split" selves: Harvey Dent/Two-Face (played by Tommy Lee Jones) and Edward Nygma/the Riddler (Jim Carrey). Reminiscent of the Vicki Vale character, Dr. Chase Meridian (Nicole Kidman) provides the superhero's love interest. Unlike Vicki, though, Chase finds Batman more sexually appealing than his Bruce Wayne persona and is drawn to the "scarred" psyche, having studied the symptoms of multiple

personalities and related psychoses herself for so many years. Completing
the group of principal players is Dick Grayson/Robin (portrayed by Chris
O'Donnell), whose thirst for justice is just as strong as his mentor's. What
is so archetypally blatant about *Batman Forever* is that each character is
exploring the persona and shadow parts of their own personality, with little
hope of ever achieving a comfortable reconciliation. "Duality is very much
the theme of this picture,"[78] to the point where the darkness of Gotham
City is interspersed with a shocking, daylight color and brightness totally
absent from the previous entries.

One major change should be addressed in this latest *Batman* film: the
replacement of actor Michael Keaton by Val Kilmer in the lead role. Some
critics have remarked that Keaton was perfect for the part, imbuing the
Dark Knight with a truly "schizoid" disposition that no one else could.[79]
Val Kilmer plays his Batman with a slightly different interpretation: he is
younger, sexier, and less cerebral than his predecessor, and he creates more
believable romantic entanglements with the female lead, Chase Meridian.[80]
These traits also allow Kilmer to be an appropriate role model for the
abandoned Dick Grayson (one could hardly say that one wanted to emulate
the Keaton portrayal). As this writer viewed Val on the screen, he could
not help but compare his Bruce Wayne to Christopher Reeve's alter ego of
Clark Kent. While Bruce was hardly a bumbling reporter, he did wear the
unmistakable glasses whenever the opportunity presented itself and elicited
the angst-ridden looks when dealing with the unapproachable female. The
similarities between the Kent and Wayne personae in *Batman Forever*
should not go unnoticed because they definitely adhere to the more traditional, comic book image of the split superhero on the screen. Let us now
examine some of the supporting characters in more depth, as their psychotic splits are just as fascinating as Batman's.

Two-Face is a villain whose disfigurement and lifestyle are done up in
Jungian ambivalency. Outwardly, Two-Face displays his dual sides for all
the world to see. His left (or sinister) facial half is the one that is horribly
distorted while the right retains the physical characteristics of his former
persona of district attorney Harvey Dent. In his novelization of *Batman
Forever*, Peter David (1995) describes Two-Face's split appearance as follows: "The right side of his face was much as it had been . . . [but] the left
side looked like a relief map of purgatory, except in this purgatory, there
would never be any redemption or forgiveness . . . just more, and greater,
insanity."[81] Because Two-Face has to endure this chimeric form, he trans-
forms everything else in the same ghastly image. The furnishings at his
criminal headquarters are split right down the middle: one side is decorated
in cheery, white contours and the opposite side in depressing black. Joining
Two-Face in his twisted campaign of crime are Sugar and Spice, an opposing pair of females who provide the appropriate sexual companionship
(i.e., normal or kinky) for each half of his personality. Even his weaponry

is an amalgamation of two different time periods: the tommy guns and get-away automobiles taken from the Depression era combined with the more high-tech gadgets of the future.[82] Given these splits, it is no wonder that Two-Face experiences a major identity crisis, at times preferring to be called Harvey and at other moments desiring the more criminal appellation.

Perhaps the most striking aspect of Harvey Dent/Two-Face's duality is that he relies on the random flip of a coin to decide most of his actions. A special significance is attributed to each toss outcome, in keeping with the Jungian concept of synchronicity. For example, "heads" might signify that Two-Face will ally himself with the Riddler in his war on Batman while "tails" might indicate that the Riddler dies for having invaded his private sanctum underneath Gotham City Bridge. The synchronous meaning derived from such "improbable, chance happenings" originally came about when Harvey was prosecuting an underworld boss.[83] He was not expecting the mobster to throw a vial of acid directly in his face during a critical part of the trial proceedings. If Harvey had stepped back, ducked, or anything else but freeze, he would have prevented his maimed condition. The reality was he did nothing and a sequence of tragedies ensued, including his birth as the highly emotive Two-Face whose twisted logic now allows him to see absolute certainty in improbabilities.[84] For instance, his crusade against Batman is predicated on the simple basis that the superhero was in the courtroom while he was undergoing his "baptism by acid" and could not save him from his kismet. Thus, the odds determined that he change his righteous, Harvey Dent nature and dedicate his life completely to "the toss," which he considers to be the only truth in the world. It is poetic justice that Two-Face falls to his death while tossing a coin that will decide his very own fate, illustrating Jung's synchronicity once more. "He who lives by the toss will most assuredly perish by it" might be a suitable motto for *Batman Forever*'s Two-Face.

Reviewers have regarded the Riddler's persona of Edward Nygma (or E. Nygma for short) to be as riveting as the Catwoman's Selina Kyle, due no doubt to actor Jim Carrey who played his pathological part as though he were in "a manic ballet . . . cavorting around like some nut Nijinsky."[85] When the audience is first introduced to Edward, he comes across as a brilliant (and quite restrained) research scientist at Wayne Enterprises who has perfected a device that can transmit television signals directly into the human brain, thereby creating the most realistic, holographic images for each viewer. Edward hopes that he has impressed his boss, Bruce Wayne, to the point where he can count on his financial backing. However, Bruce recognizes that by manipulating brain waves in this fashion, the potential exists for controlling people's minds on an almost global scale, and he turns down Nygma's proposition. This rejection is the critical turning point for Edward who decides to go into business for himself, not caring whom he harms with his invention. As actor Carrey disclosed in an interview, "Edward gets so wrapped up in Bruce Wayne's success . . . [that] he loses himself because he covets somebody else's world and somebody else's trip."[86] The respect and admiration he once held for Bruce are converted into jealousy and hatred for the man who has opposed him. Moreover, the frenzied Edward uses the technology he has developed to transfer the brain waves of all Gothamites into his skull, thereby increasing his intellectual capacity and accompanying delusional state exponentially.

Once the madness takes a firm hold, Nygma must abandon his persona and adopt a shadow disguise whereby he can vent all his frustrations, yet still be enigmatic enough (with pun intended) so as not to be identified by the one person who has thwarted his endeavors, millionaire Bruce Wayne. He decides on a leotard outfit saturated with question marks, along with a patterned jacket, eye mask, derby, and cane. The color Nygma chooses for his ensemble is very fitting: it is a fluorescent lime hue signifying the "green with envy" feeling he has for Bruce (and later Batman when he discovers the two are one and the same).[87] And so the Riddler emerges on the crime scene, intending to rule the planet with his brain drain machine. His demented plan does not succeed, and in the end it is the Riddler who falls victim to the power-hungry device and its overloaded circuits. Apparently, the raw, negative emotions he possessed made him "blind as a bat" and prevented him from foreseeing his own destiny: namely, to spend the remainder of his days locked up in a padded cell, devoid of all rationality and claiming to be Batman, with "the sleeves of his straitjacket madly flapping around like the wings of some huge bat."[88] Only in the depths of insanity could the Riddler make a connection with his hated nemesis, at the expense of sacrificing his own shadow identity forever.

Dick Grayson/Robin is directly patterned after the Bruce Wayne/Batman character, starting with his origin as a superhero. Dick loses his parents and older brother at the hands of the central antagonist (in this case, Two-Face). Throughout the first half of *Batman Forever*, the orphaned Dick struggles with the psychic trauma as best he can, pushing everyone away from his shattered universe. Bruce empathizes with the young man because they have both shared the identical experience of witnessing their own parents' deaths.[89] And so Bruce adopts Dick, hoping that in some small way he can give comfort to Grayson and prevent him from developing a split personality over the tragedy. In essence, Bruce wants to give Dick the chance he never had: to survive as a complete self, with persona and shadow intact.

As time passes, it becomes obvious that the only way Dick can cope with the loss is by creating a separate and fragmented identity in which he can heal and act out his rage toward all criminals (most especially Two-Face who robbed him of a normal life).[90] Batman, however, advises his young protégé that going after Two-Face with the sole intent of killing him will not make the suffering go away: "Killing damns you. I know. . . . You fight night after night, trying to fill the emptiness, but the pain's back in the morning. Somewhere along the way it stops being a choice."[91] Despite these words, Batman does not prevent Dick from making the decision to be his shadow partner and to pursue Two-Face since he realizes that each person is held accountable for his own existence and no one else's. And so a fellow winged companion, Robin, joins Batman not to fight crime, but to seek "a death for a death" retribution.

By the end of *Batman Forever*, the issue is resolved for Robin. As Two-Face plummets to his doom, Dick-as-Robin takes no pleasure in the event. If anything, his face displays a certain remorse over the loss of a human life. The young superhero psychologically "recovers" from the madness that has possessed him for so long, and he chooses a new goal: to bring all criminals to the courts instead of taking the law into his own hands. As Batman and Robin are seen racing side by side into the night, one can conclude that both have hardly been "cured" of the trauma that has created their shadow identities.[92] The pair still stand apart from the rest of humanity, isolated souls who crave the warmth of a normal relationship but can never obtain that inmost desire so long as they want to remain in their superhero roles. Even the title of the movie, *Batman Forever*, is a reference to both crime fighters coming to terms with their split condition and achieving a resolution of sorts: to continue the heroic battles in order to effectively contend with any recurring, depressive episodes in their fractured personaes.[93]

The *Superman* and *Batman* films remind the viewer that being an archetypal hero carries a heavy price. Although the superhero identity is perceived as a "blessing" by those people who are victimized by society's predators, it is also regarded as a "curse" by the bearer who must forever remain locked in that inadequate guise until the day he (or she) dies. One of the trends in the fantasy genre of late is to depict more ordinary mortals undergoing the metamorphosis to superhero status (*The Shadow*, 1994; *The Phantom*, 1996). The fascination with such cinematic characters is that, for all their acquired gifts, they still yearn for an "everyman" lifestyle which, sadly, they can never have. The newest *Batman and Robin* (1997) appears to have established a precedent for allowing a female (in this case, Alicia Silverstone's Batgirl) to partake of the hero's split personality, for better and for worse, as the superhero's exploits continue into the next decade and beyond.

NOTES

1. James F. Iaccino, "Jungian Archetypes in American Superhero Comic Strips: The Hero's Shadow Side," in *Understanding the Funnies: Critical Interpretations of Newspaper Comic Strips Worldwide*, ed. Ken Nordin and Gail Pieper (Lisle, IL: Procopian Press, 1997), 65, 70–72.

2. Paul Sassienie, *The Comic Book: The One Essential Guide for Comic Book Fans Everywhere* (London: Chartwell Books, 1994), 22–23.

3. Mike Benton, *Superhero Comics of the Silver Age: The Illustrated History* (Dallas: Taylor Publishing, 1991), 106; Iaccino, "Jungian Archetypes in American Superhero Comic Strips," 66.

4. Mike Benton, *Superhero Comics of the Golden Age: The Illustrated History* (Dallas: Taylor Publishing, 1992), 136.

5. Bill Boichel, "Batman: Commodity as Myth," in *The Many Lives of the Batman: Critical Approaches to a Superhero and His Media*, ed. Roberta E. Pearson and William Uricchio (London: BFI Publishing, 1991), 4–7; Sassienie, *The Comic Book*, 23–24.

6. Philip Orr, "The Anoedipal Mythos of Batman and Catwoman," *Journal of Popular Culture* 27 (Spring 1994): 176–77.

7. Benton, *Superhero Comics of the Golden Age*, 69–70.

8. Iaccino, "Jungian Archetypes in American Superhero Comic Strips," 68; Will Jacobs and Gerard Jones, *The Comic Book Heroes: From the Silver Age to the Present* (New York: Crown, 1985), 30.

9. Andy Medhurst, "Batman, Deviance and Camp," in *The Many Lives of the Batman: Critical Approaches to a Superhero and His Media*, ed. Roberta E. Pearson and William Uricchio (London: BFI Publishing, 1991), 156–58.

10. Benton, *Superhero Comics of the Silver Age*, 56.

11. Robert Bookbinder, *The Films of the Seventies* (New York: Carol Publishing Group, 1993), 237; Vincent Canby, "Review of *Superman*: Nothing 'Went Wrong,'" *New York Times*, 24 December 1978, Part II: Section 11: 1; Vincent Canby, "Review of *Superman*: Super Cast," *New York Times*, 15 December 1978, Section C15: 1.

12. Richard Meyers, *The Great Science Fiction Films* (New York: Carol Publishing Group, 1990), 110.

13. Carl G. Jung, "Archetypes of the Collective Unconscious," in *The Archetypes and the Collective Unconscious: The Collected Works*, trans. R.F.C. Hull (Princeton, NJ: Princeton University Press, 1990), 33–34.

14. Edward F. Edinger, *Ego and Archetype: Individuation and the Religious Function of the Psyche* (London: Penguin Books, 1972), 48.

15. Carl G. Jung, "The Significance of the Father in the Destiny of the Individual," in *Freud and Psychoanalysis: The Collected Works*, trans. R.F.C. Hull (Princeton, NJ: Princeton University Press, 1989), 315.

16. Meyers, *Great Science Fiction Films*, 113.

17. Robert H. Hopcke, "Archetypes and the Collective Unconscious," in *A Guided Tour of the Collected Works of C. G. Jung* (Boston: Shambhala, 1992), 16; Jung, "Psychological Aspects of the Mother Archetype," in *The Archetypes and the Collective Unconscious*, 82.

18. Carol S. Pearson, *The Hero Within: Six Archetypes We Live By* (San Francisco: HarperCollins, 1989), 33–34.

19. Bookbinder, *Films of the Seventies*, 238.

20. Robert Inchausti, "The Superhero's Two Worlds," in *The Hero in Transition*, ed. Ray B. Browne and Marshall W. Fishwick (Bowling Green, OH: Bowling Green University Popular Press, 1983), 70–71.

21. Benton, *Superhero Comics of the Golden Age*, 136.

22. Robert H. Hopcke, "Shadow," in *A Guided Tour of Jung*, 81.

23. Meyers, *Great Science Fiction Films*, 114.

24. Pearson, *Hero Within*, 40–41.

25. David Denby, "Review of *Superman II*," *New York* 14 (22 June 1981): 49; Andrew Sarris, "Review of *Superman II*," *Village Voice* 26 (10–16 June 1981): 51; Steven H. Scheuer, *Movies on TV and Videocassette* (New York: Bantam Books, 1991), 1028.

26. Meyers, *Great Science Fiction Films*, 110.

27. Carl G. Jung, "The Battle for Deliverance from the Mother," in *Symbols of Transformation: The Collected Works*, trans. R.F.C. Hull (Princeton, NJ: Princeton University Press, 1990), 303–4; Jung, "The Dual Mother," in *Symbols of Transformation*, 356.

28. Jung, "Symbols of the Mother and of Rebirth," in *Symbols of Transformation*, 255, 272.

29. Sheila Benson, "Review of *Superman II*," *Los Angeles Times*, 18 June 1981, Calendar, 1; Denby, "Review of *Superman II*," 50; Richard Reynolds, *Super Heroes: A Modern Mythology* (Jackson: University Press of Mississippi, 1992), 67.

30. Jung, "The Dual Mother," in *Symbols of Transformation*, 348–50; Hopcke, "Hero," in *A Guided Tour of Jung*, 114.

31. Douglas Brode, *The Films of the Eighties* (New York: Carol Publishing Group, 1991), 269; Meyers, *Great Science Fiction Films*, 223.

32. Jung, "Archetypes of the Collective Unconscious," in *The Archetypes and the Collective Unconscious*, 22.

33. Benton, *Superhero Comics of the Silver Age*, 107.

34. Sheila Benson, "Review of *Superman III*," *Los Angeles Times*, 17 June 1983, Calendar, 1.

35. Carl G. Jung, "The Stages of Life," in *Aspects of the Masculine*, trans. R.F.C. Hull (Princeton, NJ: Princeton University Press, 1989), 30.

36. Iaccino, "Jungian Archetypes in American Superhero Comic Strips," 65.

37. Jung, "Stages of Life," in *Aspects of the Masculine*, 33.

38. Robert Asahina, "Review of *Superman III*," *New Leader* 66 (27 June 1983): 22.

39. Hopcke, "Shadow," in *A Guided Tour of Jung*, 81.

40. Carl G. Jung, "Wotan," in *Civilization in Transition: The Collected Works*, trans. R.F.C. Hull (Princeton, NJ: Princeton University Press, 1990), 192.

41. Carl G. Jung, "On the Nature of the Psyche," in *The Basic Writings of C. G. Jung*, trans. R.F.C. Hull (Princeton, NJ: Princeton University Press, 1990), 94.

42. Carl G. Jung, "Definitions, under Self," in *Psychological Types: The Collected Works*, trans. R.F.C. Hull (Princeton, NJ: Princeton University Press, 1990), 431.

43. Benton, *Superhero Comics of the Silver Age*, 102, 107.

44. Anne Billson, "Review of *Superman IV: The Quest for Peace*," *Monthly Film Bulletin* (September 1987): 283; Mike McGrady, "Review of *Superman IV: The Quest for Peace*," *Newsday*, 25 July 1987, Part II, 7; Scheuer, *Movies on TV and Videocassette*, 1028.

45. Jung, "The Sacrifice," in *Symbols of Transformation*, 431–32.

46. Jung, "The Dual Mother," in *Symbols of Transformation*, 347–48.

47. John Marriott, *Batman: The Official Book of the Movie* (New York: Bantam Books, 1989), 86–89.

48. Ibid., 8; Iaccino, "Jungian Archetypes in American Superhero Comic Strips," 70.

49. William Uricchio and Roberta Pearson, "I'm Not Fooled by That Cheap Disguise," in *The Many Lives of the Batman: Critical Approaches to a Superhero and His Media*, ed. Roberta E. Pearson and William Uricchio (London: BFI Publishing, 1991), 183.

50. Jim Collins, "*Batman The Movie*: Narrative and the Hyperconscious," in *The Many Lives of the Batman: Critical Approaches to a Superhero and His Media*, ed. Roberta E. Pearson and William Uricchio (London: BFI Publishing, 1991), 168.

51. David Denby, "Review of *Batman The Movie*," *New York* 22 (17 July 1989): 46; Orr, "The Anoedipal Mythos of Batman and Catwoman," 169–70; Peter Travers, "Review of *Batman Returns*: Bat Girls on the Line," *Rolling Stone*, 9 July 1992, 109.

52. Roberta Pearson and William Uricchio, "Notes from the Batcave: An Interview with Dennis O'Neil," in *The Many Lives of the Batman: Critical Approaches to a Superhero and His Media*, ed. Roberta E. Pearson and William Uricchio (London: BFI Publishing, 1991), 19; Bill Zehme, "Review of *Batman: The Movie*," *Rolling Stone*, 29 June 1989, 41.

53. Uricchio and Pearson, "I'm Not Fooled by That Cheap Disguise," 198.

54. James F. Iaccino, *Psychological Reflections on Cinematic Terror: Jungian Archetypes in Horror Films* (Westport, CT: Praeger Publishers, 1994), 167–68.

55. Zehme, "Review of *Batman: The Movie*," 42.

56. Collins, "*Batman The Movie*: Narrative and the Hyperconscious," 167–68.

57. Jenette Kahn, "Tribute," *Detective Comics* 599 (April 1989).

58. Ken Hanke, "Review of *Batman The Movie*," *Films in Review* 40 (October 1989): 480; Mike McGrady, "Review of *Batman The Movie*," *Newsday*, 23 June 1989, Part III, 3; Uricchio and Pearson, "I'm Not Fooled by That Cheap Disguise," 198–99.

59. Benton, *Superhero Comics of the Golden Age*, 70; Kim Newman, "Review of *Batman Returns*," *Sight and Sound* (August 1992): 48.

60. Craig Shaw Gardner, *Batman Returns* (New York: Warner Books, 1992), 4.

61. Richard Blake, "Review of *Batman Returns*: Menagerie à Trois," *America* 163 (22 August 1992), 89.

62. Mindy Newell, *Catwoman* 4 (New York: DC Comics, 1989): 16; Orr, "The Anoedipal Mythos of Batman and Catwoman," 181.

63. Carol S. Pearson and Katherine Pope, *The Female Hero in American and British Literature* (New York: R. R. Bowker, 1981), 18–25.

64. Hopcke, "Hero," in *A Guided Tour of Jung*, 114; Jung, "Symbols of the Mother and of Rebirth," in *Symbols of Transformation*, 259–61.

65. Barbara Cramer, "Review of *Batman Returns*," *Films in Review* 43 (October 1992): 338.

66. Gardner, *Batman Returns*, 89–90.

67. Richard Alleva, "Review of *Batman Returns*: 'Meow!' She Roared," *Commonweal* 119 (14 August 1992): 30.

68. Gardner, *Batman Returns*, 119.

69. Alleva, "Review of *Batman Returns*," 30.

70. Orr, "The Anoedipal Mythos of Batman and Catwoman," 180.

71. Pearson, *Hero Within*, 89–90.

72. David Denby, "Review of *Batman Returns*," *New York* 25 (13 July 1992): 63–64.

73. Blake, "*Batman Returns*," 89.

74. Gardner, *Batman Returns*, 236–37.

75. Peter Travers, "Review of *Batman Returns*," *Rolling Stone*, 23 July 1992, 111.

76. Pearson and Pope, *Female Hero*, 103–20.

77. Orr, "The Anoedipal Mythos of Batman and Catwoman," 181.

78. Berthe Roegger, "Review of *Batman Forever*: Batman Reborn," *Sci-Fi Entertainment* 2 (June 1995): 41.

79. Pauline Kael, "Review of *Batman: The Movie*: The City Gone Psycho," *New Yorker* 10 (July 1989): 84; Marriott, *Batman*, 38–39.

80. Jack Kroll, "Review of *Batman Forever*: Lighten Up, Dark Knight!", *Newsweek* 125 (26 June 1995): 54; Ralph Novak, "Review of *Batman Forever*," *People Weekly* 43 (26 June 1995): 21.

81. Peter David, *Batman Forever* (New York: Warner Books, 1995), 41.

82. Roegger, "Review of *Batman Forever*: Batman Reborn," 44–45.

83. Carl G. Jung, "Appendix: On Synchronicity," in *Synchronicity: An Acausal Connecting Principle*, trans. R.F.C. Hull (Princeton, NJ: Princeton University Press, 1991), 115.

84. Jung, "Exposition," in *Synchronicity*, 32–33.

85. Kroll, "Lighten Up, Dark Knight!," 54.

86. Will Murray, "Review of *Batman Forever*: Riddler Forever?" *Starlog* 218 (September 1995): 28.

87. Bruce Bibby, "Review of *Batman Forever*: Riddle Me This, Batman," *Premiere* 8 (May 1995): 59.

88. David, *Batman Forever*, 245.

89. Bibby, "Review of *Batman Forever*: Riddle Me This, Batman," 57–58; Marc Shapiro, "Review of *Batman Forever*: Robin Forever," *Starlog* 217 (August 1995): 28.

90. Michael Brody, "*Batman*: Psychic Trauma and Its Solution," *Journal of Popular Culture* 28 (Spring 1995): 175–76.

91. David, *Batman Forever*, 174.

92. Brody, "*Batman*," 176.

93. Novak, "*Batman Forever*," 21.

7

The *Indiana Jones* and *Highlander* Chronicles: Quests for the Holy Grail Archetype

Just one aspect of the archetypal hero will be considered in this chapter: his (or her) acquisition of a marvelous treasure that will transform the self as well as the world. Many of the great grail stories of legend relate how the heroic seeker can be spiritually renewed and given new life once that sacred object is in his possession. Before we proceed with our archetypal interpretation of the *Indiana Jones* and *Highlander* film sagas, we should spend a few moments mentioning the key elements in some of the grail myths.

INTEGRAL COMPONENTS OF THE GRAIL MYTHS

In the Fisher King legends of the twelfth century, the kingdom is ruled by a monarch who was severely wounded in the groin. Since he is not a fertile ruler, his entire kingdom is a wasteland in serious need of renewal. "The crops are dying, the monasteries are empty, and the people are depressed."[1] All the king can do is fish all day, hoping that someone will come to make him and his people whole again. The wandering Parsifal arrives at the Grail Castle wherein dwells the Fisher King along with several sacred objects (including a chalice, a bloodstained lance, and a shallow dish). Since the young Parsifal does not know their intended function, he is unable to assist the wounded monarch until several years later when he has acquired sufficient knowledge. Upon his return, he takes the spear and touches the Fisher King's genitals with the bloody tip, thereby healing the ruler of his injury. At that same moment the entire kingdom is restored to its former beauty and glory. In some of the myths, Parsifal takes the place of the transformed "Grail King" to become the new guardian of the sacred treasures. The paradoxical part of the story is that the king never realized he had the power to cure himself in his very own castle. Only an outsider was able to answer the timeless question, "Whom do these grail objects truly serve?"[2] The reply is, of course, the very people to which they have been entrusted.

Many of the objects in the Fisher King tale can be associated with Jesus Christ's crucifixion. The cup, which served as the goblet during the Last Supper, was supposed to contain some of Christ's blood which he shed on the cross. Along with the chalice was the dish which had held Jesus's final meal, a simple fare of bread.[3] Finally, the bloodstained lance was originally used by one of the Centurion guards to pierce the side of the crucified Jesus in order to ascertain that he had expired. It should be pointed out that not all grails are so intimately connected to the Christian savior. In tracing the origins of grail tradition, John Matthews (1990) provides an entire list of sacred treasures that hold some special significance. Some accounts describe an emerald jewel, which fell from the dethroned Lucifer's crown, that had the power to cast an enlightened, godlike status upon the bearer; still others reveal that one of the progeny of Adam and Eve, Seth, was given a magical cure by God allowing humanity to rid itself of all its "sinful" sicknesses; Celtic tradition depicts an ancient cauldron with the properties of restoring life and bestowing rare favors upon the holder; and alchemic writings indicate that the philosophers' stone was able to transmute base metal into pure gold.[4] Even with this wide assortment of supernatural objects, the one most associated with the grail is the Christian chalice, often referred to as the Holy Grail.

The quest for the Holy Grail is the basis of the popular Camelot story. The Knights of the Round Table, headed by King Arthur, experience a common vision of the Grail floating on a beam of light during the Pentecost celebration. All the knights take a solemn pledge to seek out the holy object and, if possible, bring it back to Camelot whereupon the kingdom will become the New Jerusalem, or earthly Paradise. The quest is not successful for many of the knights: most are killed in their search or die in their attempt to retrieve that most precious object. Only three, who are pure of mind and heart, actually accomplish the task. One of the three, Sir Galahad, dies "in ecstasy" after encountering the Grail; another, Sir Perceval (sometimes referred to as Parsifal), decides to remain at the Castle of the Grail to become its new ruler; and finally, Sir Bors returns to Camelot "to tell of the miracles" before setting out on a new crusade.[5]

At this point, one might inquire what is so special about the Holy Grail that knights would devote their entire lives to finding it. From an archetypal perspective, the Grail represents a lasting covenant between God and man through the continued presence of Christ within the chalice. Similar to the Jungian mandala, Christ symbolizes the complete self, "a glorified man . . . unspotted by sin," to which all should aspire.[6] Edward Edinger (1972) further remarks that the blood of Christ is the life of the human soul and that it is a divine source of nourishment for those who sip the contents of the Grail. Thus, the very essence of the cup is "life-sustaining energy" which can feed millions and cause a spiritual renewal of mind as well as body.[7] If we had the chance, many of us would seize the opportunity to transcend the limitations of the flesh by partaking of the eternal Grail, and the knights were certainly no exception to the norm. Given this mythic overview, let us now look at some film portrayals of grail-related objects, beginning with the popular heroic-adventure trilogy, *Indiana Jones*.

RAIDERS OF THE LOST ARK: THE KNIGHT BEGINS HIS QUEST

Susan Aronstein (1995) regards the three films, *Raiders of the Lost Ark* (1981), *Indiana Jones and the Temple of Doom* (1984), and *Indiana Jones and the Last Crusade* (1989), collectively, as the exploits of a knight who rescues maidens and liberates people from tyrannical rule before undertaking the most heroic quest of all: the search for the Holy Grail itself.[8] If one searches deeper, though, each movie can be regarded as a journey toward a sacred object that will elevate its principal character, Indiana Jones, to a more spiritual level than the physical one of simple "fortune and glory." As the knights were transformed by their quest, Jones has changed (for the better) by the end of each journey. This is perhaps the strongest power of grail treasures: to make each seeker more chivalrous and honorable—the very precepts to which all knights, past and present, should adhere.[9]

The first movie, *Raiders of the Lost Ark*, starts off at a rapid pace, with a character sketch of the "pre-knightly" Jones right after the opening credits. The date is 1936 and Indiana (portrayed by Harrison Ford) is searching for an idol in the jungles of South America. As soon as he gets possession of the golden object, he loses it to his adversary Belloq (Paul Freeman). Both men are "flawed" in the sense that they will do anything to obtain the idol—even desecrate another culture's temple to plunder its treasures. One reviewer notes that Jones and Belloq have the same egotistical character (at least initially): they can benefit most handsomely by cashing in on their prize.[10] Since Belloq has the idol, Jones perceives him to be the "winner" and concedes his defeat until the ensuing bout, which is not long in coming.

Indiana's entire attitude toward the next grail object he sets his sights upon, the Ark of the Covenant, is especially disturbing. Rather than heeding the advice of his friend Marcus (played by the late Denholm Elliott), who believes that there might be some great spiritual force residing within the Ark which the Nazis might be able to use to their advantage, Indiana regards the container of the Ten Commandments as nothing more than a find "of great historic and cultural significance."[11] He even tells Marcus that the American Army Intelligence will probably pay a generous price for its retrieval. Because Indiana scoffs at the mystical powers of the Ark, he is not connected to anything (or anyone) sacred. He does not carry "the voice of God" within his soul, and so most of his life is spent wandering from one expedition to the next, with the one constant being the terrible loneliness and isolation he feels because he is so removed from others.[12]

The failed relationship he had with a fellow archaeologist's daughter, Marion Ravenwood (Karen Allen), attests to the fact that Indiana does not want to get too close to another. He regards people like the objects that he seeks, to be used and then discarded when their usefulness has ended. The now adult Marion discloses to Jones that she loved him and he just tossed her aside on his way up the professional ladder to success. All he can say is that he is terribly sorry this happened, but he will not admit his responsibility for taking advantage of a teenage girl's first romantic encounter. Just as Marion has learned to hate him over the years, the audience comes to loathe the insensitive side of Indiana Jones. We wish he was "the knight in shining armor," ready to marry the maiden who has been pining for him. Instead, Indiana comes across as an ignoble brute who only desires the medallion Marion has acquired in order to identify the exact location of the Ark. That is the primary reason for his return visit to her bar, and it is, at best, an exploitative one.

Unlike those knights of legend, Indiana places Marion's life in jeopardy one time after another. Our "pre-hero" is so preoccupied with his goal of obtaining the Ark that he inadvertently leads the Nazis straight to the maiden's door, and later he allows them to abduct her in the most public of places, a busy Cairo street.[13] *Raiders of the Lost Ark* proves to be an interesting inversion of the typical Arthurian romance in which the central figure is the "worthless protector" and the maiden is the "gutsy, Amazonian warrior." Marion can drink the rowdiest of her customers under the table, and she even knows how to handle a weapon (a quality most fairy tale princesses do not possess); in fact, she shoots one of Indy's assailants point-blank in the head.[14] But for all her brashness and ingenuity, Marion is still victimized by the evil forces of Germany because she has been entrusted to a mere apprentice, Indiana Jones, who has not yet mastered the knightly code of proper heroic conduct.

As the movie unfolds, Indiana does metamorphose into a true hero, but it is not a simple conversion. He first has to experience the "loss" of Marion (he believes that she has perished in an explosion and holds himself accountable for her "death"). Then Indy must confront his doppelganger, the evil Belloq, a second time. The conversation between the two is most illuminating as it sheds some light on what Indy really values in life. As Belloq explains with such insight, "Archaeology has always been our religion, our faith . . . the historic relic, the quest—it is like a virus in your blood . . . [that is] the vice we have in common."[15] Jones has to admit to himself that he and Belloq share the same shadow nature when it comes to coveting any precious grail object. If unchecked, this tragic flaw in Indy might push him over the edge and make him as villainous as Belloq.

Luckily, Jones does not become a reflection of Belloq but attains a true heroic status. The turning point comes when he must face his worst shadow fear in the pit where the Ark is buried. The ground is infested with venomous snakes of all shapes and sizes. For centuries, snakes (as well as serpents) have been regarded as "favorite symbols for describing psychic happenings that suddenly dart out of the unconscious."[16] While their presence might free up dangerous and powerful instincts from the shadow side of our personality, they can also provide us with the necessary knowledge and wisdom to advance to new levels of existence.[17] Navigating through the snake-filled terrain can be considered a mixed blessing for Indy. One wrong move and he will most certainly die; however, if he can manage to survive in this archetypal underworld, he will learn to appreciate human life more fully. The wisdom imparted by the snakes is immediately displayed by Indy when he recovers Marion (who is thrown into the pit with him) and hugs her *with feeling*. She matters more to him than the Ark which is taken away by Belloq and his Nazi associates. Perhaps Marion is the greatest grail of them all since she "opens up" Indy to "something good within his core" which he can now actualize and give freely to others.[18]

Of course, Jones does not give up his quest for the Ark, but his approach to the sacred object has become ennobled, thanks to his newfound appreciation for Marion. Indy will not allow the Germans to use the Ark for their own nefarious purposes for he recognizes the awesome, godlike power contained within it. He would rather have the Americans keep the Ark in a safe place where it can do less harm. Indiana's patriotism is so strong that it propels him to engage in one knightly feat after another, from wrestling with Germany's mightiest warriors in hand-to-hand combat to stopping an enemy convoy by first leaping onto the lead truck from horseback and then hanging from its underside until he can successfully incapacitate the driver. We are able to cheer for Indiana because he is one of the "good guys," fighting to preserve American democracy from the international forces of tyranny.[19] Some have even compared Indy to the political figure of Ronald Reagan in that his "holy mission" is similar to Reagan's stand on foreign policy which, in essence, stated that the United States would remain a beacon for freedom in the world only if its leaders did not waver in their convictions but remained strong and upright both in word and deed.[20] Indy is able to move beyond his own simple, egocentric desires of possession and self-gratification and perceive the more global issues at stake should the Ark fall into the wrong hands. And it is this macrocosmic (almost presidential) thinking that makes Indy the perfect candidate to bring the Ark back to his kingdom of America.

As in many grail adventures, a final showdown between the knight and his shadow counterpart must ensue before the prize is won.[21] In *Raiders of the Lost Ark*, Belloq and Jones confront each other one last time on an isolated Mediterranean island, a location the Germans have chosen to release the energies of the Ark in the hopes that they will be able to control the forces before conferring them onto their leader, Adolf Hitler. Belloq manages to gain the upper hand and captures both Indy and Marion and allows them to witness the opening of the Ark before their intended demise. Belloq's victory is short-lived, however. Once the Ark's seal is broken, "the light of creation" streams forth and pierces Belloq and the other raiders with its penetrating brilliance.[22] Convinced that the grail object holds a supernatural force beyond all comprehension, Jones warns Marion to keep her eyes shut and not to look in the direction of the Ark—no matter what. Indy's advice saves them both, and order to the world is restored after the Ark magically reseals itself.

Raiders of the Lost Ark's archetypal knight recognizes his most grievous sin of possessing grail objects and, in the epilogue, counsels the intelligence officers about the dangers involved if they "blindly" try to examine the Ark's secrets. Like Indy, we are able to see the true meaning of the grail. Put simply, we can be spiritually transformed only if we abandon our greedy, materialistic desires. As John Matthews and Marian Green (1986) suggest, this grail experience must be made continually conscious to ourselves and others around us if it is to have lasting benefits.[23] For our hero, Indiana Jones, the quest for the Ark would be only one in a series of journeys toward other sacred objects and further self-enlightenment.

INDIANA JONES AND THE TEMPLE OF DOOM: THE KNIGHT REJUVENATES A WASTELAND

The second *Indiana Jones* feature, *Temple of Doom*, is actually a prequel to *Raiders of the Lost Ark* with the time period set one year earlier (i.e., 1935).[24] This is not only of chronological importance, but also of archetypal significance. The Jones character cast in *Temple of Doom* is the pre-knight, "a mercenary out for his own gain . . . uncontrolled by any sort of chivalric code."[25] He has not yet had the Ark encounter; therefore, he views archaeological objects solely in terms of their cash—not religious—value. Since Indy is rarely depicted in his professorial garb as the esteemed Dr. Jones, one even questions whether he appreciates the historic import of the artifacts he unearths.

When the audience first sees Indy at Shanghai's Obi Wan Club, he is attired in a white dinner jacket with accompanying vest, bow tie, and a red carnation in his lapel. Though the image is very debonair, Jones's motives are not.[26] He has been hired by a despicable crime boss, Lao Che (Roy Chiao), to retrieve the ashen remains of Emperor Nurhachi, the first warlord of the Manchu dynasty, in exchange for a priceless diamond. Indy does not really give a damn who possesses Nurhachi's urn; all he cares about is the payment for the services he has rendered. But, he has seriously miscalculated the intentions of Lao Che. Upon delivery of the urn, Lao Che double-crosses Jones, poisoning his drink so that there are no witnesses to the sordid transaction. What follows is utter chaos: the nightclub turns into a war zone with Indy trying to obtain the vial that contains the antidote to the poison while dodging bullets, knives, and other assorted weapons.[27] He manages to retrieve the vial, yet he is doggedly pursued by Lao Che's minions through the back streets of Shanghai as well as up in the sky over the Indian continent before parachuting out in a rubber raft with his newly acquired companions, singer Willie Scott (Kate Capshaw) and the precocious preteen, Short Round (Ke Huy Quan).

There is little doubt that this opening to *Temple of Doom* is a cinematic treat for the old-time, movie serial aficionado.[28] On a more profound level, however, the film sends another message. Dr. Jones is out for himself, and he places those around him in continual danger as he proceeds to take what he can get—by legal or crooked means. The rendition of Cole Porter's "Anything Goes" (sung by Willie at the nightclub) typifies the creed to which Indy has dedicated his pre-*Raiders of the Lost Ark* existence. It proves to be a dangerous one to follow as some of the club patrons are injured or killed, including his best friend, Wu Han (David Yip). Critics have regarded the Indiana Jones character as a fatally flawed individual who is so ungovernable that he can destroy others as well as himself should he embrace the lifestyle of the "outlaw."[29] From this perspective, the adventures that transpire can be construed as lethal traps which Indy has inadvertently set by his own misguided philosophy. Even in sleep, there await numerous perils for Jones and his crew (e.g., the airplane and jungle sequences), so long as the leader of the ragtag group does not aspire to anything higher or more noble of purpose.

The golden opportunity does present itself to Indy rather unexpectedly upon his arrival in the village of Mayapore. The elderly tribal chieftain explains that a dream portended Jones's coming and that "the outsider" would help his people recover the sacred stone, Sivalinga, which was ransacked from their shrine. This grail object apparently blessed the villagers with good luck; after Sivalinga was taken, "the wells dried up and the river turned to sand . . . [then] the crops were swallowed by the earth and the cows turned to dust . . . [finally the plunderers] stole their children and took them [and the stone] to Pankot Palace."[30] The chieftain believes that their god, Krishna, has listened to his prayers and sent Indy to them in their most desperate hour. Though the old man acknowledges the value of Jungian synchronicity, Indy does not.[31] He discounts the words of the chief as nothing more than primitive superstition, and he plans to leave the Fisher King wasteland in the morning.

But, another meaningful coincidence presents itself to the narrow-sighted Jones that night: one of the local children returns to the village after making his escape from Pankot Palace. In his hands he holds a fragment of parchment that depicts Sivalinga as one of the Sankara stones of legend—an incredibly potent talisman that has great mystical (not to say market) value.[32] Although Indy reaches a critical decision to embark on a new quest to Pankot Palace, he hardly regards it as a holy mission of God (or Krishna). Instead, it is journey that will line his pockets with ready cash should he find Sivalinga. Like Parsifal, he does not yet recognize the spiritual, rejuvenative force buried within the stone—so blinded is he by his own capitalistic urges of "fortune and glory."

In the Palace of Pankot, Indy and crew discover a series of underground tunnels which lead to the Temple of Doom. Here they witness a number of "sadistic . . . and oppressively ugly" actions committed by the Thuggees, a resurrected cult group devoted to the pagan god Kali.[33] Human hearts are yanked out of chests by the high priest Mola Ram (Amrish Puri), before the still animated bodies are thrown into the fiery bowels below. The abducted children of Mayapore are also treated in a brutal fashion: they are shackled and severely whipped by the Thuggee guards and are forced to use their bare hands to dig into the rock to find the missing Sankara stones. (Once the set of five is obtained, Mola Ram intends to rule the planet with his insane religion) Indy cannot tolerate these obscenities any longer, and he attempts to free the innocent boys and girls from the yoke of human slavery, even if it means abandoning his egocentric quest for Sivalinga. Thus begins the "eye-opening" journey that will move Indiana Jones out of his mercenary lifestyle into the mode of the hero.

Like *Raiders of the Lost Ark*, *Temple of Doom*'s passage is not an easy one for Indy. He must confront his inner demons once again, only this time it is his "dark self" that he must face.[34] The Thuggees capture Jones and bring him to Mola Ram, who forces him to drink a foul-tasting liquid referred to as "the blood of Kali" (which is the antithesis of the life-giving, Christian substance[35]). After the poison penetrates his system, an immediate change comes over the archaeologist. He willingly becomes a true convert to the Thuggee religion, and he obeys the orders of Mola Ram without question or hesitation. James Kahn's (1984) description of this sequence is most fitting: "His [Jones's] eyes, normally so deep, so clear, flecked with coppery gold, crystal-pure—his eyes had undergone some indescribable transformation. Something about them was opaque now. Tarnished . . . cold. He was lost."[36] Many knights to be, including Parsifal, must encounter their doppelganger self (or Black Knight) before they can partake of the grail mystery. And it is a gut-wrenching, tormenting type of experience for them as they come to realize they possess a "death-dealing" evil that can be just as great as the forces they are trying to vanquish—if left unchecked.[37] Harrison Ford's cinematic portrayal of "turning toward the shadow side" in *Temple of Doom* appears to be compatible with these grail accounts.

Apparently the intended, sacrificial offering of Willie into the fiery pit by Mola Ram does not phase Indy as he remains unmoved by the proceedings. Just when all looks hopeless (for both the lead female and the potential hero), Indy's young sidekick manages to snap him out of the zombie trance. Of course, Short Round uses a very persuasive technique: a torch applied directly to Professor Jones's chest.[38] But it is Short Round's words, "I love you," that carry the real magic, returning Indy back to his familiar persona. As mentioned in the analysis of *Raiders of the Lost Ark*, people like Marion can be grails just as much as revered objects, so long as they can give others a meaning and value to their existence.[39] For Indiana Jones, the love of another person given freely and without restrictions proves to be the most powerful sorcery in that it elevates him to a new level much more humanitarian in scope. As Indy hugs the boy in appreciation for what he has done, the audience is able to register the emotion as the first caring feeling the man has actually elicited toward another in the entire movie. And we, like Jones, experience a sense of pleasure that the struggle with the shadow side has led to a most desirable outcome for our new knight in shining armor.

In the final "roller coaster ride" minutes of *Temple of Doom*, everything falls into place.[40] Indy liberates the children and vanquishes Mola Ram with a little help from the Sivalinga stone. The object literally burns the hand of the Thuggee high priest while Jones explains in the Hindu dialect that he has betrayed Krishna. Mola Ram's fall to his doom is fitting, but even more so is Indy's ability to snatch Sivalinga in midair and not experience the same deadly burns from touching the stone. He now knows the true power of the grail: it will bring life to all those who believe in its magic. When Jones and company return to Mayapore, they find that the barren countryside has been restored to its former splendor (in Fisher King style): "Trees budded beside streams that flowed clear and bright. Flowers were trying to bloom. And peasants were tilling their fields [once more]."[41] Indy does not seem surprised by the topographical transformation since he has encountered one of a deeper and even more spiritual nature in the course of his quest. Although the temptation of personal fortune and glory might persist in Indy's psyche and lead him on the wrong path again in *Raiders of the Lost Ark*, there is every assurance that the young knight will try to recapture that sacred contact with the Sivalinga stone in whatever future grail objects he pursues with a passion, from the Ark of the Covenant to even the Holy Grail itself.

INDIANA JONES AND THE LAST CRUSADE: THE KNIGHT
GOES AFTER THE GREATEST GRAIL OF THEM ALL

In *Last Crusade*, two opening vignettes clearly reaffirm the pre-knightly
disposition of Indiana Jones. A young Indy (portrayed by the late River
Phoenix) is after the precious Cross of Coronado; unfortunately, looters
lay claim to the artifact and manage to sway the local law officials to their
side. Though Indy loses the battle to another "Belloq" (who sports a highly
distinctive fedora upon his head), he does not abandon the pursuit. If anything, he is encouraged by the unnamed villain to give chase, and he receives the fedora as a token of his adversary's respect and admiration for
what he has almost accomplished that day. Approximately thirty years
later, the more mature Indy is able to retrieve the Coronado Cross and
bring it back to the university's museum where he is gainfully employed as
a professor of archaeology.[42] Indiana succeeds in this second outing primarily because he has become his own worst shadow enemy. He has mod-
eled his actions after Fedora (for lack of a better name) and so remains
unaffected by the number of people who perish as a direct result of his
personal vendetta. Even Jones's dress resembles that of the mercenary's,
right down to the felt hat he proudly displays as part of his accepted,
criminal heritage. Indiana appears to have taken a step backward from the
end points of *Raiders of the Lost Ark* and *Temple of Doom*, relishing the
"code of the self" over the more knightly virtues befitting a nobleman of
the court.

What makes *Last Crusade* the most memorable entry in the film trilogy
is that it continually contrasts Indy's baser motives with those of his father's, Professor Henry Jones (played by Sean Connery). When we are first
introduced to the older Jones, he is engrossed in a piece of parchment which
will lead him to the precise location of the Holy Grail. Not even the young
Indy's latest adventure with the Coronado Cross can distract the elder from
his work. Ironically, we never get a chance to see the father's visage because
the camera remains on Indiana throughout the first vignette. The direction
executed by Steven Spielberg is done in a deliberate fashion: the boy is so
preoccupied with his own materialistic desire to possess objects that he does
not take the time to appreciate the father's higher "quest of spiritual enlightenment [and understanding]."[43] This opening sequence sets the stage
for the later conflicts that transpire between father and son.

From an archetypal analysis, many knights-to-be (as well as mythological
heroes) are fatherless. Without the presence of that parental figure in their
lives, such heroes have to make their own way, meaning that they have to
become independent and take charge of their own destiny. Sometimes, they
might set their ambitions too high, resulting in many failures and far too
few successes.[44] While the character of Indiana Jones does have a father,
he still feels the latter's absence in his development. And like other knights-

to-be, Indy is constantly on the lookout for a substitute father who can provide him with the direction he sorely needs.[45] Sadly, it is the Belloqs and Fedoras of the world whom Indy encounters and patterns his lifestyle around rather than his own flesh-and-blood "Grail-King."

The only saving grace for Jones is that his friend Marcus Brody (reprised by the late Denholm Elliott) accompanies him throughout the *Last Crusade* and offers him some fatherly wisdom that will help him find the now missing family member as well as recover the Grail.[46] That the elderly Professor Jones has been kidnapped while continuing his lifelong search for the sacred chalice reinforces the view that Indy is fatherless to an even greater extent than ever before since there now exists the possibility that the "old man" might have died. While in this vulnerable state, Indy begins to ask Marcus some serious questions, such as, "Do you believe the Grail actually exists?" Marcus's answer is an insightful one which our hero must reflect upon throughout the movie: "The search for the cup of Christ is the search for the divine in all of us. I know. You want facts. But I don't have any for you, Indy. At my age, I'm willing to accept a few things on faith. I can feel it more than I can prove it."[47] For Indy to admit that some basis exists for the Grail legend is to acknowledge that his father had dedicated his career to something very valuable, in fact, the most precious of all artifacts. One can understand why Indiana is reluctant to accept the position advanced by Marcus; to do so would involve a radical reorientation of his philosophy toward archaeology. The discipline might indeed be more a search for truth rather than what he has naively accepted for so many years: the examination of scientific fact.

When Indy rejoins his father (who is alive and finally visible to the audience), the reunion is hardly a joyous one. Henry mistakes him for one of his captors and smashes a vase over his head. Although it is an accident, perhaps the elder considers his offspring more like the villains of the tale for having gone his own way than following in the former's footsteps. Certainly, Henry treats Indy as a child when it comes to dealing with the mysteries of the Grail. That is why he calls his young and inexperienced son "Junior" time and time again. Indy is offended by the label and rejects it with the remark, "Don't call me Junior."[48] His refusal to accept the name is symbolic of his refusal to accept the teachings of the old man. However, the events that unfold would seem to indicate that the parent does know more than the son, confirming Jung's view that the archetypal father is possessed with a spirit that can guide the hero on the correct path, especially through his admonishments and criticisms.[49]

First off, Henry points out to Junior that the woman he has slept with, Dr. Elsa Schneider (Alison Doody), is really a spy sent by the Nazis to recover his most important work, the Grail diary. Indy does not heed his father's warning, and sure enough Elsa pockets the diary right before his unbelieving eyes. Second, Henry is able to extricate both of them from a

Nazi stronghold by simply sitting down in a chair and reflecting on their predicament; as he begins to lean backward, a trigger mechanism is activated which opens up part of the floor, revealing a ramp that leads them both to the outside courtyard. Indy is amazed by the good fortune as he has usually relied on his knuckles and brashness to get him out of dangers instead of the mental abilities exercised by his dad. Third, after they have made their escape, Henry has to instruct Junior as to the importance of the Grail quest. It is not to obtain eternal life for the self, but to prevent the armies of darkness from prevailing over the entire globe with its power. Indy scoffs at the explanation, relating that he has never understood his father's obsession with the Grail. He even punctuates his comments with a blasphemous "Jesus Christ" which not only offends the father, but also shows his ignorance to the real meaning behind the Grail; namely, to reflect and magnify God's glory—not one's own (or, in this case, Indy's fortune and glory).[50]

After more adventures involving the Nazis, father and son are able to pool their resources and establish that the Grail is buried somewhere in the valley of Hatay. The trail leads them to a majestic temple wherein await three challenges for any knight bold enough to possess the mystical cup. Indy is reluctant to continue the quest, especially when he witnesses several Nazis fail the first of the three tests and die. However, the American traitor Donovan (Julian Glover) forces Jones to make the crucial decision by shooting his father point-blank in the chest. Indy realizes that he must abandon all logic and make the necessary act of faith. He must believe in the healing power of the Holy Grail if the elder is to survive.[51] And so he enters the Grail cave ready to face the deadly booby traps, armed only with his father's diary of knowledge (which he now must accept as the truth). It should be noted that our hero is without his favored whip since he knows that his intellectual abilities are needed to solve the Grail mystery instead of his physical prowess.

Each challenge Indy faces involves an alchemic work, a deciphering of clues that will lead him to a "greater development of his [own] consciousness," so that he is in the proper state of mind to receive the Grail.[52] The first test involves Indy's kneeling down so that the "Breath of God" (i.e., a razor-sharp pendulum) does not decapitate him. The second task, "proceeding in the footsteps of the Word of God," requires even greater powers of discernment. Indy must correctly spell God's name, Jehovah, beginning with the Latin letter "I" so that he can hopscotch over the correct, alphabetically labeled stones to safety. The final (and most demanding) test requires Indy to place his complete faith in the Almighty and leap onto an invisible bridge which spans a deadly chasm. Following the "Path of God," he arrives at the Grail chamber where he is greeted by an ancient guardian who confers the well-deserved status of knighthood upon him for being successful in his quest.[53]

Before the Keeper of the Grail can give Indiana the sacred treasure, Donovan intrudes upon the scene and seizes the shiniest cup encrusted with the most colorful stones from an altar of assorted chalices. In many respects, Donovan resembles the pre-knightly Indy who is seeking only his own immortality. Such an egotistical desire proves to be the villain's undoing. After he drinks from the wrong chalice, Donovan literally ages to death. This sequence would suggest that there are "black [or anti-] Grails" which bring about destruction instead of creation.[54] Fortunately, Indy does not make the same mistake as Donovan. Exercising his newfound wisdom, he chooses a simple, wooden vessel which might have been owned by a carpenter's son, and he allows his father to sip of its life-giving fluids after testing the contents himself. The result is miraculous: Henry Jones's wound quickly heals to the point where he can get up and stand with some assistance from Indy and Marcus. The professor does not seem to show any surprise in his amazing recovery as he has always accepted as truth that the Holy Grail contained these renewing energies.

The question is then posed by the father: what has Indiana learned from this ultimate quest? Though the son cannot provide a response to the elder, Indy's actions betray his inner state of mind. By allowing the Grail to fall into a magical abyss, he has obtained the greatest prize of all: his own father's illumination.[55] With that newly acquired insight, the knight is bestowed the worthy title of Henry Jones Junior (which elevates him above the more commonplace designation, Indiana, which was shared by the family mongrel). Comparable to the ending of the Fisher King tale, the Junior Jones has at long last attained the status of the Senior Jones and will be able to transmit that inherited wisdom effectively to a new generation of students, having realized that there are more important goals in life than the simple acquisition of physical objects.[56] *Last Crusade* concludes the trilogy on an optimistic note, with the "continuity of kingship" (as well as scholarship) being maintained in the Jones's lineage.[57] The sacred quests would seem to be over as both father and son have drunk from the Holy Grail and have reached their absolute fulfillment.

THE *HIGHLANDER* TRILOGY: AN OVERVIEW

The sword-and-sorcery set of *Highlander* tales also involve a search for the grail archetype. Unlike the *Indiana Jones* chronicles, the sacred object is not something that has a physical presence; rather, it lies within the very soul of its principal character, Conner MacLeod (Christopher Lambert), who is ready to emerge at the time of "The Gathering."

Some opening comments are in order to help orient the reader to the multiple (and sometimes confusing) timelines presented in each of the *Highlander* stories. Since our earliest history, a race of immortals has coexisted with the human species. By experiencing a mortal death and surviving, these superhuman creatures (who look just like us) can live countless generations. However, other immortals can kill them by severing their heads from the shoulders and absorbing their life essence in a ritual termed "The Quickening."[58] The rules followed by this race are simple and direct: (1) fighting is necessary so that there are few to covet "the prize" on the day of the Gathering; (2) claiming sanctuary on holy ground will temporarily halt the battles; and (3) procreation is not an option (although one can have sexual relations) to ensure that a proper balance exists between death and regeneration. What that ultimate grail encounter will be remains a mystery in keeping with the assorted mythologies, but should an evil immortal claim the prize, then death and devastation will be wrought upon the entire planet.[59] It is hoped that someone pure of heart and mind will survive the Quickenings so that order can be restored to the universe once more. Conner MacLeod is one of these latter immortals whose complex lifespan is depicted in the *Highlander* trilogy (to date).

HIGHLANDER: THE HUNT BEGINS FOR THE PRIZE

The first *Highlander* (1986) film provides the necessary historical background for the two ensuing sequels in a series of flashbacks interspersed throughout its first half. Before becoming an immortal, Conner MacLeod and his clan waged a fierce battle with the Black Knight, Kurgan (Clancy Brown), and his minions across the Scottish Highlands in 1536. Unfortunately, MacLeod was slain by the invader, only to find himself reborn in a perfect, unblemished state. Believing that this miracle was the devil's work, Conner's people banished him from his home of Glenfinnan. Alone and dejected, Conner chanced upon an elderly immortal, Juan Sanchez Ramirez (Sean Connery), who instructed him in the ways of the immortals.[60] Soon, MacLeod was prepared to take on any of those who desired his head, but Kurgan proved to be a formidable opponent. In the dead of night, the Black Knight beheaded Ramirez and vowed he would seek out MacLeod across the centuries until there would be only one of his race left (namely himself) to inherit the spoils of the Gathering. Thus, the motivation was established for the anticipated duel between these two immortals in the present-day time line.

While the *Highlander* story is hardly an original one, it does contain some central ingredients of the grail myth. First, Juan Ramirez typifies the Merlin figure: he possesses "hidden knowledge" about the race of immortals and is, moreover, a "seer" of MacLeod's future.[61] Ramirez prophesies that Conner will contend with Kurgan at the time of the Gathering, but that he himself will be one of those who will "fall by the wayside . . . [having] lived too long already."[62] Second, the reference to Kurgan as the Black Knight is in keeping with the Fisher King legend in which Parsifal meets the dreaded Vassal (who goes by the same appellation). Both

MacLeod and Parsifal are the victors of their sword fights with the sinister doppelganger. However, one change should be noted with respect to Parsifal's battle. Unlike MacLeod, Parsifal does not slay his Black Knight; rather, he merely wounds him so that the shadow self which Vassal represents can be more effectively integrated into Parsifal's personality.[63] Finally, as in so many knightly tales (see Gawain's adventures[64]), there is a comely *Highlander* maiden who needs to be rescued from the clutches of the principal villain. In this case, it is a contemporary forensics specialist, Brenda Wyatt (played with a good deal of pluck by Roxanne Hart). Brenda reminds MacLeod of his lost love, the bonny Heather, who was brutally raped by Kurgan over 400 years ago.[65] Conner hopes to rekindle that romance as soon as his rival is finally disposed of and the prize is won.

Before mentioning what that sought-after grail entails, the archetypal import of the immortal's sword (incorporated in all three of the *Highlander* films) should be addressed. According to Emma Jung and Marie-Louise von Franz (1986), the sword

> denotes strength, power and, in that [Arthurian] age more particularly, chivalry. . . . As the weapon especially characteristic of heroes or knights, the sword is often very closely connected with its owner, as if were a part of him . . . having a name and a personality all its own.[66]

MacLeod's blade certainly fits this description. His sword is no ordinary one; it resembles one used by the Samurai in the Middle Ages, but its pieces can be dated as far back as 500 B.C. and the metal appears to be folded at least 200 times over, making it almost impervious to breakage. The magic inherent within MacLeod's sword cannot be denied, when one considers that Juan Ramirez was its previous owner.[67] It is an instrument that can bring forth the redemption of the entire world by the mystical spilling of the Black Knight's blood at the time of the Gathering. The lance that penetrated Christ's side at the crucifixion also served a similar fashion: the drawing forth of the Savior's blood so that all humans would be delivered from sin.[68]

Like Christ, Conner experiences a resurrection of his own upon Kurgan's beheading. He is literally lifted into the air, more alive than ever before as the power of the Final Quickening courses through him. Novelist Jennifer Roberson (1996) best describes the *Highlander* experience as an overfilling of souls, of "those he had killed . . . [of] heads and hearts and brains and bodies—toomany toomany toomany—all clamoring for comprehension."[69] During this transformative process, MacLeod screams out in joy (as well as in pain) that he knows everything and is everything; these statements are indicative of the omniscient, godlike state that has been attained by the last of the immortal knights. Many of the legendary heroes relate similar encounters with the Holy Grail. One in particular, Sir Lancelot, experiences a vision in which a priest approaches the altar of the blessed vessel and is smitten down by the breadth of God. The man cannot rise as he has lost all power of movement. Even the senses of sight and hearing abandon the priest, so consumed is he by the presence of the Lord Jesus.[70] Once MacLeod touches ground again, he too has a rapturous blackout as his "new" body attempts to compensate for the divine energy flowing through it.

Christopher Lambert's closing narration, while brief, provides some insights as to how exactly his *Highlander* character has been physically and spiritually altered by the Gathering. One of the grail gifts Conner has inherited is his ability to sense what people are thinking all over the world. Thus, his messianic goal is to assist the members of the human race in understanding each other better and, in so doing, help them reach their fullest potential. But the greatest (and most precious) gift bestowed upon MacLeod is the elusive mortality he has desired for so many centuries. Now he can have children and grow old with his beloved Brenda by his side. Upon first glance, one might think that the first *Highlander* film has a fairy tale ending;[71] however, Juan Ramirez's final words resonate a different interpretation. The message that he delivers to MacLeod's inner self is a powerful one: "Use the [grail] power well . . . and don't lose your head." As long as humility is exercised in the use of the gifts, MacLeod will enjoy a full and rich life on the planet. But if supreme egotism overtakes him, then surely he will fall like Kurgan—only this time it will be his own hubris (not another immortal) which will be the ultimate destroyer.[72] Given this epilogue, the stage would be set for the darker mood of the first sequel, *Highlander 2: The Quickening* (1990) where a new, and somewhat more disturbing, image of the mortal MacLeod is portrayed in search of the grail once again.

HIGHLANDER 2: IMMORTALITY IS ONE'S CURSE (OR BLESSING) FOR ABANDONMENT OF THE PRIZE

While *The Quickening* is faster paced than its predecessor in furthering MacLeod's odyssey on Earth,[73] it does suffer from one principal weakness: it destroys a substantial part of the immortal mythos already established by the original *Highlander* writer, Gregory Widen. The origins of Conner and Juan Ramirez are transplanted to the distant planet of Zeist where the two have been designated criminals for opposing the dictatorship of General Katana (Michael Ironside). Banished to our planet nearly 500 years ago, the pair are condemned to an existence of immortality until just one exiled Zeistian remains to inherit the "prize" (in this case, a mortal release from eternal life or a return to Zeist fully exonerated of all wrongdoing). While this more futuristic *Highlander* premise is an interesting one to consider, there remain some unanswered questions: Why is Earth chosen as the penal planet (unless our race shares some kinship with the Zeistian one)? If General Katana remains in charge of Zeist's one world government, would not a continual stream of insurrectionists be sent to Earth making it next to impossible to ever reach the time of the Gathering? And finally, why would the last immortal desire to return to his homeworld, given the sorry state of affairs already present there? Fans of the first *Highlander* feature and adapted television series (1992 to 1998) became so adamant about the flaws in this story line that a return to the basics occurred in *Highlander 3*.[74] Moreover, a renegade version of *The Quickening* immediately became available which tastefully deleted all references to the planet Zeist and included additional film footage to ensure proper continuity in the *Highlander* film trilogy.

Despite this limitation, *The Quickening* does manage to offer some fresh material on Conner's life as a mortal in the final days of one millennium and the beginning of another. By 1999 Conner has developed a shield that can protect the human race from the slowly deteriorating ozone layer. At this time, he is full of life and energy, basking in the aftereffects of the Gathering. Every human admires him for saving their world from the sun's harmful rays, and he is hailed as the New Age messiah. But by 2024, MacLeod is a totally different individual. He is characterized as a tired, old man who has lost his passion for everything except his own egocentric interests, including listening to opera music.[75] His wife, Brenda, has perished, leaving the man more alone than ever. Perhaps it was this loss that set MacLeod on the path of self-destruction.

In keeping with this newly emerging personality pattern, Conner has abandoned all responsibility for his technological creation. The shield has now been taken over by a multinational corporation which extorts countries into believing they still require the protection, even though the ozone layer has miraculously reformed around the earth. One terrible (and totally unforeseen) side effect of the shield's use is casting the world into a state of perpetual darkness—devoid of all light as well as energy.[76] One might say that MacLeod's opus reflects his own troubled psyche: the creator's mind is not in harmony with his machine, and so both are emitting damaging waves to all living things.[77] As an irate citizen remarks to Conner before she smashes a bottle over his head, "Did you ever think about what you did?" Her statement is designed to induce a self-reflective state in our hero; instead, it barely registers in Conner's muddled brain. Surprisingly, the once immortal has changed into something even worse than Kurgan (at least the Black Knight and others like him were true to their nature[78]). MacLeod does not hold himself accountable to anyone, not even himself, for the troubles inflicted upon humanity and therein lies his fault. He is failing to live up to his grail potential and is at a critical juncture where he must decide what to do with the few remaining days he has left to live.

The reversion back to immortality seems the appropriate punishment for Conner since he has abused the resources he has been given. Ironically, it is the evil General Katana who is instrumental in MacLeod's conversion. He has ordered two underlings to kill the Highlander (for reasons unknown). However, the assassins are effectively beheaded by MacLeod, and the ensuing Quickenings cause a cellular regeneration in Conner: in the old man's place is a virile, young immortal ready to take on any diabolical Zeistians. With the reclaimed sword at his side, he calls upon his dead mentor, Juan Ramirez (reprised by Sean Connery), to assist him in his new mission: the destruction of the Shield Corporation as well as his misused brainchild.

While some critics were confused by Ramirez's suddenly returning to life with his head intact, let alone MacLeod regaining his lost immortality, there is definite symbolism behind these actions.[79] Our hero has gone through a Jungian rebirth to be perfected once again. The first perfection was Conner's acquisition of the prize (as so impressively depicted at the end of the original *Highlander* movie). However, as Jung notes, just because the grail has been reached does not mean that further improvements are no longer required in one's psyche.[80] And so, by the time of *The Quickening*, a second perfection is in order; Conner needs to be reborn in the immortal state so that some appreciation of the grail prize can be regained. Thus, the life-death-rebirth cycle for most heroes would seem to be a recurring, never-ending one—including that of the Highlander.[81] The return of Ramirez can be explained by the same logic. How can an immortal ever die if he has tasted life to the fullest? True, Kurgan had taken Ramirez's head before the appointed period, but not his immutable soul. It is that impervious element that Conner MacLeod retrieves in the form of his past mentor who is strategically placed by his side to show him, in true master-apprentice fashion, the "error of his mortal ways."

One should not dismiss the positive connotation of the sword which MacLeod carries in his reborn state. It reflects certain cognitive aspects of its owner: a keen mind, a sharp intellect, and an "intuitive" understanding for things not so easily grasped.[82] This "ability to be decisive and discriminating . . . to say no and yes and move ahead with life"[83] was something lacking in the mortal MacLeod, and so the sword was not a visible component of the man's makeup. However, once the transformation back to immortality occurred, then the blade (and its associated attributes) became an integral part of the Highlander. Conner is now able to perceive just how deadly the shield is when placed in the wrong hands, and he is able to make hard decisions that will ultimately benefit mankind and restore the race (and himself) to a "bright and sunny" future. Ramirez too can be regarded as a personification of the sword's most positive features: he can bring discriminating thought and judgment to bear on the difficult situation in which MacLeod has placed the entire planet.[84] Together with sword and mentor, a more than likely possibility exists that Conner will annihilate what Ramirez refers to as "his monstrosity" (i.e., the life-draining shield).

The final half of *The Quickening* focuses on the two immortals penetrating the corporation's defenses and dealing with Katana (who has allied himself with those human greed mongers). Although MacLeod succeeds in his plan, it can be accomplished only by Ramirez sacrificing his life essence for the greater good. But, a new hope is generated from the death of the mentor. As the shield collapses in the wake of Katana's beheading, MacLeod is told by the spirit of Ramirez that the real prize is his immortality and that he should regard it as a blessing, not a curse, sent from God.

The major strength of *The Quickening* lies in its reorientation of the grail mystery—from coveted mortality to savored eternal life. And MacLeod does indeed rediscover the grail. (Actually, the prize was never lost; it was just hidden from view.) As soon as all the negative emotions connected with Conner's earthly existence were purged, then it could be uncovered from within his very core.[85] Maybe there is some merit in having the Highlander be an extraterrestrial after all. As a Zeistian, he can more easily free himself from the fleshy restraints and dedicate his "new life" to something other than before—whether it be on Earth or his true home. The ability of the grail to transform one into an entirely different being with a new direction and purpose is what awaits all seekers,[86] and Conner MacLeod has reached that next level of reality in his knightly quest.

HIGHLANDER 3: THE KNIGHT CONTINUES HIS QUEST AD INFINITUM

Highlander 3: The Sorcerer (1995) underwent a title change (to the unnumbered *Highlander: The Final Dimension*) before the film officially opened, primarily because of its uneven links with the original feature as well as *The Quickening*. Though *The Final Dimension* was supposed to be a sequel to the first movie and a prequel to the second,[87] Conner MacLeod maintains his immortality throughout the various time lines and never changes—for the better or the worse. Therefore, exactly what the grail prize consists of in this final chapter is even more enigmatic than ever before! In this respect, the third *Highlander* is not as significant as the prior works, but for the sake of some coherence it will be examined.

To summarize the opening of *The Final Dimension* (which is one of the best parts), MacLeod seeks out the sorcerer Nakano in the mountains of Japan to guide him in his path as an immortal. Conner has just recently lost both his wife, Heather, and Ramirez to Kurgan and requires the appropriate direction from Nakano. Taking him on as his student, Nakano continues the instruction started by Ramirez and forges a magical "sword of power" for Conner so that he can be adequately prepared to do battle with a foe even mightier than Kurgan: the Egyptian Pharaoh Kane (played

by Mario Van Peebles). Before MacLeod has an opportunity to experience
even one Quickening, Kane invades Nakano's sanctum and beheads the
sorcerer who offers up his own life to the gods so that the Highlander can
escape. Kane is able to absorb all the powers of illusion from the dead
magician, but the energy surge is so great that it brings down the entire
mountain, burying the evil immortal until the end of the twentieth century.
The tomb is then uncovered by contemporary Japanese who are attempting
to locate a site for their nuclear power plant; their drilling attempts reac-
tivate Kane who designs his vendetta against MacLeod, the only "pure"
immortal that can stop him from dominating the entire world.[88]

While this plot is a basic rehash of the first *Highlander* (right down to
the death of MacLeod's teacher by a Kurgan-like copy),[89] the figure of Kane
possesses the additional qualities of the Jungian trickster, making him the
darkest of all the shadow knights with which MacLeod must contend. He
can magically teleport himself from Japan to New York City in the blink
of an eye. In addition, Kane can induce all sorts of visual hallucinations in
the victims he has targeted, constructing a very grim reality for them out
of their innermost fears. But the Black Knight's greatest power is his
"morphing" capability which the film effectively utilizes (thanks to the genius of screenplay writer Paul Ohl).[90] Unlike other critics, this author was
delighted to see Kane change from a bird of prey to an exact double of
MacLeod to even Conner's latest flame, Alex Johnson (Deborah Unger), as
these transformations were found to be compatible with the most primitive
of trickster figures. Jung discloses that the trickster's shape-shifting sets him
above other humans while at the same time creates an inferior status because of his inability to regulate one dominant identity amidst all the other
assumed personalities.[91] Kane is one of those "divided souls." We never
know his human life story or how he became an immortal; rather, we are
bombarded by one identity shift after another until we learn that Kane
cannot control these changes, so consumed is he by the alluring power of
the trickster.

Based on his fragmented self, there is little doubt that Kane will eventually lose his duel with the more stable Highlander. This becomes a certainty after his initial skirmish with MacLeod, in which Conner's sword is
broken at the hilt. Instead of killing MacLeod then and there, Kane allows
him to live until their next encounter. This lack of foresight on the part of
the shape-shifter allows MacLeod to fashion another sword from the mystical metal from which the first was forged, thereby fulfilling the Fisher
King prophecy: "Whosoever succeeds in joining the broken sword together
[which was split in the middle] will be the rightful and predestined heir of
the Grail."[92] And so, in the final confrontation between the two immortals,
MacLeod is the victor. Just before Conner strikes the decapitating blow,
he slices Kane literally into two pieces; this action not only reaffirms the
split nature of the trickster but also shows the audience that Kane is not

worth saving as he laughs off the injury with the comment, "Oooh . . . that was very unsportsmanlike."[93] For Kane, all existence is one big game in which the stakes are one's immortal soul. Conner, on the other hand, perceives something more in life: it should be cherished to its fullest, not devalued as a sport. In the end, Conner's philosophy is the one that prevails.

Even though *The Final Dimension* never addresses just what MacLeod has won by his victory, at least two grail possibilities can be considered. The first is that he is at peace with himself and has abandoned his warrior ways, now that he is the last immortal on the planet. The second (and more interesting) one is that he has formed a human family with Alex and an adopted son, John, in the Highlands of Scotland. MacLeod has let others into his life once again, and while they will suffer the mortal frailties of age and death, he will still love them and enjoy their presence for however brief a time. The last chronicle of the *Indiana Jones* saga also highlighted the search for a loved one, Indy's father and, ultimately, the reestablishment of the Jones family.[94] Maybe this is what the grail truly represents after all. It is not something physical—an Ark or lost mortality—but an acquired wisdom which will allow us to appreciate the divinity in significant others as Conner and Indy have discovered by the end of their adventures.

Plans are already under way to film a fourth *Highlander* feature with Christopher Lambert playing the lead role one more time.[95] With the success of the television version, however, a more logical choice would be to have Adrian Paul in the next installment since the small screen cousin of Connor's, Duncan MacLeod, has not yet experienced his grail encounter. Whoever is selected for the next movie, one can be sure that the plot will revolve around the day of the Gathering and the prize which is rightfully earned, for the grail archetype will never die so long as there are knights in the world who want to embark on the most sacred of all quests.

NOTES

1 Richard Rohr, *Quest for the Grail* (New York: Crossroad Publishing, 1994), 57.

2. Ibid., 151–52.

3. Carol S. Pearson, *Awakening the Heroes Within: Twelve Archetypes to Help Us Find Ourselves and Transform Our World* (San Francisco: HarperCollins, 1991), 50.

4. John Matthews, *The Elements of the Grail Tradition* (Rockport, MA: Element Books, 1990), 3, 11, 52–54.

5. John Matthews, *At the Table of the Grail: Magic and the Use of Imagination* (New York: Routledge and Kegan Paul, 1987), 6–7; Matthews, *Grail Tradition*, 5, 104–10.

6. Carl G. Jung, "Christ, A Symbol of the Self," in *Aion: Researches into the Phenomenology of the Self: The Collected Works*, trans. R.F.C. Hull (Princeton, NJ: Princeton University Press, 1990), 37.

7. Edward F. Edinger, *Ego and Archetype: Individuation and the Religious Function of the Psyche* (London: Penguin Books, 1972), 227–35.

8. Susan Aronstein, "Not Exactly a Knight: Arthurian Narrative and Recuperative Politics in the *Indiana Jones* Trilogy," *Cinema Journal* 34 (Summer 1995): 4.

9. Matthews, *Grail Tradition*, 104; David Sterritt, "Review of *Raiders of the Lost Ark*," *Christian Science Monitor* 73 (18 June 1981): 18.

10. Peter Biskind, "Blockbuster: The Last Crusade," in *Seeing Through Movies*, ed. Mark Crispin Miller (New York: Pantheon Books, 1990), 144.

11. Campbell Black, *Raiders of the Lost Ark* (New York: Ballantine Books, 1981), 48.

12. Pearson, *Awakening the Heroes Within*, 129.

13. Aronstein, "Not Exactly a Knight," 14.

14. Andrew Kopkind, "Review of *Indiana Jones and the Temple of Doom*," *The Nation* 238 (9 June 1984): 713; Ralph Novak, "Review of *Indiana Jones and the Temple of Doom*," *People Weekly* 21 (4 June 1984): 12.

15. Black, *Raiders of the Lost Ark*, 103.

16. Jung, "Gnostic Symbols of the Self," in *Aion*, 186.

17. Jung, "The Structure and Dynamics of the Self," in *Aion*, 244–45.

18. Rohr, *Quest for the Grail*, 108–10.

19. Aronstein, "Not Exactly a Knight," 15; Douglas Brode, *The Films of the Eighties* (New York: Carol Publishing Group, 1991), 58.

20. Robert Dallek, *Ronald Reagan: The Politics of Symbolism* (Cambridge: Harvard University Press, 1984), 59; Mary Stuckey, *Playing the Game: The Presidential Rhetoric of Ronald Reagan* (New York: Praeger, 1990), 61.

21. Rohr, *Quest for the Grail*, 123–26.

22. Black, *Raiders of the Lost Ark*, 175.

23. John Matthews and Marian Green, *The Grail Seeker's Companion: A Guide to the Grail Quest in the Aquarian Age* (Wellingborough, Northhamptonshire, England: Aquarian Press, 1986), 19.

24. Michael Buckley, "Review of *Indiana Jones and the Temple of Doom*," *Films in Review* 35 (August-September 1984): 426.

25. Aronstein, "Not Exactly a Knight," 9.

26. James Kahn, *Indiana Jones and the Temple of Doom* (New York: Ballantine Books, 1984), 4.

27. Richard Corliss, "Keeping the Customer Satisfied: Review of *Indiana Jones and the Temple of Doom*," *Time* 123 (21 May 1984): 82; Jack Kroll, "Review of *Indiana Jones and the Temple of Doom*: Indy Strikes Again," *Newsweek* 103 (4 June 1984): 78.

28. Buckley, "Review of *Indiana Jones and the Temple of Doom*," 426.

29. Aronstein, "Not Exactly a Knight," 9, 26 (note 5); Peter Travers, "Movie Reviews of Heroes: Macho Under Fire," *Rolling Stone*, 19 October 1989, 27.

30. Kahn, *Indiana Jones and the Temple of Doom*, 56.

31. Pauline Kael, "Review of *Indiana Jones and the Temple of Doom*: A Breeze, a Bawd, a Bounty," *New Yorker* 60 (11 June 1984): 100.

32. Kahn, *Indiana Jones and the Temple of Doom*, 59–60, 77–78.

33. David Denby, "Review of *Indiana Jones and the Temple of Doom*: Lost in the Thrill Machine," *New York* 17 (4 June 1984): 73.

34. Moishe Postone and Elizabeth Traube, "Review of *Indiana Jones and the Temple of Doom*," *Jump Cut* 30 (March 1985): 13.

35. Edinger, *Ego and Archetype*, 229.

36. Kahn, *Indiana Jones and the Temple of Doom*, 149.

37. Matthews, *Grail Tradition*, 95; Rohr, *Quest for the Grail*, 125–26.

38. Philip Strick, "Review of *Indiana Jones and the Temple of Doom*," *Films and Filming* 358 (July 1984): 19.

39. James F. Iaccino, *Psychological Reflections on Cinematic Terror: Jungian Archetypes in Horror Films* (Westport, CT: Praeger, 1994), 66.

40. Tom O'Brien, "Review of *Indiana Jones and the Temple of Doom*," *Commonweal* 111 (15 June 1984): 375.

41. Kahn, *Indiana Jones and the Temple of Doom*, 213–14.

42. Richard Blake, "Knight Errand: Review of *Indiana Jones and the Last Crusade*," *America* 160 (17–24 June 1989): 591; Rob MacGregor, *Indiana Jones and the Last Crusade* (New York: Ballantine Books, 1989), 3–42.

43. Aronstein, "Not Exactly a Knight," 19.

44. Emma Jung and Marie-Louise von Franz, "Perceval's Early History According to Chretien de Troyes," in *The Grail Legend*, trans. Andrea Dykes (Boston: Sigo Press, 1986), 45–46.

45. Georgia Brown, "Review of *Indiana Jones and the Last Crusade*," *Village Voice* 34 (30 May 1989): 57; E. Jung and von Franz, "Perceval's First Visit to the Grail Castle," in *Grail Legend*, 73–76.

46. Tom O'Brien, "Facts of (Ghetto) Life: Review of *Do the Right Thing* & *Indiana Jones and the Last Crusade*," *Commonweal* 116 (14 July 1989): 403.

47. MacGregor, *Indiana Jones and the Last Crusade*, 56.

48. Ibid., 106, 109.

49. Carl G. Jung, "The Phenomenology of the Spirit in Fairytales," in *The Archetypes and the Collective Unconscious: The Collected Works*, trans. R.F.C. Hull (Princeton, NJ: Princeton University Press, 1990), 208, 217–22; E. Jung and von Franz, "Perceval's Further Adventures," in *Grail Legend*, 264, 274.

50. E. Jung and von Franz, "The Redemption of the Grail Kingdom; Perceval's End," in *Grail Legend*, 295; Rohr, *Quest for the Grail*, 152.

51. MacGregor, *Indiana Jones and the Last Crusade*, 188.

52. E. Jung and von Franz, "Perceval's Task," in *Grail Legend*, 111–12.

53. Aronstein, "Not Exactly a Knight," 23–24.

54. Matthews, *Grail Tradition*, 91, 100.

55. MacGregor, *Indiana Jones and the Last Crusade*, 215.

56. Rohr, *Quest for the Grail*, 154.

57. E. Jung and von Franz, "The Redemption of the Grail Kingdom," in *Grail Legend*, 296–97.

58. Jason Henderson, *Highlander: The Element of Fire* (New York: Warner Books, 1995), 6.

59. Garry Kilworth, *Highlander: The Movie* (London: HarperCollins, 1996), 114–15, 124; Tim Pulleine, "Review of *Highlander*," *Monthly Film Bulletin* (August 1986): 236.

60. Henderson, *Highlander: The Element of Fire*, 8–10; Kilworth, *Highlander: The Movie*, 84–102.

61. E. Jung and von Franz, "The Figure of Merlin," in *Grail Legend*, 348; E.

Jung and von Franz, "Merlin as Medicine Man and Prophet," in *Grail Legend*, 360–62.

62. Kilworth, *Highlander: The Movie*, 115.

63. E. Jung and von Franz, "Perceval's Further Adventures," in *Grail Legend*, 255, 275.

64. E. Jung and von Franz, "Gauvain's Adventures," in *Grail Legend*, 228–29.

65. Kilworth, *Highlander: The Movie*, 221–22, 252.

66. E. Jung and von Franz, "The Sword and the Lance," in *Grail Legend*, 79.

67. Kilworth, *Highlander: The Movie*, 141–42, 161.

68. E. Jung and von Franz, "The Sword and the Lance," in *Grail Legend*, 92–93; Rohr, *Quest for the Grail*, 113.

69. Jennifer Roberson, *Highlander: Scotland the Brave* (New York: Warner Books, 1996), 196.

70. Matthews, *Grail Tradition*, 112.

71. Jung, "The Phenomenology of the Spirit in Fairytales," in *The Archetypes and the Collective Unconscious*, 251–52.

72. Kilworth, *Highlander: The Movie*, 247–51.

73. Marc Shapiro, "Battle of the Immortals: Review of *Highlander 2*." *Starlog* 185 (December 1992): 35; Marc Shapiro, "The Immortal Man: Review of *Highlander 2*," *Starlog* 174 (January 1992): 49.

74. Leah Rozen, "Review of *Highlander 2: The Quickening*," *People Weekly* 36 (25 November 1991): 22; Jenny Turner, "Review of *Highlander 2: The Quickening*," *Sight and Sound* (June 1991): 48.

75. Shapiro, "The Immortal Man: Review of *Highlander 2*," 51.

76. Turner, "Review of *Highlander 2: The Quickening*," 47.

77. Carl G. Jung, "Religious Ideas in Alchemy: The Psychic Nature of the Alchemical Work," in *Psychology and Alchemy: The Collected Works*, trans. R.F.C. Hull (Princeton, NJ: Princeton University Press, 1991), 255–74.

78. Henderson, *Highlander: The Element of Fire*, 48.

79. Tom Tunney, "Review of *Highlander 3: The Sorcerer*," *Sight and Sound* (March 1995): 38; Turner, "Review of *Highlander 2: The Quickening*," 48.

80. Jung, "Gnostic Symbols of the Self," in *Aion*, 212–13.

81. Jung, "Concerning Rebirth," in *The Archetypes and the Collective Unconscious*, 141.

82. E. Jung and von Franz, "The Sword and the Lance," in *Grail Legend*, 80–83.

83. Rohr, *Quest for the Grail*, 112.

84. E. Jung and von Franz, "The Table, the Carving Platter and the Two Knives," in *Grail Legend*, 171.

85. Matthews, *Grail Tradition*, 117.

86. Ibid., 121; Pearson, *Awakening the Heroes Within*, 50.

87. Tunney, "Review of *Highlander 3: The Sorcerer*," 38.

88. Shapiro, "Battle of the Immortals: Review of *Highlander 2*," 35; Dan Yakir, "Raising Kane: Review of *Highlander 3*," *Starlog* 210 (January 1995): 36–37.

89. Shapiro, "The Immortal Man: Review of *Highlander 2*," 71.

90. Stephen Holden, "Review of *Highlander: The Final Dimension*," *New York Times*, 28 January 1995, 16; Leah Rozen, "Review of *Highlander: The Final Dimension*," *People Weekly* 43 (13 February 1995): 27–28.

91. Jung, "On the Psychology of the Trickster-Figure," in *The Archetypes and the Collective Unconscious*, 255, 263–64.

92. E. Jung and von Franz, "Perceval's Further Adventures," in *Grail Legend*, 288; E. Jung and von Franz, "The Sword and the Lance," in *Grail Legend*, 81.

93. Yakir, "Raising Kane: Review of *Highlander 2*," 66.

94. Blake, "Knight Errand," 591.

95. Shapiro, "The Immortal Man: Review of *Highlander 2*," 71.

8

The *Omen* Trilogy: The Growth of the Demon Child Archetype

The original intent of this chapter was to analyze the *Phantasm* series with respect to Jung's child-god archetype. The first *Phantasm* (1979) had all the ingredients of the typical fantasy, including Stuart Kaminsky's (1988) surrealistic images of mad dwarfs, flying silver balls, driverless hearses, vibrating space gates, and the sinister figure of the "Tall Man" who presided over a fiery, interdimensional underworld.[1] Even the title itself, *Phantasm*, was able to elicit all sorts of dreamlike apparitions in the viewer before the story actually unfolded on the screen.[2] Unfortunately, the sequels (*Phantasm II*, 1988, and *Phantasm III: Lord of the Dead*, 1993) did not follow the blueprint already laid down by writer-director-producer Don Coscarelli and made one wonder whether the entire episode was no more than the psychotic visions of a troubled teen who never recovered from the deaths of his parents and older brother. In addition to the confusing format, the *Phantasm* trilogy never reached a mainstream audience and remains a cult series (at best) with which many fantasy fans are unfamiliar. Given these inherent problems, it was decided to select another film package that was more archetypally suitable for the unit.

The Omen movies appear to have enough fantastic scenes in them to please any horror or science-fiction aficionado; however, they are all nicely strung around the general theme of Satan's son's coming of age to rule over the planet.[3] One can immediately detect an inversion of the child-god image to that of a maturing demon-child who continues to grow more and more in each successive sequel. With this new archetype in mind, let us look at how the horror genre has successfully integrated some of its contents into the fantasy world of the deadly child.

THE OMEN: THE DEMON CHILD EXPERIENCES HIS FIRST TEMPER TANTRUMS

The opening minutes of *The Omen* (1976) reveal the interesting origins of the devil's child. The mating of Satan with a jackal results in an unearthly offspring, which is born and then given to a U.S. diplomat, Robert Thorn (Gregory Peck), and his wife, Katherine (Lee Remick), who have just lost their own child in the delivery room. The couple are grateful to take care of the newborn (who is later christened Damien), little realizing just what type of creature they will be rearing. While the entire premise might sound ludicrous, producer Harvey Bernhard never depicts the actual birth of the son of Satan on the screen; instead, he relates the incident via the dialogue of some secondary characters (including one Father Brennan who witnessed the cryptic event and cannot live with the secret).[4] In this way, the viewer must accept the idea that the devil has created his own image on earth so that everything else in the trilogy proceeds in a logical fashion. The end result is a fast-paced series that manages to sustain one's curiosity throughout the duration, perhaps even more so than its prototypic predecessors, *Rosemary's Baby* (1968) and *The Exorcist* (1973).[5]

Despite *The Omen*'s rather hurried presentation of Damien Thorn's roots, the Jungian imagery remains one of the film's most salient features. Contained in chapter 13 of the Book of Revelations is a description of the Antichrist: he is referred to as "the Beast" who bears a birthmark of three "sixes."[6] Damien (played quite menacingly by child star Harvey Stephens) not only has that mark on his forehead, but his birth occurs at six in the morning on the sixth day of the sixth month—confirming that he will be the one to initiate the dreaded Apocalypse upon the world. Given this Biblical context, the demon child clearly possesses a nature unlike other humans. To paraphrase Jung, his psyche is animalistic, primordial, and monstrous to behold. It further contains within its very core an awesome supernatural element, setting the bearer apart from all others.[7]

Because Damien is so different, he can be likened to an "orphan" who has no home on Earth. As C. Kerenyi (1993) notes, the archetypal child is often portrayed as an abandoned foundling who has been expelled from heaven and must endure his "primal solitude" without parents or friends. Such an elemental being will be exposed to all sorts of dangers and persecutions in this vulnerable state. But if it can survive, then it will have accomplished something truly godlike.[8] With respect to *The Omen*, Damien has no biological mother he can call his own. Moreover, his biological father is residing in another dimension entirely (i.e., the underworld). The only one he can rely on is Mrs. Baylock (Billie Whitelaw), a sinister governess whose primary charge is to protect him from those who might eventually discover his identity.

This is not to say that Damien is entirely helpless. While he needs Baylock's help, he effectively demonstrates his own powers on more than one occasion. When displayed, however, they are typically accompanied by a fierceness and rage so incredibly savage that pain, suffering, and even death will be the eventual outcome. (This would reinforce the Jungian interpretation of the primordial child's being depicted as an inhuman, with a soul more akin to an animal's and with instincts just as deadly.[9]) For instance, Damien's nanny, Chessa, is hypnotized by a wild mastiff to take her own life during the boy's fifth birthday party. The way she commits the suicide is especially brutal: she hangs herself from the rooftop of the Thorn estate in front of the astonished celebrants while yelling out, "Look here, Damien . . . it's all for you!" Rather than averting his eyes from the grisly event (like the others around him), the demon child gazes in a transfixed fashion at the lifeless body of Chessa and then acknowledges the dog with "a garish grin" and a friendly shake of the hand.[10] These actions are indicative not only of the boy's ruthless disposition, but also of his mystical link with the barbaric world of the primitive (in this case, represented in the form of a rabid, shadow animal).[11] The child's association with the wild dogs is so strong in the film that one of the mastiffs serves as his protector, and a pack of the fierce creatures is commanded by Damien in a later sequence to attack Robert Thorn at the gravesite where his real son is buried.

Although Damien is not physically present at Father Brennan's untimely fate, he is again connected through the harsh winds and electrical storms that pummel the guilt-ridden priest into submission. Just when it looks as though Brennan has evaded nature's cruel touch by finding sanctuary at a church, a lightning bolt suddenly issues forth from the clouds and strikes a pole atop the building, loosening it from its moorings. As the beam falls down, it seems almost guided by an invisible hand to seek out the priest and skewer him right into the very ground. A curious photographer, Keith Jennings (David Warner), is also disposed of by an unseen force that releases the brakes of a truck and sends its deadly contents—plates of glass—directly at the unsuspecting man. Before Jennings can cry out, the sharp objects slice his head from his shoulders, killing the man instantly.[12] The agent responsible for these gruesome murders is, of course, Damien. Though he never directly touches his victims, his demonic spirit infects each with disastrous consequences.[13] This interpretation is compatible with the Jungian description that the immaterial "spirit" can often taken the form of a boy and can act out the child's malice through such natural elements as wind, storms, and even animal figures. Jung speculates that the most corrupt of all the "spirits" is the devil himself; since Damien is related to that ancient character by blood, he is capable of tapping into that supernatural realm whenever he so desires and, through his will, can eliminate anyone with ease.[14]

As *The Omen* proceeds to its inevitable conclusion, Damien is able to play more of a participant role in the injuries instead of remaining an "innocent" observer on the sidelines. Presumably this is a result of Robert and Katherine's figuring out who he really is and what danger he represents to the entire human civilization.[15] In a series of stages, Damien tears down Katherine's defenses one by one until she lies crippled and helpless before the forces of evil. First, he mauls her when the Thorns go to All Saints Church to attend a wedding; the child experiences such uncontrollable fits that they leave the scene, but not before his fingers rip into Katherine's face dangerously close to one of her eyes. Soon afterward the boy instigates a pack of baboons at a local zoo to attack their vehicle. All Katherine can do is to look on as the blood-crazed monkeys pound their bodies into the car, trying to penetrate the interior. Luckily, she manages to escape the danger by pressing down on the accelerator pedal with all her might. Her anxiety attack, however, is so severe that she requires psychological counseling. (Kathy embraces the therapeutic help even more when she discovers that she is pregnant again.) Finally, in the film's most riveting sequence, Damien uses his tricycle to hit the stool which Katherine is standing on and causes her to fall over the balcony railing. By the time Robert finds her crumpled body in the foyer and takes her to the hospital, he is informed by the staff that they have lost their second child as a result of the supposed "accident."[16] While Katherine has barely survived the encounter, her mental and physical condition have been so deleteriously affected that Mrs. Baylock is able to put "the finishing touches" onto her fate with little opposition. There is no doubt that this "small boy" exercises a gigantic power for destruction: he can challenge the strongest of adult foes and break them apart like twigs if they get in his way.[17]

On the other hand, Robert Thorn is a different type of adversary than Katherine. He is more removed from the home situation, and he does not share the same worries as his wife about Damien's strange behavior (until it is much too late[18]). Even when the exorcist Bugenhagen (Leo McKern) relates the procedure by which the demon must be slain, Robert is hesitant to accept the holy daggers from the man. He cannot envision putting any child (let alone his own) on an altar and piercing him with the seven knives that will purge the spiritual essence of evil from the boy. It is Robert's sympathy for Damien's human persona that proves to be his ultimate undoing.

By the time Thorn has deciphered all the clues and has led Damien to All Saints Church to be sacrificed, he still cannot take it upon himself to plunge the first dagger into the boy's chest. Screenplay writer David Seltzer captures this moment both in film and in the derived text: "The boy had been jostled into wakefulness and stared up at him with innocence in his eyes. . . . 'I hurt . . . Daddy' the child whimpered. 'Don't look at me,' Thorn [replied as he] raised the stiletto high above him."[19] So moved is Robert by Damien's pain that he hesitates for several seconds, giving the police sufficient time to track his location and shoot him down before he can kill the boy. One might ask why Thorn cannot commit the exorcism, especially after Damien has murdered several people close to him (including his wife, Kathy). If one views Damien as the archetypal Antichrist, however, then everything makes sense. The demon child is "a perverse imitator of Christ's life," meaning that he can appear angelic and pure to those around him while concealing his depraved nature.[20] Robert is easily swayed by Damien's "childlike" exterior and does not see the inner psyche of the shadow beast. This can be considered *The Omen*'s fatal attraction: one is drawn into the apparently innocent and helpless world of the child, thereby becoming trapped forever.

No one is immune to Damien's powers of deception. By the end of the film, the president of the United States has taken custody of the lad, falling under his spell just like those before him. And so the prophecy forecast in the Book of Revelations seems to be coming to fruition: the devil's child will rise from the "eternal sea" of politics with the intent of creating armies of destruction around the world.[21] The two remaining *Omen* sequels focus on this satanic plan, engineered by Damien, in greater detail.

DAMIEN—OMEN II: THE DEMON CHILD ENTERS PUBESCENCE WITH RAGING HORMONES

At the start of *Damien—Omen II* (1978), we find that the boy (now portrayed by Jonathan Scott-Taylor) has advanced in years and is approaching his thirteenth birthday, which some have considered the rite of passage into the more powerful realm of the adolescent.[22] He has left the comfortable confines of Washington, D.C., for his uncle's home on the outskirts of Chicago, Illinois. There Richard Thorn (William Holden) grooms both Damien and his own offspring, Mark (Lucas Donat), to take over his own multinational conglomerate, Thorn Industries. Of course, the corporation would serve as the perfect vehicle for Damien in his quest for world domination, perhaps even more so than the fairly obvious Oval Office which would attract any number of assassins and terrorists who would try to prevent the boy's rise to the top.[23] This modification in the original Seltzer screenplay makes for a far better story line, and having Damien come of age allows the primordial child to develop further his budding talents—to the detriment of not just the Thorns and their associates but of all humanity.

The favored creature throughout *Omen II* is not the four-legged type; instead, it is a sinister raven which scans its surroundings and intended victims with piercing, malevolent eyes.[24] Like the mastiff in *The Omen*, the bird symbolizes the subhuman, animalistic nature of the demon child.

Many fairy tales relate that the raven is one of the devil's common guises; through this shape, the dark trickster is able to extend his vision and power on earth.[25] The ability of flight gives the bird another edge; no one can ever contain or imprison it for it can simply fly away to seek out a higher perch. The connection between Damien and the raven is made especially evident when the adolescent stares at a school bully, Teddy (John J. Newcombe), with the same birdlike eyes before flinging the ruffian's body against a door. And there is the painting on Yigael's Wall in the Holy Land which depicts the Antichrist as Damien with serpent locks for hair and a familiar friend in his hands: the raven, of course.

In the first hour of *Omen II*, the black bird is present at every killing (which is hardly coincidental as it is the metamorphic form of Damien Thorn himself). Sometimes it just watches the events unfold from a safe vantage point, such as when Bugenhagen (Leo McKern) is buried alive in the ruins of a temple or corporate executive Atherton (Lew Ayres) drowns in the icy Wisconsin waters. At other times, the raven inserts itself directly into the scene, much to the dismay of those it has targeted. Typically the female characters suffer the most from the bird's wrath. As the cantankerous Aunt Marion (Sylvia Sidney) reads her Bible in bed, Damien's familiar soars into the room and lands atop her bedpost, frightening the poor woman to death. The "best" attack is reserved for photojournalist Joan Hart (Elizabeth Shepherd). When Hart discovers that Damien is the Antichrist, the raven is sent on a mission by the boy: to seek out the woman and dispose of her. It accomplishes its objective almost in Shakespearean style. The bird lands atop Hart's head and pulls out strands of hair from her scalp before plucking out the sensory organs she has most need of in her profession: her eyes. Then it flies to a nearby tree to observe the grisly incident that is to follow. The already blind woman hears the sound of a diesel engine and attempts to hail the truck's driver for help. But the eighteen-wheeler cannot brake in time and it squashes Hart like a bug, much to the delight of the raven, which utters a "single loud shriek . . . before melting away into the darkening autumnal sky."[26]

While the winged messenger is meting out its punishments, Damien is undergoing a startling revelation of his own. He is beginning to discover who he really is. Unlike the original *Omen*, in which the child displays an all-knowing (and quite devilish) smile, the older boy generates a sneer at best and oftentimes cannot attribute a source to his strange gifts.[27] For this reason, writer and producer Harvey Bernhard included a number of the devil's disciples in the plot so that Damien might receive the proper schooling in the ways of evil. Most occupy high positions of power or, if not, remain in close proximity to the boy and attend to his every want, (including the Thorn chauffeur and Richard's second wife, Ann). Two of the more prominent satanists are Thorn Industries second in command Paul Buher (Robert Foxworth) and Sergeant Neff (Lance Henriksen) of the Da-

vidson Military Academy which Damien attends. Both advise the adolescent on more than one occasion that the time will come when the entire
world will recognize his true greatness. Though the boy is confused by their
words, he is told to consult the Book of Revelations to learn more about
himself and his destiny.

As Damien reads that particular section of the Bible and then uncovers
the devil's birthmark of 666 under his scalp, his whole life undergoes a
radical turning point. He races out to the waterfront and, looking up at
the darkening sky, exclaims, "Why . . . why me?" to the heavens before
collapsing in a heap.[28] From a Jungian perspective, the nearby waters signal
a birth which is transpiring: in this case, it is the rise of consciousness from
the shadow depths of the unconscious.[29] Prior to this moment, Damien was
closely allied with the animal psyche and was not fully aware of his own
self. Now he is able to detach himself somewhat from the instinctual sphere
of the beast (as well as the innocence of the child) in order to develop a
stronger, more liberating identity.[30] Buher's remark that "the man will put
away childish things" nicely illustrates this transformative experience. That
Damien is not happy about the internal change taking place merely reinforces just how sensitized he is to all the elements, both good and bad, of
his Antichrist psyche. But, he does come to adopt them as part of his new
personality almost immediately. When his cousin Mark asks if everything
is all right that same night, Damien replies ever so matter of factly, "I'm
okay . . . now," confirming his acceptance of the transfiguration.

Interestingly, the raven never makes a reappearance after this pivotal
sequence in the film. It was not an oversight on the part of the producer;
rather, the bird (and all that it represents) has been integrated into Damien's
conscience so that he can start dispensing his own cruelties without the
need of another agent. All Damien has to do is stare at the person with his
bird-of-prey eyes, and the marked individual will suffer a horrible death.
Such fates include being crushed by a runaway train, asphyxiated by poisonous fumes, and sliced in half by an elevator cable. Although the adolescent has managed to resolve his identity crisis, it is mankind's misfortune
to be forever plagued by this cognizant demon.[31]

The final portions of *Omen II* deliver the "gloom and doom" message
of Biblical prophecy most emphatically, especially when familial members
like Mark and Richard Thorn fall under Damien's all-encompassing fury.
That the young Antichrist decides to murder his cousin Mark against the
visually spectacular backdrop of a "snow-blanketed Wisconsin forest" is
significant.[32] The autumn and winter seasons have always been associated
with the death of particular gods as well their eventual renewal in the
periods that are to ensue (i.e., the spring and summer months).[33] Antihero
Damien also enacts this death-rebirth cycle. As he so callously severs a
number of arteries from Mark's brain, resulting in Mark's excruciatingly
painful death, the demon god destroys whatever humanity remains that

links him to our species. In the aftermath of the tragedy, a new and more powerful Damien emerges with fire burning brightly in his eyes and a rage stronger than any hormonal reaction could produce. The bestial wail emitted by Damien over Mark's lifeless body signifies the death of his human persona and the realization that he is doomed to be a pure and utter savage. Joseph Howard's novelization of *Omen II* verifies this interpretation. He describes the attack on Mark as an animalistic one, in which "the dreadful beak and claws of the invisible bird tore at his [Mark's] head . . . and cleaved his skull until blood began to drip from his nostrils, from his eyes, even from his ears."[34] The internalization of the raven form in Damien has already been referenced and validates what the Antichrist has intentionally become: the Beast made flesh.

How Damien deals with his foster father, Richard, is in keeping with his expanded awareness of what he truly is, and it brings an appropriate closure to this first *Omen* sequel. The adolescent is able to take over Ann's mind, forcing her to plunge the seven daggers intended for his demise deep inside her husband's body. The expression which Richard conveys to his wife before he expires is one of complete surprise for he has terribly underestimated the boy's abilities. After Ann commits the crime, Damien seeks out the adjacent boiler room and causes the furnace to explode with ease, trapping the poor woman in the resultant conflagration. The demon is able to walk away from the scene completely unscathed, reminding the viewer of the scene in which Damien was first introduced, when he was also seen moving away from flames, in this instance a large bonfire in the middle of the vast lawn of the Thorn estate.[35] One might say Damien has come full circle: he has returned to the starting point, but he is finally capable of creating the hellish underworld on earth himself instead of relying on others for help and protection.

Damien actually smiles at the end of *Omen II*, pleased with what he has accomplished. He takes delight in his orphan state, relishing the feelings of abandonment and isolation connected with being parentless.[36] Unlike the first *Omen*, Damien prefers to be on his own, and, in this respect, will be capable of achieving so many "divine" feats once he reaches manhood.[37] By the time of *The Final Conflict—Omen III* (1981), he will be in charge of Thorn Industries and will engage in a political path which will take him straight to the presidency of the United States.

THE FINAL CONFLICT—OMEN III: THE DEMON CHILD ATTAINS ADULTHOOD AND BECOMES MUCH MORE THAN A MAN

At age thirty-two, Damien Thorn (Sam Neill) is already exercising a corporate viciousness by thriving on the misfortunes of others (i.e., the poor and downtrodden) around the world, all for the sake of expanding his own empire. It would seem that there is nothing that can stop him in his quest for global domination. He is able to use his childhood familiar, a Rottweiler guard dog, to hypnotize the current ambassador of Great Britain (Robert Arden) into taking his own life so that Thorn can assume his diplomatic seat. Moreover, Damien is able to sway the president (Mason Adams) into allowing him to be the head of the United Nation's Youth Council as well as endorsing his upcoming candidacy for the U.S. Senate.[38] One of the characteristics of Damien's personality, which is manifested in *Omen III*, is his smug self-assuredness: he can obtain whatever he desires, and he uses people, even the most prestigious in the country, as pawns for his own gain.

What was sorely missing in the first two *Omen* films was an extensive, psychological profile of the Antichrist, which this one more than sufficiently provides. On a televised talk show with interviewer Kate Reynolds (Lisa Harrow), Damien presents his rather cynical views on parental education. He relates, "We ply them [the young] with our values. We indoctrinate them with our mediocrity until finally they emerge from their brainwashing as so-called fully fledged citizens . . . clipped, impotent, but above all safe."[39] By being head of the Youth Council (and one day of the world), he hopes to bring the power back to that unappreciated segment of the population. When later asked by the spellbound Kate why he has never married, Damien remarks that he is too much of a skeptic and that there is little time to engage in such pursuits.[40] Consistent with his given nature, he cannot place his faith or trust in anyone but himself; if he did so, it would be an admission that he still requires others (particularly the comfort of a mate) in order to survive.

Damien is not without his passions, however. One burning desire is to prevent the Second Coming of the Messiah, even if it means slaying every male infant born on that fateful day, March 24. Naturally, the event is heralded by a trinitary alignment of stars which Damien telepathically senses along with his dog.[41] Not only does the return of the Christ figure present an obstacle to Thorn's plans, but the being's very divinity also saps him of some of his supernatural powers (hence the reason for the widespread infanticides).

At times the Antichrist demonstrates an almost maniacal obsession with his counterpart, outweighing any other pressing priority or concern. For example, on the uppermost floor of his estate, Damien has a black chapel which houses only one object: a life-sized, naked figure of Christ wrapped around the cross in a perverse posture of the crucifixion. Whenever he feels troubled, Thorn visits the room and talks to the statue as though it were something alive. His monologues are quite intriguing because they reveal the beliefs he holds dear to his soul.[42] According to Damien, hell is not a place located in the bowels of the earth; instead, it is "the leaden monotony" of Judeo-Christian existence. This despicable lifestyle can change if people are allowed to embrace the raptures of his father's kingdom. Then and only then will a heaven on earth be experienced in which there will be an everlasting paradise of pain and a total purification of evil. (He reiterates his position to Kate right before he engages in a brutal type of love-making with her which resembles more of a rape than an affectionate type of bonding.)

When he poses such questions to the Christ replica as "What can you offer humanity [that I cannot]," Damien can be likened to the Jungian image of archaic man in all his glory. As already discussed in chapter 3, this primordial version of the modern-day human possesses a "pre-logical" state of mind whereby everything, even the remotest of occurrences, is perceived as having an apparent purpose and direction. Congruent with archaic man's egocentric view of reality, Damien regards his "morality" as the only right one; any other is considered evil and poses a threat to his continued well-being.[43] That is why he rejoices when he grasps the head of the Christ statue and attempts to drive the crown of thorns deeper into the lifeless skull. Although the effort injures his own palms, Damien believes he has caused actual harm to his nemesis. One of the assertions espoused by archaic man is that any action, no matter how slight, must produce a significant reaction in the world.[44] Clearly, Damien Thorn follows this guiding principle laid down by his ancestor. As the statue bleeds with his own blood, it looks almost as if red tears are flowing from the eyes of the "stricken face."[45] The Antichrist hopes that what he has wrought in the unhallowed chapel will lead to his final victory over the Messiah in the days ahead.

While Thorn puts his plan of infant killings into motion, a band of Benedictine monks from Subiaco, Italy, are working behind the scenes to destroy the demon once and for all. Each armed with one of the seven holy daggers of Meggido, they pursue a deadly game of cat and mouse with Damien.[46] Unfortunately, the priests do not realize that the tables have been turned on them and they are, in fact, the ones being hunted by the devious Damien.

Two sequences in which Damien eliminates several of his antagonists display how he has evolved from the childlike figure of *Omen I* and *Omen II* to the more efficient, adult "killing machine" of *Omen III*. In the first incident, Brothers Paolo and Martin think they have slain Thorn with their daggers; however, they quickly discover that a spell has been cast over them by the Antichrist and that it is Brother Matteus who has fallen by their hand. The two monks are so shocked by their actions that they allow the shadow trickster to seal them in a deep well where they will spend their remaining days "wailing and gnashing their teeth." The second set of murders surpass the first as they revolve around a fox hunt already in progress. This time, the holy men (in this case, Brothers Simeon and Antonio) assume they have outsmarted Damien by luring him away from the main hunting party. What happens instead is that their animals lash out at them with a vengeance. One stare from Damien and the horse on which Simeon is riding unexpectedly rears, sending the man over a parapet to his death. Brother Antonio meets an even grimmer fate: with the simple command, "Take him," Damien directs a pack of foxhounds to rend the holy man apart.[47] Although this scene is reminiscent of the dog attack in the first *Omen*, there is a major difference in this version. Thorn is now seen to be orchestrating the entire assault, showing just how much strength he has acquired from his "wonder years" to the end point of his maturation cycle.[48]

The inverted Sermon on the Mount is a further indication that Damien's might is spreading globally. He soars down to his "Disciples of the Watch" via helicopter and instructs them to seek out and destroy the Nazarene child so that they will inherit his father's paradise on earth. The followers embrace Damien's words by yelling back in a deafening chorus, "We hear and obey." What is of interest is the particular constituency of the group; though most are faceless, some are quite respectable members of the community.[49] There are priests, nurses, even boy scouts who have given their allegiance to Thorn and sacrificed the ideals of their given professions. They justify the despicable acts they commit (drowning babies in baptismal fonts, suffocating newborns in hospitals by turning off the oxygen supply) by their wanting to share in the power and glory of the Antichrist.

Even with his disciples' help, the Herod-like scheme concocted by Damien seems to be backfiring. As he informs his assistant, Harvey Dean (Don Gordon), the Messiah continues to elude him. His hypersenses can detect the godly presence, to the point where his own energies are being depleted by the "parasitic monster" which continues to live and grow in some still hidden location.[50] This might explain why Damien cannot perceive the danger which Kate Reynolds represents to his existence. Ordinarily, Thorn should have a keen sense of direction and purpose similar to the archetypal primitive who relies greatly on his sensory organs for his own survival.[51] However, his counterpart is robbing him of those archaic gifts, and so he cannot see what will transpire when he converts Kate's son, Peter (Barnaby Holm), to his cause.

To get Peter back at any cost, the "nonpracticing" Kate has decided to ally herself with the head monk, Father DeCarlo (Rossano Brazzi), who has managed to stay on the sidelines throughout the entire story. Together, they lure Damien to a deserted cathedral where supposedly the Christ child is. Peter is bright enough to suspect that this is a trap; Damien, on the other hand, dismisses the idea since he believes Kate would never intentionally harm her son by deceiving someone of his stature. As it turns out, it is the Antichrist himself who causes Peter's death by using the boy's body as a shield against the dagger which DeCarlo thrusts at him. This miscalculated act leads to Damien's downfall when Kate picks up the stiletto in the confusion and plunges it into his back with as much force as she can muster.

The dying Thorn has not considered just how powerful the love bond is between mother and child (having been deprived of that experience altogether). The parent-child association can be so spiritual and divine in nature that it can conquer anything and even bring the archetypal "God down from heaven" to rule on earth.[52]

This is exactly what happens at *Omen III*'s conclusion. Kate holds Peter's lifeless shell close to her in a warm, loving embrace, and at that same moment the mystical figure of Christ appears, shining forth with rays of love for all mankind. The only remark which Damien can utter before he dies on the steps of the altar is that the Nazarene has won nothing in this "final conflict" between good and evil. But he has, and it is that the primordial emotion of love can bind people more closely together and make them survive dangerous encounters with the most despicable of demons who would seek to prey on that communal force.[53] And so, in Damien's place, a new energy permeates the universe—an energy that will allow the children of humanity to grow in more positive, not negative, directions.

THE *OMEN* CHILD NEVER DIES

Audiences, who wished for an ending with a darker tone, did not find much merit in *Omen III*'s optimistic message.[54] To satisfy the popular sentiment, several projects were developed which continued *The Omen* saga both in novel and film. Approximately one year after the novelization of *Omen III*, a new story was conceived by Gordon McGill which centered on the unholy offspring of Damien Thorn and Kate Reynolds. In this outing, appropriately entitled *Omen IV—Armageddon 2000* (1982), the nameless "Boy" is about to set the entire world afire in a nuclear holocaust of Biblical proportions. Recognizing that the entire human race will be exterminated in the process, one disciple of Thorn's Inner Circle manages to kill the child before the insane plan can be realized.[55] While the story line resembles the earlier movie treatments, McGill was able to bestow an adult-like wisdom upon the Boy, reminding the reader that the archetypal child can possess a higher level of consciousness than the ordinary mortal (making the figure a very powerful one with which to contend).[56]

Omen veteran producer Harvey Bernhard always intended to do a film treatment for a fourth episode of the popular series, and after a decade of waiting he was given the go ahead by Fox Studios to oversee a television movie of the week which, regrettably, became a sanitization of his original screenplay meant for the big screen.[57] Still, *Omen IV: The Awakening* (1991) did introduce some novel elements into the Thorn legacy which deserve mentioning. First and foremost, a child of the opposite gender, Delia (Asia Vieria), was now given the lead role. Thanks to the acting talents of Vieria, Delia was played with a memorable animus-assertiveness. The close-ups on her frowning face, in particular, imparted a menacing aura which oftentimes went unnoticed by her concerned, quite naive foster parents. In addition, Bernhard was allowed the opportunity to depict a satanic version of the Virgin Mary's immaculate conception. Through the fictitious process of "foetus papyraceus," Delia was able to carry her twin brother's embryo in her womb for a number of years, until the time was right for it to be implanted in her foster mother, Karen (Faye Grant), so that it could mature and be delivered in the natural way.[58] By *Omen IV*'s climax, both Delia and her newborn sibling, Alexander, are in a position to inherit vast riches and influential power. Although a follow-up movie was never made, the *Omen* series was able to end its run the way it began: with the archetypal children of the devil once again executing the mightiest misdeeds on the planet. The full-circle pattern of the films is in keeping with the Jungian view that the primordial youngster will be eternally present; humanity might come and go, but the child will never die so long as there is an incompleteness in the world which requires development and eventual wholeness.[59]

NOTES

1. Stuart M. Kaminsky, *American Film Genres* (Chicago: Nelson-Hall, 1988), 132.

2. Scot W. Horton, "Review of *Phantasm*," *Phantasm LP Soundtrack* (Burbank, CA: Varese Sarabande Records, 1979): Back Record Sleeve.

3. William K. Everson, *More Classics of the Horror Film: Fifty Years of Great Chillers* (New York: Carol Publishing Group, 1990), 210.

4. David Seltzer, *The Omen* (New York: Signet, 1976), 60–62.

5. Robert Bookbinder, *The Films of the Seventies* (New York: Carol Publishing Group, 1993), 149; Vincent Canby, "Review of *The Omen*: Hollywood Has an Appealing New Star—Old Gooseberry," *New York Times*, 25 July 1976, Part II: 13: 1; Richard Eder, "Screen Review: *Omen* Is Nobody's Baby," *New York Times*, 26 June 1976, 16: 1.

6. Seltzer, *The Omen*, 181.

7. Carl G. Jung, "The Psychology of the Child Archetype," in *The Archetypes and the Collective Unconscious: The Collected Works*, trans. R.F.C. Hull (Princeton, NJ: Princeton University Press, 1990), 161, 166.

8. Carl Jung and C. Kerenyi, "The Primordial Child in Primordial Times," in *Essays on a Science of Mythology: The Myth of the Divine Child and the Mysteries of Eleusis*, trans. R.F.C. Hull (Princeton, NJ: Princeton University Press, 1993), 27, 30–31, 36–37.

9. Jung, "The Psychology of the Child Archetype," in *The Archetypes and the Collective Unconscious*, 163.

10. Seltzer, *The Omen*, 20.

11. Carl G. Jung, "Symbols of the Mother and of Rebirth," in *Symbols of Transformation: The Collected Works*, trans. R.F.C. Hull (Princeton, NJ: Princeton University Press, 1990), 237–39.

12. Seltzer, *The Omen*, 108–9, 184–85.

13. Bookbinder, *Films of the Seventies*, 149.

14. Jung, "The Phenomenology of the Spirit in Fairytales," in *The Archetypes and the Collective Unconscious*, 208–17.

15. Canby, "Review of *The Omen*: Hollywood Has an Appealing New Star," Part II: 13: 1.

16. Seltzer, *The Omen*, 42–45, 68–70, 119–22.

17. Jung and Kerenyi, "The Primordial Child in Primordial Times," in *Essays on a Science of Mythology*, 41–42.

18. Eder, "Screen Review: *Omen* Is Nobody's Baby," 16: 1.

19. Seltzer, *The Omen*, 196–97.

20. Carl G. Jung, "Christ, A Symbol of the Self," in *Aion: Researches into the Phenomenology of the Self: The Collected Works*, trans. R.F.C. Hull (Princeton, NJ: Princeton University Press, 1990), 42; Jung, "The Historical Significance of the Fish," in *Aion*, 110.

21. Canby, "Review of *The Omen*: Hollywood Has an Appealing New Star," Part II: 13: 1.

22. Vincent Canby, "Review of *Damien—Omen II*: Born unto a Jackal," *New York Times*, 8 June 1978, Section C6: 5.

23. Vincent Canby, "Review of *Damien—Omen II*: On Keeping the Scenery in Its Place," *New York Times*, 18 June 1978, Part II: 17: 4.

24. Joseph Howard, *Damien—Omen II* (New York: Signet, 1978), 9.

25. Jung, "The Phenomenology of the Spirit in Fairytales," in *The Archetypes and the Collective Unconscious*, 235–36, 240; Jung, "The Sign of the Fishes," in *Aion*, 72.

26. Howard, *Damien—Omen II*, 85.

27. Canby, "Review of *Damien—Omen II*: Born unto a Jackal," Section C6: 5.

28. Howard, *Damien—Omen II*, 130.

29. Jung, "The Dual Mother," in *Symbols of Transformation*, 325–26.

30. Jung, "Symbols of the Mother and of Rebirth," in *Symbols of Transformation*, 235–36.

31. Canby, "Review of *Damien—Omen II*: Born unto a Jackal," Section C6: 5; Richard Combs, "Review of *The Final Conflict—Omen III*," *Monthly Film Bulletin* (October 1981): 198.

32. Canby, "Review of *Damien—Omen II*: On Keeping the Scenery in Its Place," Part II: 17: 4.

33. Jung, "Symbols of the Mother and of Rebirth," in *Symbols of Transformation*, 236–37, 267–68.

34. Howard, *Damien—Omen II*, 169–70.

35. Ibid., 15–16.

36. Jung and Kerenyi, "The Primordial Child in Primordial Times," in *Essays on a Science of Mythology*, 36–37; Carol S. Pearson, *The Hero Within: Six Archetypes We Live By* (San Francisco: HarperCollins, 1989), 27–29.

37. Jung, "The Psychology of the Child Archetype," in *The Archetypes and the Collective Unconscious*, 177–81.

38. Combs, "Review of *The Final Conflict—Omen III*," 198; Carrie Rickey, "Review of *The Final Conflict*," *Village Voice* 26 (25–31 March 1981): 38; David Sterritt, "*The Final Conflict*," *Christian Science Monitor* 73 (7 May 1981): 19.

39. Gordon McGill, *The Final Conflict* (New York: Signet, 1980), 70.

40. Ibid., 56.

41. David Ansen, "Review of *The Final Conflict*," *Newsweek* 100 (30 October 1981): 83; Joseph Gelmis, "Review of *The Final Conflict*," *Newsday* 20 October 1981, Part II: 10; Archer Winsten, "Review of *The Final Conflict*," *New York Post*, 20 October 1981, 41.

42. McGill, *The Final Conflict*, 80–82; John Paul Ward, "Review of *The Final Conflict*," *Films in Review* 32 (May 1981): 312.

43. Carl G. Jung, "Archaic Man," in *Modern Man in Search of a Soul*, trans. W. S. Dell and Cary F. Baynes (San Diego, CA: Harcourt Brace Jovanovich, 1990), 126–28.

44. Ibid., 132–33.

45. McGill, *The Final Conflict*, 82; Ward, "Review of *The Final Conflict*," 312.

46. Ansen, "Review of *The Final Conflict*," 83; Winsten, "Review of *The Final Conflict*," 41.

47. Gelmis, "Review of *The Final Conflict*," Part II: 10; Rickey, "Review of *The Final Conflict*," 38.

48. Jung and Kerenyi, "The Primordial Child in Primordial Times," in *Essays on a Science of Mythology*, 38–39.

49. Combs, "Review of *The Final Conflict—Omen III*," 198.

50. McGill, *The Final Conflict*, 96.

51. Jung, "Archaic Man," in *Modern Man in Search of a Soul*, 129; Jung, "Psychology and Literature," in *Modern Man in Search of a Soul*, 163–64.

52. Jung, "The Hymn of Creation," in *Symbols of Transformation*, 63–64.

53. Ibid.; Jung, "The Song of the Moth," in *Symbols of Transformation*, 85–86.

54. Sterritt, "Review of *The Final Conflict*," 19; Ward, "Review of *The Final Conflict*," 312.

55. Gordon McGill, *Omen IV—Armageddon 2000* (New York: Signet, 1982), 207–15.

56. Jung, "The Psychology of the Child Archetype," in *The Archetypes and the Collective Unconscious*, 169.

57. Mark Kermode, "Review of *Omen IV: The Awakening*," *Sight and Sound* (December 1991): 45.

58. Ibid., 44–45.

59. Jung, "The Psychology of the Child Archetype," in *The Archetypes and the Collective Unconscious*, 177–79.

Part Three

A Jungian Analysis of Television Archetypes

9

Shadow Pursuers: Fanatical Figures in *The Fugitive, The Incredible Hulk, Starman,* and *The Pretender*

As we have already discussed in chapters 3 and 4, the shadow archetype can take the form of an entire species inimical to humankind or can devour anything unlike itself throughout the cosmos. In the medium of the small screen, a different and more popular image of the Jungian shadow has been displayed to viewers over the last three decades. This concluding chapter will examine the enduring television archetype of the shadow pursuer as well as why new generations are able to identify with such fanatical figures whose all-consuming obsession is the capture of their intended prey.

THE FUGITIVE: THE PROTOTYPE FOR THE SHADOW PURSUER IS LAID DOWN

September 17, 1963, was a significant date in television history. That evening the first episode of *The Fugitive* aired, and the brief, but informative, opening narrative provided by William Conrad disclosed the key elements of the memorable plot. Dr. Richard Kimble (played in low-key style by David Jannsen) is wrongly accused of killing his wife, Helen. Actually, a fiendish-looking one-armed man has committed the crime and is seen by Kimble as he returns home later that evening. Since no one believes the doctor's story, he is sentenced to die in the electric chair. En route to the death house, Kimble manages to escape from one of the law officials, Lieutenant Philip Gerard (Barry Morse), after their train derails. Thus was born a four-year, televised manhunt as Gerard relentlessly pursued Kimble from rural town to big city while Kimble searched for the real perpetrator who would clear his name of the misdeed.[1]

As noted by *The Fugitive*'s creator, Roy Huggins, Richard Kimble represented an archetypal Everyman who was fighting for his life, against impossible odds, to remove the stain of "guilt" from his person. Audiences were inclined to "root for the [very personable, even charming] underdog," even though Kimble did commit a felony by failing to acknowledge the decision of the courts and by fleeing from the police.[2] An even more fascinating character than the doctor stands out in this author's mind; namely, Lieutenant Gerard. Although he appeared in only about a third of the episodes, the presence of Gerard lurking in the corners was always perceived as a palpable threat to our hero. The lieutenant, who interprets the law by the book, is not in a position to question the decision of a jury; his sole function is to make sure that the legal process is carried out to the best of his ability. As an instrument of the law, Gerard holds himself responsible for Kimble's escape and, hence, must track "the Fugitive" down so that the justice system can continue to operate the way it was intended.[3] That he never regrets what he is doing throughout the entire length of the series is compatible with his mission. The lieutenant maintains an ever-present impartiality to the Kimble case and does not allow his personal feelings to interfere with the job he has been assigned. If Richard Kimble symbolizes the dissenter, Philip Gerard is the spokesperson for the entire judicial organization of which that dissenter is still a part. Such opposite characters enabled the writers of *The Fugitive* to present the age-old theme of "individual freedom versus dependency on the State" in a fresh perspective.[4]

Of course, Gerard does show an almost maniacal obsession in his quest to find Kimble. When the role was first being conceived, it was intended that the part be played in an "over the top, Captain Ahab" style with plenty of snarls and snappy comebacks. Finally, actor Barry Morse was able to bring a more workable and sophisticated approach to the lieutenant, due no doubt to his acquaintance with Victor Hugo's epic novel *Les Misérables* (1862). Hugo's classic tale revolved around a reformed thief, Jean Valjean, who could not escape his past so long as Inspector Javert was there to remind him of his crimes. Morse patterned his character after Javert's, to the point where even the name "Gerard" phonetically resembled the relentless nemesis of the French hero.[5] As Philip Gerard evolved in the course of the four years that *The Fugitive* aired, so did his fixation on capturing Kimble. By the final episodes, the older detective had to rely on glasses to discern his prey and had to shift his preference from left-hand usage to right; despite these physical disabilities, Gerard never abandoned his crusade and remained steadfast in his adherence to the "code." One was left wondering at times whether the shadow pursuer should have been insti-

tutionalized as he had devoted so much of his life (and energies) to capturing someone who was blameless of any wrongdoing.

The two-part resolution to this melodrama, appropriately entitled "The
Judgment," did bring an effective closure to the series. When Gerard finally
catches up with Kimble and arrests him at the end of Part One, there is no
sense of satisfaction on the officer's part. If anything, there is grim remorse.
He even apologizes to the doctor for doing what has to be done. Kimble's
response is no less striking: he accepts the circumstances and allows himself
to be taken away by the lieutenant instead of opposing him. The civility
shown on the part of both pursuer and pursued would suggest that the
hunt was never a savage one. Instead, it was a "gentlemanly quest between
two opponents who had come to respect each other."[6]

By Part Two Gerard has decided to give Kimble a twenty-four-hour reprieve to find the elusive, one-armed man, even though he believes the
search to be a fruitless one. Gerard may have broken his own code which
he has rigorously observed for so long, but he feels that it is one last act
within his power to grant. After all, the fugitive has given his word that
he will submit to the legal process once the reprieve has expired—which is
a major victory for the lieutenant and the system he embraces. The final
minutes of this episode find Jannsen tracking down his quarry at an abandoned amusement park, and Morse accepting the plausibility of the doctor's story by giving Kimble his own gun (after being wounded by the
one-armed man).[7] When the confession is delivered by the murderer, the
running stops for Kimble as he is exonerated of the crime. It is only then
that Gerard shakes hands with the cleared man, saying nothing further. In
the eyes of the officer, Kimble's status has changed and so his mission has
come to an end. One almost feels sorry for Gerard at the close; unlike
Kimble, who rejoins his family and is able to return to his former lifestyle,
the lieutenant is by himself—divorced from all others and no doubt significantly changed by the pursuit that has consumed his entire being.

Since the time of *The Fugitive*, a number of television shows have tried
to emulate the basic story of a shadow pursuer in search of a wandering,
oftentimes afflicted, protagonist. More times than not, science-fiction and
fantasy series have provided the perfect vehicle for casting their hunter and
hunted as "bigger than life" characters who either have the technological
resources to stalk their prey or are endowed with exceptional powers to
elude their dogged predator. *The Immortal*, *Werewolf*, *Stephen King's
Golden Years*, *The Visitor*, and *Dark Skies* are just a few of the entries that
have followed the Gerard-Kimble prototypic mold closely. We will be examining several noteworthy shows extending from the 1970s into the
1990s, with a particular focus on how the stalker has been portrayed
throughout each series' run. First on our agenda is the very popular superhero program *The Incredible Hulk* (1977–1981), which endured almost
as long as *The Fugitive*.

THE INCREDIBLE HULK: THE SEARCH IS ON FOR THE MISUNDERSTOOD BEAST

The major question posed in *The Incredible Hulk* was what would happen if a scientist was able to tap into the hidden strengths shared by all mortals. For Dr. David Banner (played by the late Bill Bixby), the answer becomes a living nightmare. He unknowingly exposes himself to a high-intensity beam of gamma radiation which affects his DNA so that in moments of rage or anxiety, he literally metamorphoses into a primitive, uncontrollable brute (Lou Ferrigno).[8] Wanting to rid himself of this "shadow" side, Banner enlists the help of fellow scientist Elaina Marks (Susan Sullivan); unfortunately, their efforts prove futile, and the doctor is left to search for the elusive cure for his condition throughout the course of the series.[9]

What really sustained the *Incredible Hulk* was the side plot involving a reporter from *The National Register*, one Jack McGee (Jack Colvin), who wants (more than anything else) to interview the reluctant Banner about his secret experiments. McGee is not a person who gives up easily, and when the creature is first spotted, he comes to the doctor with many questions about the "big, greenish-tinged Hulk" but receives few answers. The final third of the pilot movie concentrates almost exclusively on McGee and his attempts to discover the connection between Banner and the creature. When the scientist finds him nosing around the laboratory, he forcibly ejects the reporter from the premises. In the scuffle, McGee spills a bottle of flammable liquid which causes the entire facility to explode, leaving Elaina Marks dead and a grieving Hulk at her side. In a situation similar to that of Inspector Gerard, McGee wrongly accuses the creature of killing Drs. Marks and Banner (Banner's body cannot be found), and he notifies the local law enforcement agencies of the situation. Hence, the hunt is on for the Hulk with a persistent, *Fugitive*-style reporter following the trail so that he can deliver "the story of the century" to his editor as soon as the beast is captured and tried for his crimes.[10]

One might say that Jack McGee is his own worst enemy. Due to his inquisitive nature, he is indirectly responsible for the death of Elaina Marks in the opening episode. The fact that Jack does not even consider this possibility but instead blames the Hulk for the "accident" reflects the grievous sin committed by all shadow pursuers. According to Jung, the more negative features of one's shadow are sometimes projected onto others so that the person can deny himself "those [very] nasty, unsavory qualities" that constitute his inner personality.[11] Shadow pursuers like McGee are unable to admit their own faults; rather, they attribute personal defects to others so that they can elevate their position in society.[12] In the case of McGee especially, the process of shadow projection is quite strong since he works for a less than reputable publication which appeals almost exclusively to the checkout-line market. And so we have a reporter who wants to expose the truth behind the murders of the scientists, yet has devoted his life to a perpetual falsehood by not acknowledging who the real agent is (i.e., himself).

By *The Incredible Hulk*'s second season, Jack McGee realizes that most of the authorities do not believe his story. Some even treat him as a buffoon in public gatherings. On occasion we see Jack's own boss and fellow columnists talking down to him. While the *National Register* has indicated that it will give ten thousand dollars to the person who can supply McGee with the necessary information leading to the Hulk's capture, the promise remains an empty one and is used only as a publicity stunt to gain a broader reader base. Given these circumstances, the only logical recourse for Jack is to trap the creature himself so that he can vindicate his quest to those multitudinous doubters in the world. He seeks out a big game hunter in Chicago, Illinois (of all places), from whom he acquires curare-dipped darts that will temporarily paralyze the Hulk without causing permanent injury to the beast's nervous system (refer to the "Stop the Presses" episode). By the end of the second year, McGee also adds a net formed of the strongest metal links to his slowly growing arsenal of anti-Hulk deterrents (as depicted in "The Confession" episode).

Perhaps McGee's best weapon is the knowledge he possesses about the creature's metamorphic capabilities.[13] How he comes by this information is revealed in the pivotal two-parter entitled "Mystery Man." McGee has been stranded with his quarry out in the middle of a raging forest fire, but he does not suspect his traveling companion is the Hulk or, for that matter, Dr. David Banner. The doctor/Hulk has received facial burns from a very severe automobile accident and needs to wear a complete head mask so that the skin can heal properly. The disguised Banner also has suffered a form of traumatic amnesia and requires the help of McGee (of all people!) to fill in the gaps as to why he might have been involved at a Hulk sighting. That Banner saves McGee who is trapped in the raging fire is not unexpected; that Banner needs to change into the creature to do it is an interesting plot twist developed by the series' frequent writer and producer, Nicholas Corea. Though the Hulk's human identity remains concealed from his shadow pursuer in keeping with the premise of the comic book story line,[14] Jack has finally figured out why his prey has been such an elusive one. The Hulk has the Jungian trickster's ability to alter its shape so that it can merge with the human crowd, hence making it more difficult to track down.[15] McGee devotes himself to a new task by the conclusion of "Mystery Man"—to incapacitate the beast when it is in human form. The only puzzle which requires deciphering on Jack's part is figuring out who the man is behind the Hulk. One might say that Banner has pulled the best tour de force on the reporter in this string of episodes. He has kept the illusion alive that the Hulk has killed the doctor, and he has never compromised himself by admitting that the Hulk is the doctor, only that the Hulk is someone else—referred to from this point on in the series as the enigmatic "John Doe."

"Mystery Man" contained some interesting (if not memorable) pieces of dialogue between the hunter and the hunted which fleshed out both characters considerably and ensured *The Incredible Hulk*'s survival for another few seasons on the small screen. Banner asks McGee why he wants the Hulk so badly. The reply is reflective of the reporter's rather vain, egocentric nature: "Because the Hulk means escape. I can get off *The Register*, get my own column back, write real stories. Be somebody!"[16] Taking the side of the creature for the moment, David reminds Jack of the many heroic things it has accomplished since it made its first appearance (even McGee has composed some stories highlighting the Hulk's positive actions). But the reporter cannot be dissuaded from his pursuit. He is quick to point out that one's existence is made up of choices involving "you or the other guy." For Jack, the bottom line is that the Hulk needs to be sacrificed so that he can, ultimately, get ahead and do something meaningful with his life. Such self-righteous denial of one's own shadow side is what makes the pursuer a terribly misguided individual who cannot perceive the harm he is doing to others and, most of all, himself by engaging in the hunt so blindly.[17]

An episode from the third year, "Proof Positive," followed up on this theme by devoting itself solely to the character of Jack McGee and his personal crusade against the Hulk. This was the only story that did not feature Bill Bixby and used a stand-in for the concluding, metamorphic sequence from human to Hulk. Jack's all-consuming obsession with the creature has finally taken its toll on the man. He has missed several other, equally important, assignments for the *Register*; he has been experiencing recurring and vivid nightmares in which the Hulk crushes him in those massive, superstrong hands; and he even daydreams about the monster as a result of his run-down, stressed-out condition. His behavior has been triggered by the acquisition of a new editor by the tabloid, Patricia Steinhauer (Caroline Smith), who wants to eliminate the trash and devote her energies to reporting the real, hard-hitting news. Jack's weekly feature on the Hulk is one of those columns that will be dropped as a result of Steinhauer's dictates; thus, the pursuer suddenly finds himself without a purpose in life. In McGee's distorted mind, the enemy has expanded to include anyone who does not believe in the Hulk (and there are plenty of individuals at his workplace who can now be regarded with suspicion and paranoia, not the least of whom is his new editor-in-chief).

The crisis reaches a resolution of sorts when McGee convinces Steinhauer that the Hulk actually exists. He brings her to a reported sighting, where both of them witness the transformation from man into monster. Redeemed in the eyes of his boss, Jack regains his column, but his fixation remains as he is seen running off on another lead by the end of the episode. Attending to the viewpoint of the shadow pursuer for at least several of the episodes appears central to the hunter-quarry plot, and *The Incredible Hulk* was not the only series that had this recurring focus.[18] *The Fugitive* also had its share of plots that revolved around Lieutenant Gerard and his obsession with Kimble. In "Never Wave Goodbye," the detective tries to communicate, albeit unsuccessfully, to his wife and son that his prolonged absences are necessary so that a wrongdoer can be brought to justice. A subsequent two-parter, "Landscape with Running Figures," relates what this manhunt has done to the pursuer's family. While Philip Gerard has not yet reached the limits of his endurance, his wife Marie is dangerously close to a mental breakdown over the man "who's never there." Clearly, Gerard loves his wife and does not want the marriage to end; on the other hand, he cannot abandon his quest for the fugitive.[19] Both McGee and Gerard seem to be "at odds with themselves." They still desire human contact and relationships with significant others; however, the hunt to which they have dedicated themselves has made them wanderers who travel their paths, for the most part, alone and in a state of unfulfillment.[20]

Our psychological analysis of Jack McGee would not be complete without considering *The Incredible Hulk*'s fourth-season entrees, "Prometheus: Parts One and Two." Series creator Kenneth Johnson, who remained with the show throughout its entire airing, mainly in the role of executive producer, decided to answer (in a roundabout way) the fans' most asked question, "Would the Hulk ever be captured by McGee?"[21] The reporter himself responds in the opening minutes of "Prometheus" that perhaps this might be the time "we'll finally get him." As the story unfolds, though, it is not the lone pursuer who is able to contain the creature, but an even more powerful governmental organization (referred to by the title name) which is devoted to tracking down any extraterrestrial life form not conforming to our own. The Prometheus unit succeeds in its task only because Dr. Banner is not entirely himself; he has been affected by mysterious rays emanating from a crashed meteorite that leaves him in a half-human, half-Hulk form. The chimeric Banner has only rudimentary intelligence and limited strength, making him an easy prey for the collective hunters who transport him to their hidden mountain base in central Colorado for further scrutiny. Of course, the plot would not be complete without the presence of Jack McGee. He is able to penetrate the defenses by attiring himself in the appropriate garb and passing himself off as one of the organization's military leaders. Sadly, McGee attains the same status as Banner when he is detected: a victim to be used so that the secrets of the monster can be revealed and eventually tapped into by our very own government.

"Prometheus," one of the most creative and highly innovative story lines of its time, employed elements of fantasy and "big brother" conspiracy rather nicely into the continuing *Hulk* saga. (Subtle precursors of the more contemporary series, *The X-Files*, can be detected in these episodes.) However, one should not ignore the deeper, Jungian message of collective shadow powers which are much deadlier and fearful to behold than those of simple-minded pursuers. Organizations resembling Prometheus are dangerous in that they destroy the individuality of their members, robbing them of all responsibility and leaving an anonymous "mass" of people who blindly follow those in charge.[22] Although a "think tank" of scientists is employed at Prometheus, the ones ultimately leading the group are working behind the scenes. That they remain hidden from view is significant as they represent all the dark, unseen forces of the Jungian unconscious waiting to be unleashed upon the world.[23] By observing the day-to-day operations via satellite transmissions, the nameless ones are able to deploy effectively their Army-like minions at just the right moment to deal with any conceivable threat to world security.

Into this harsh environment comes Jack McGee, who believes he can dupe the group long enough so that he can get his story published on the Hulk's confinement. However, the lone pursuer has terribly underestimated the Prometheus unit. Once the chimeric creature breaks out of its laser prison by pounding its fists through the floor and escaping through the tunnels, guards are ordered to use any force necessary to restrain the beast. Jack is the only one who disagrees with this policy, but his words go unheeded. As a result, Banner returns to his savage, mightier form and levels the entire headquarters before departing. (Apparently removed from the meteorite's influence, the good doctor is at last freed from his half-state.) The conclusion of the two-parter shows viewers that there is another, nobler side to hunter Jack McGee. He is able to maintain his individuality against the repressive system, and he takes the side of David Banner, not wanting "the Everyman" to be in shackles and chains for the rest of his life. Like many other *Hulk* tele-tales, "Prometheus" is charged with emotions, especially when Jack helps the re-formed Hulk escape.[24] By switching his allegiances (without any hesitation on his part), the reporter might have reached the point of recognizing the dark side of his own self and how the pursuit has tainted his soul. Or the heroic action might just reflect a payback for all the times the creature saved him. One never knows what Jack McGee was truly capable of achieving because the show was abruptly canceled by the CBS Network before a satisfactory ending could be filmed.[25] Apart from a cameo appearance on one of the later NBC made-for-television movies (*The Return of the Incredible Hulk*), McGee would never return to finish the chase he started years ago.

STARMAN: THE HUNT CONTINUES FOR THE ELUSIVE, DNA-SWAPPING ALIEN

The ABC television series *Starman* (1986–1987) was based on the earlier motion picture by the same name, and so a brief explanation of the movie plot is in order. A shapeless emissary from another world crash-lands its craft in Wisconsin and then assumes the human form of the deceased Scott Hayden (Jeff Bridges) by cloning his DNA from a lock of hair contained within a family album. Naturally, the widowed Jenny (Karen Allen) is stunned to see her "husband" still alive. After the alien convinces her about its true identity, they both embark on a cross-country trip to Arizona where a rescue ship is scheduled to appear in three days.[26] It is imperative that the creature make this deadline; otherwise, it will have to sacrifice the physical shell and die. Along the way, both "Scott" and Jenny fall in love and conceive a hybrid embryo—much to the delight of Jenny who always desired a child of her own. But an ever present danger follows them. Government agents and SETI (Search for Extra-Terrestrial Intelligence) operatives are tracking the alien's movements in the hopes that they can catch up with the visitor before it departs. The head of the team, George Fox (Richard Jaeckel), wants to do more than just ask the Starman simple questions, however. His intentions are to take the "thing" back to Washington and dissect it piece by piece in order to obtain information on this newest menace threatening the world's security.[27] So the race is on to Arizona, with Fox's helicopter gunships closing in at the same time that the other-worldly ship is making its intended rendezvous with the "man from the stars."

Bridges's rather innocent, yet charming, portrayal of the alien is in sharp contrast to Jaeckel's more experienced role of the bureaucratic chief who barks out orders to his inferiors every chance he can get. For all his administrative background, though, George Fox will ultimately fail in his task to entrap the visitor. His "bounty hunter mentality" does not allow room for morality and other ethical deliberations.[28] Simply put, Fox has an assignment to complete for the government, and he must do it without question or hesitation on his part. Because of his tunnel-vision view of reality, the shadow pursuer seems incapable of learning anything from the Starman. Yet, the viewer is greeted in one scene after another by the alien's very caring and steadily growing human nature. Fox is not a witness (and probably would show no desire to be one) to the number of miracles performed by this interdimensional traveler. For instance, Starman resurrects a dead deer that has been shot by a hunter because he cannot stand to see any life form extinguished in so vicious a manner. Likewise, after crashing through a road block, he heals Jenny's mortal wound for much the same reason. The man from the stars has something to teach Homo sapiens about its own brutish shadow and what might happen if it is not held in check.[29] Agent Fox definitely typifies the worst in the species, and yet there are those like Jenny who represent humanity's best members. She not only survives, but is also blessed with a part of the Starman's more advanced, spiritual core at the conclusion of the film.[30] It seems a shame that the Starman's pursuers have not opened their eyes as well to the good emanating from the alien. If they did, they might perceive more similarities than differences between the two races.

The *Starman* series takes place fifteen years later, when the visitor's son, Scott (C. B. Barnes), activates a sphere entrusted to him by his mother, Jenny, who has left the boy in an orphanage and has hidden herself from the ever watchful eyes of the SETI organization. The "call" from Scott's glowing, silver orb is picked up light years away by the Starman. Having achieved the capability of surviving on our planet, the traveler clones a new body: that of a late photojournalist, Paul Forrester (Robert Hays), who perished while on assignment.[31] The new "Paul" immediately seeks out his son, but the reception is not what he expects. Scott feels betrayed by the man who walked out on him years ago and does not understand why he has returned. But Paul does not give up on the adolescent, and by the end of the first episode (entitled "The Return"), they both make a pact to search for the whereabouts of their missing family member, Jenny Hayden.[32]

"The Return" also marks the reappearance of NSI (National Security Intelligence) operative George Fox (now played with suitable histrionics by Michael Cavanaugh). The pursuer's thinning hair and bad heart condition are a testament that the man has changed physically over the years—and not for the better. Fox is still consumed by one goal: he has to find the visitor and any inhuman offspring it created before the entire world is besieged by the growing alien threat. His ranting and raving to his superiors about the "bloodthirsty killer" that destroys human bodies and then replicates them for its own sinister purposes is a sight to behold. In spite of his hysterics, George Fox is able to convince the leaders of the country that his pursuit has merit, and he quickly receives the manpower he needs to accomplish his mission. Maybe it is Fox's projection of his own dark hatreds and prejudices onto the vulnerable Starman that ultimately sways the group to which he reports. After all, who would not want to exterminate a lesser, more inferior race if it could mean the elevation of the human one to godhood status?[33] Obviously, the right buttons are pushed, and Fox is given the go-ahead to bring in the despicable creature and its brood for further study.

Unlike McGee and Gerard, whose actions speak louder than their words, George Fox lives up to his namesake by using his silver tongue to persuade others to accept the lie he believes about the Starman. As Jung discloses, shadow pursuers who have this particular talent are able to "meet with astounding success [at least] for a short spell. . . . It is part and parcel of their make-up to be plausible and to be taken seriously by a wider public."[34] In the pilot, Paul Forrester's reporter-girlfriend, Liz Banes (Mimi Kuzyk), falls under Fox's control when she discovers that her lover is acting differently after he comes back from his fateful photo shoot. Dazzled by the government man's talk of world security, Liz leads Fox right to "Paul" and Scott placing both their lives in immediate danger. A later episode,

"Society's Pet," revolved around the same theme, only this time it was a relation of Scott's who did the actual betraying. Antonia Wayburn (portrayed by Janet Leigh) desires more than anything else to get her nephew away from Paul so that she can raise the boy in the style and class to which she is accustomed.[35] She would even sell her soul to the devil, or in this case George Fox, to attain her goal. It is only after she finds out that the slick government agent wants Scott as well as Paul that Antonia has a change of heart and decides to side with the Starman against Fox and his band of storm troopers. Interestingly, most of the informants on the series experienced this eye-opening conversion; they recognized their own shadow faults and corrected the circumstances for the benefit of the two fugitives, Paul and Scott.[36] Sadly, Starman's pursuer comes away from these events unshaken and all the more determined to catch his elusive prey.

Fox did manage to lay his hands on the alien in several of the episodes before the show was put on hiatus and was eventually canceled after only a single season. In the pivotal "Fever" teleplay, General Wade has decided to shut down the "Project: Visitor" program unless agent Fox can obtain some incontestable evidence that such a creature actually exists. One of those wondrous, synchronous moments occurs for George when Paul literally falls into his lap. The Starman has been trying to battle a simple cold, but because his blood has not developed any antibodies to ward off the infection during his short stay on our planet, he succumbs to the fever and is raced to the local hospital. The physician in charge, Dr. Dukow (Marta DuBois), is quite puzzled by the man's condition and even more so by his strange blood type. Fox obtains a sample of blood to take back to his superior as undeniable proof of the alien's presence. One of the best scenes of the *Starman* series involves Fox's explaining to Dr. Dukow that her patient is not a "he" but an "it" that requires some physical intervention to sustain the body, at least until "it" can be transported to Washington. Dukow is shocked by Fox's insensitivities to the human she is treating; in her eyes, the agent before her is more of an "uncaring thing" than the creature who lies in a near death, comatose state. Again, the shadow pursuer transplants everything "dark and imperfect" within himself onto another (in this case, an innocent visitor from beyond our solar system) in order to avoid facing up to his own inadequacies and inferiorities.[37] Interestingly, Fox puts the doctor on the right track by suggesting an intrusive treatment of some type. Dukow reasons that a blood transfusion from Paul's offspring should be effective because the youngster's system already contains the necessary antibodies. Sure enough, Paul is cured and is subsequently escorted out of the hospital by Dukow before Fox can recapture him. Though George is able to keep the Visitor project running a few more months, he regards the incident overall as another failure so long as his "shadow-alien" continues to be let loose upon the world.

Likewise, in the "Grifters" episode, Paul is jailed as a result of his run in with two scam artists (David Doyle and Eric Server), where he meets an elated Fox who cannot believe the lucky hand fate has dealt him. The dialogue between the hunter and his prey make this episode a memorable (if not insightful) one; highlights of their conversation appeared as part of the opening titles for the remaining stories.[38] Fox literally bombards the Starman with his barrage of questions: "How many more of you are out there?"; "How deeply have you infested us?"; and "How many will have to be excised to save our planet?" Paul's reply is loaded with meaning: "After all these years, is that all you want to ask me?" Clearly, George Fox is not willing to change his bigoted views. If anything, he wants the visitor to corroborate them so that his pursuit can finally be validated (most of all in his own eyes). It appears that the government man cannot get out of his red tape mind-set to ask Paul the real reason for his return.[39] He might be quite surprised to learn that the Starman is similar to any human father who has feelings of love and affection for his son and who will do anything to protect his offspring from harm—even cross great distances (or, in this case, galaxies) to ensure that essential contact is maintained. Seen in this perspective, Paul's mission is not to destroy life, but to create it and then be responsible for it.[40] Poor George Fox should be pitied for not reaching out to the man from the stars with open arms instead of clenched fists and gun in pocket.

After receiving word that the series would be canceled with no hope of a reprieve at the eleventh hour, executive producers James Henerson and James Hirsch decided to write a two-part teleplay ("Starscape") that would bring some closure to Starman's search for Jenny Hayden. In essence, the plot would try to rekindle the intergalactic romance between the alien and his human mate which viewers found so appealing in the original movie, only this time two different actors (Robert Hays and Erin Gray) would evoke feelings of tenderness and sweetness in the other.[41] Part One, which proceeds at a rapid pace, starts with Paul and Scott tracking down an artist who goes by the alias of Karen Isley. What interests the pair is the starscape she has painted: it is the precise constellation that Paul calls home. While Scott is sidetracked by some relatives of Karen's who wish to keep her identity secret, Paul manages to find the woman eking out an existence as a hermit in the wilderness of northern Arizona. In stages, he teaches Karen Isley (a.k.a. Jenny Hayden) to trust and love him all over again. By Part Two Paul believes that Jenny is strong enough to handle the real reason he has reentered her life. (It should be remembered that the Starman has cloned a new body which Jenny had never encountered prior to this moment.) The news does not come as a complete shock since she has detected something magical and very familiar about this stranger from the very beginning. She even looks forward to seeing her son, Scott, again now that she has Paul to help her through any crisis.

Just when it looks like a happy ending is on the horizon for the trio,

George Fox intrudes upon the scene to claim the prize he has been denied all these years. With tranquilizer gun in hand, he immobilizes both Paul and Scott and takes them to the mysterious Building 11, which houses the remnants of Paul's first spacecraft. There the pair are poked and prodded from head to toe under the supervision of Fox who watches with grim satisfaction from an upper observation window. Eventually, Paul extricates himself and his son from their confinement, but not before the shadow pursuer gains the upper hand and threatens to shoot Forrester should he decide to leave the base. Before he can carry out the execution, Fox suffers a major heart attack and falls to the floor, overcome by the pain. Paradoxically, it is Starman who saves the man's life by using his mystical powers of healing, which he channels through his silver sphere to George's failing organ, strengthening the heart beats almost immediately. Needless to say, the military doctors are stunned that Fox has a clean bill of health and suffers no lingering aftereffects of the seizure. There is, however, no cure for the agent's obsession with Paul. He is bent on tracing the whereabouts of the fugitive alien by the conclusion of the two-parter, even if it means placing his own life in jeopardy once more. For George (as well as any other determined shadow pursuer), psychic change is not feasible unless he "accepts himself in all his wretchedness . . . [and begins to realize] he is the oppressor of the person he condemns."[42] By not considering the possibility that the extraterrestrial might have been responsible for his recovery, Fox fails to attain an "unprejudiced objectivity" and would rather maintain a lie of his own making in the final minutes of the series.

And what of the recovered Jenny Hayden? She has left both Paul and Scott, knowing that George Fox will hunt her down and use her as "bait" to get to her lover and son. Though Jenny's motives might be questionable, her intuitions about the pursuer are right on the mark. The government man will never call off the chase, until all three of them are sacrificed for the "higher good" of world security. In many respects, Starman is still the innocent clone of fifteen years ago.[43] By bringing Fox back from the dead, he has allowed the pursuit to continue and has forced Jenny into hiding, perhaps never to return. While technologically advanced, the race to which Starman belongs still has a lot to learn about the devious nature of humans, especially those of single-minded shadow pursuers engaged in their high-stakes games.

THE PRETENDER: THE MAN OF A THOUSAND PROFESSIONS MEETS HIS MATCH

In the most contemporary television series to date, *The Pretender* (which premiered in the fall of 1996 and is still in production), we have elements reminiscent of both *The Incredible Hulk* and *Starman* but with some new twists. Here the wanderer is a middle-aged man named Jarod (Michael T.

Weiss) who has "the ability to insinuate himself into any walk of life, to literally become anyone [by simply digesting the information about the designated profession]."[44] Ever since Jarod's childhood, his impressive talent has been exploited by a top-secret organization referred to as the Centre. After nearly thirty-three years of confinement, the "Pretender" breaks out of his prison to discover who he is and if any of his family members are still alive. Jarod's psychiatric mentor at the Centre, Sydney (Patrick Bauchau), is concerned for his well-being and hopes that he will return of his own accord. But the one assigned to the case, Ms. Parker (played by Andrea Parker), has different feelings about Jarod.

She has been recalled from the Centre's corporate section to track down the runaway; once she retrieves (or preferably eliminates) him, then she can concentrate on her own career goals. To paraphrase Ms. Parker's sentiments in the opener, Jarod is a Frankenstein monster that must be disposed of promptly. This arrogant thinking is typical of the Amazon warrior, an emerging female role model in the cinematic world who is not afraid to express her animus side if it means coming out the winner in a battle.[45] Apart from the gender change, there is another important variation with *The Pretender*'s shadow pursuer. She is not engaged in the hunt to obtain kudos from the Centre. Unlike McGee and Fox, who desired the recognition of their affiliated organizations (i.e., the media and government), Ms. Parker wants to disassociate herself from this menial job as soon as possible. It is her autonomous nature that makes her a fascinating predator and will, ultimately, lead her on a course in direct opposition to her superiors.[46]

In most of the episodes, the Pretender assumes a variety of disguises to bring prominent evildoers to justice.[47] In the pilot, Jarod becomes a surgeon to flush out an incompetent member of the team who frequently operates while under the influence of alcohol. Similarly, in the "Virus Among Us" teleplay, Jarod assumes the false identity of a virologist to expose the unbalanced leader of an infectious disease research center who has been mutating strains to near lethal levels. But what, ultimately, made the show a critical success was the "contest of wits" between the Pretender and his attractive pursuer, Ms. Parker. Almost every show involves Jarod leaving a variety of clues for Ms. Parker to follow in order to give her the false impression that she will catch him. Yet, our hero is always two steps ahead of her, exercising his creative powers to the fullest when dealing with his adversary.[48] The end result is that Ms. Parker comes away from each close encounter emotionally frustrated and visibly disappointed while a gleeful Jarod welcomes the opportunity to continue playing the game as a more than willing participant.

Perhaps the best example of how the Pretender actually turns the tables on his hunter is illustrated in the aforementioned "A Virus Among Us" episode. Jarod has set an elaborate trap for the unsuspecting Parker: he has extracted the sticky substance from over 100 roach motels and has coated his entire apartment with the powerful adhesive. When Ms. Parker and her Centre minions arrive, their shoes become literally glued to the floor. While they are trying to extricate themselves from their predicament, a video re-cording of Jarod is activated. The professorial image on the screen, com-plete with suit, bow tie, and egghead-style glasses, announces that class is in session and that today's topic is "How to Catch That Most Elusive Bug: The Roach." Ms. Parker all too readily picks up on the demeaning remark and in her distraught state pushes one of the agents onto the bed. But only half his body falls down, leaving the other half still plastered to the floor. The contorted position of the subordinate, coupled with Jarod's video smile, make the pursuer even more frantic, but she can do nothing except wait for Sydney to send in reinforcements from the Centre. Clearly, Jarod is a different type of prey than David Banner or Paul Forrester. With his intellectual prowess and other extraordinary gifts, he is able to outwit the shadow pursuer on more than one occasion.[49] Most of all, it is Jarod's take charge attitude that provides a welcome change from all the other passive and highly vulnerable hunted figures (including the prototypic *Fugitive* character).

Of the numerous shadow hunters on the small screen, *The Pretender*'s is probably the most emotive. At times Ms. Parker loses control, yelling at Sydney and his associates with such passion that one can almost feel the Centre's walls vibrate as well as the heat that emanates from her almost inhuman stares. As Jung mentions, once the shadow is released in full force, all those uncontrollable affects race madly to the surface to find expression. Reason and intellect will be the first to suffer from such "shadow attacks," leaving the person in the dominant, feeling mode of the primitive.[50] This is not to say that the individual rarely benefits from these freed-up emotions. One immediate advantage is that the person is better connected with his (or her) hidden half and, hence, can experience life much more sensually and keenly than ever before.[51] Several teleplays, which devoted their entire subplot to such "positive feeling moments" in the life of Ms. Parker, are worthy of discussion, if for no other reason than that they provide the reader with a more in-depth look at the shadow pursuer's motives and desires.

"The Better Part of Valor" is a fascinating excursion into Ms. Parker's past loves and her current romantic entanglement. An old flame, Michael Patrick (Anthony Starke), reenters Ms. Parker's life to light up her days and nights with nonstop hunger and lust. The change in the hunter is im-mediately evident to Sydney: she comes to work with a smile affixed to her face, ready to make coffee for her "boys" who have been up all night in their latest search for Jarod. But the transformation is a brief one, like the affair she is having with Michael. When she discovers that her lover has been working for one of the Centre bosses, Dr. Raines, in order to ascertain how she is proceeding with the "Pretender" case, Ms. Parker becomes so angry that she soon has Michael in an uncompromising position on the floor (with her heel embedded in his chest, no less). To reduce the impact of the betrayal, Ms. Parker tells Michael that "she was faking each and every orgasm."[52] As she storms out of the room, the viewer is left with ambivalent feelings toward the pursuer who appears so much warmer and more caring in this episode than in previous ones in her "Ms. Freeze" persona.

"Ranger Jarod" allowed actress Andrea Parker to impart more substance to her character than ever before. For the first time, Jarod experiences feelings of love for his partner, Nia (Elpidia Carrillo), who is conducting a mountain search for a missing ornithology student. Interestingly, the one at the Centre who is most shocked at this strange turn of events is Ms. Parker. In a series of childhood flashbacks, she recalls particular moments when she was drawn to the mysterious boy at the Centre named Jarod. She remembers whispering her first name only to Jarod in private and even giving him a kiss full on the lips. Most of the episode presents Ms. Parker in this reminiscing state until she finally meets Nia. Her animus then comes out "like a jealous lover," and she sizes the woman up, possibly hoping someday to compete with her for Jarod's affections.[53] Ms. Parker has kept her intense passion for the Pretender repressed for such a long time because she dare not admit the bond she holds with the man in fear that it will prevent her from performing her job (i.e., to capture her past boyfriend). And so Ms. Parker prefers to be completely possessed by the animus spirit, to the point of losing her femininity and all aspects of her womanly persona.[54] Jung best explains it in his discussion of relationships with the complementary gender: they are typically "full of animosity . . . [and] very often run their course heedless of the human performers, who afterwards do not know what happened to them."[55] So it is with Ms. Parker, who cannot provide an adequate description of what she has felt with Jarod and who would rather focus on her target from a dispassionate viewpoint than continue to dwell on the perplexing matter. Thus we leave the hunter where she started, tracking her goal but with a bit more hesitancy and confusion in her overall makeup.

Given this symbiotic connection between Jarod and Ms. Parker, it was inevitable that the series' executive producers (Steven Long Mitchell and Craig W. Van Sickle) would compose a story around both characters being entrapped by a crazed Marine Patrol officer who is responsible for killing a number of Haitian refugees in the Florida Keys and is considering a similar fate for our protagonist and antagonist. The appropriately named "Keys" teleplay marked a turning point in the hunt between Jarod and Ms. Parker since the two have to rely on each other to extricate themselves from their confinement and rescue a little girl who is dying from a high fever while simultaneously finding a safe haven from a raging hurricane that has blown into their vicinity.[56] Jarod even saves Ms. Parker's life before the villain of the tale can shoot her. When she inquires why he did this, the reply is a simple one: "Because I remember the little girl who gave me my first kiss." Though the hunter is grateful to Jarod, she ends the conversation by announcing that the chase will continue until he is brought back to the Centre, either willingly or by force. One aspect of Parker's psyche appears to have undergone a metamorphosis. She no longer entertains the idea of killing her prey, now that she considers him an integral part of her past life (and maybe her present one as well).

If Jarod is searching for any surviving family members, his complement is also undertaking a quest of her own: to find out why her own mother supposedly killed herself at the Centre. A number of *Pretender* episodes ("Mirage," "Keys," "Unhappy Landings," and "Baby Love") involve her deciphering clues leading up to her mother's "suicide." The pieces of the puzzle that she puts together lead her to the conclusion that Mrs. Parker was trying to rescue several children (including Jarod) who were abducted by the Centre, but she was silenced before she could successfully execute her plan. It is ironic that the hunter has to rely on the prey to provide her with the necessary background information and appropriate documents to make the case that her superior, Dr. Raines, was more than peripherally involved in her mother's death. Jarod helps Ms. Parker for an obvious reason. If he can convince her that the people she works for are not above eliminating people for the higher good of the Centre, then maybe the relentless pursuit will stop one day (at least he hopes so).

The archetypal mother figures prominently in the lives of both Jarod and Ms. Parker, linking the two inexplicably together. Not only is Jarod seeking his real mother and lost childhood (with its associated dependencies),[57] but so is Ms. Parker—only in her situation she is recovering her "maternal" image and suppressed femininity. It is hardly coincidental that Andrea Parker portrays both mother and daughter since Jung contends that every woman contains elements of the offspring in herself and vice versa.[58] Unfortunately, for the shadow hunter, the animus' ruthless will to power wins out so that she is not in a position to "live for others" and sacrifice her very being as her mother had done.[59] One might say that Jarod and Ms. Parker represent two sides of the same coin, a Yin/Yang duality of needy anima and dominating animus, respectively, who require each other to complete themselves.

In the first season finale, "The Dragon House," the chase between hunter and hunted follows a new direction as another Pretender is introduced into the story line. Posing as an FBI agent, Jarod is on the trail of a murderous sociopath, Kyle (Jeffrey Donovan), whom he recognizes as his childhood companion at the Centre. Why Kyle has chosen a criminal path instead of Jarod's more noble (and colorful) career is best explained by the Centre's psychiatrist, Sydney, who relates that the notorious Dr. Raines had been conducting some secret experiments on the young abductees years ago. Through an intensive conditioning procedure, one of the boys was purged of all moralistic principles, and he acquired the skills and thought processes of an assassin (including the ingrained phrase, "I decide who lives and dies") before taking it upon himself to venture out into the world. Now Raines wants the grown-up Kyle back so that he can remove certain brain areas through laser surgery and reprogram the man's deadly impulses to eliminate more important targets, such as political figures and world leaders. Eventually, Raines catches up with his creation and, with the assistance of several armed operatives, returns him to the Centre. But the plot is far from over. Jarod learns that Kyle is, in reality, his younger brother. After recovering from his initial shock, Jarod decides to rescue his relative—even if it means placing his own life in jeopardy.[60] Thus, the hunted goes back to the Centre (and Ms. Parker) in the hopes of liberating his own flesh and blood from the very facility that robbed him of his childlike innocence.

That Jarod has an evil brother with the same talents and abilities fits in with many religious myths, including the story that God had two sons, an elder one named Satan and a younger one, Christ.[61] Later Grail King legends also explained the wounding of the monarch by an "invisible and sinister brother" who aspired to the former's kingdom and lands.[62] One constant remains throughout these accounts: good and evil are intimately connected and can never be separated. While Kyle dismisses the idea that his soul can be saved by Jarod, he wants to locate his parents just as much as his brother and that goal alone makes both Pretenders kindred spirits. Sadly, Kyle never gets the opportunity to start his search. Right after Jarod frees him from the Centre, a team of FBI officials corner Kyle and, in the ensuing shoot-out, explode the vehicle in which he is trapped.

By the end of the cliff-hanger, Jarod comes face to face with his mom (Kim Meyers) and his younger sister, Emily. Though the reunion is a brief one, the likelihood exists that the Pretender will be able to link up with his family someday (probably in the final episode of the series). And some poetic justice is delivered to the despicable villain of the tale, Dr. Raines. An unidentified person punctures Raines's portable oxygen tank with a bullet, causing the man to suffer first degree burns throughout his entire body. The closing minutes of "The Dragon House" reflect the theme of this chapter. Jarod makes a phone call to Sydney and, with gusto, dares the mentor to catch him if he can. This statement brings the major plot element back into focus. The chase with Ms. Parker and the rest of the Centre will continue, so long as Jarod continues to display his stubborn defiance against the shadow hunters who would like nothing better than to suppress those individualistic qualities for the benefit of the collective.

Shows like *The Incredible Hulk*, *Starman*, and *The Pretender* will always fascinate audiences by the very fact that one man is fighting the system and winning every day he can prolong the struggle and endure. The Jack

McGees, George Foxes, and Ms. Parkers of the world will always be there around every corner to spring their traps, but they will fail so long as human beings exercise their option to oppose group conformity and be true to their own nature.

NOTES

1. Ed Robertson, *The Fugitive Recaptured: The 30th Anniversary Companion to a Television Classic* (Los Angeles: Pomegranate Press, 1993), 13.

2. Leonard H. Goldenson with Martin J. Wolf, *Beating the Odds* (New York: Charles Scribner's Sons, 1991), 5–10.

3. Robertson, *The Fugitive Recaptured*, 35–36.

4. Carl G. Jung, "After the Catastrophe," in *Civilization in Transition: The Collected Works*, trans. R.F.C. Hull (Princeton, NJ: Princeton University Press, 1990), 201.

5. Steven Eramo, "Barry Morse: Space Refugee," *Starlog* 221 (December 1995): 49.

6. Robertson, *The Fugitive Recaptured*, 177.

7. Ibid., 177; Eramo, "Space Refugee," 49.

8. James F. Iaccino, *Psychological Reflections on Cinematic Terror: Jungian Archetypes in Horror Films* (Westport, CT: Praeger Publishers, 1994), 86–87.

9. Stuart M. Kaminsky and Jeffrey H. Mahan, *American Television Genres* (Chicago: Nelson-Hall, 1988), 123–24.

10. Pat Jankiewicz, "Review of *The Incredible Hulk*: Time of the Green," *Starlog* 204 (July 1994): 76; Mark Rathwell, *The Incredible Hulk FAQ Version 2.4*, http://www.uoguelph.ca/%7Emrathwel/Hulk/faq.html (1996): 2.

11. Robert H. Hopcke, "Shadow" in *A Guided Tour of the Collected Works of C. G. Jung* (Boston: Shambhala, 1992), 82.

12. Carl G. Jung, "The Shadow," in *Aion: Researches into the Phenomenology of the Self: The Collected Works*, trans. R.F.C. Hull (Princeton, NJ: Princeton University Press, 1990), 9.

13. Iaccino, *Psychological Reflections on Cinematic Terror*, 86.

14. Mike Benton, *Superhero Comics of the Silver Age: The Illustrated History* (Dallas: Taylor Publishing, 1991), 80.

15. Ibid., 79; Hopcke, "Trickster," in *A Guided Tour of Jung*, 122.

16. Rathwell, *The Incredible Hulk FAQ Version 2.4*, 5–6.

17. Jung, "The Fight with the Shadow," in *Civilization in Transition*, 225.

18. Don E. Peterson, "Review of *Alien Nation*: Bright Horizon," *Sci-Fi Entertainment* 2 (February 1996): 53.

19. Robertson, *The Fugitive Recaptured*, 45–46, 119–20.

20. Carol S. Pearson, *The Hero Within: Six Archetypes We Live By* (San Francisco: HarperCollins, 1989), 67–72.

21. Peterson, "Review of *Alien Nation*: Bright Horizon," 53, 79.

22. Jung, "Epilogue to 'Essays on Contemporary Events,'" in *Civilization in Transition*, 229–30.

23. Jung, "The Fight with the Shadow," in *Civilization in Transition*, 221.

24. Jankiewicz, "Review of *The Incredible Hulk*: Time of the Green," 75.

25. Rathwell, *The Incredible Hulk FAQ Version 2.4*, 8–9.

26. Rex Reed, "Review of *Starman*," *New York Post*, 14 December 1984, 43; David Sterritt, "Review of *Starman*," *Christian Science Monitor* 76 (31 December 1984): 18.

27. David Ansen, "Review of *Starman*: At Long Last?" *Newsweek* 104 (17 December 1984): 81; Sheila Benson, "Review of *Starman*," *Los Angeles Times*, 13 December 1984, Calendar, 1; Richard Combs, "Review of *Starman*," *Monthly Film Bulletin* (May 1985): 163.

28. Leo Seligsohn, "Review of *Starman*," *Newsday*, 14 December 1984, Part III: 9.

29. Ansen, "Review of *Starman*: At Long Last?" 81.

30. Reed, "Review of *Starman*," 43.

31. Brian Lowry, "Robert Hays: *Starman* About Town," *Starlog* 114 (January 1987): 18; Vicki Hessel Werkley, *The Starman Episode Synopsis*, http://www.calweb.com/~smccrory/stepguide.html (1993): 1.

32. Margaret Ronan, "Television Program Review: *Starman*," *Scholastic Update* 119 (23 February 1987): TE8.

33. Jung, "After the Catastrophe," in *Civilization in Transition*, 203.

34. Ibid., 204, 206.

35. Werkley, *The Starman Episode Synopsis*, 3.

36. Jung, "Epilogue to 'Essays on Contemporary Events,' " in *Civilization in Transition*, 228.

37. Carl G. Jung, "The Problems of Modern Psychotherapy," in *The Practice of Psychotherapy: The Collected Works*, trans. R.F.C. Hull (Princeton, NJ: Princeton University Press, 1990), 58–59.

38. Werkley, *The Starman Episode Synopsis*, 5–6.

39. John Nangle, "Review of *Starman*," *Films in Review* 36 (March 1985): 183.

40. J. Hoberman, "Review of *Starman*," *Village Voice* 30 (25 December 1984): 67.

41. Ansen, "Review of *Starman*: At Long Last?" 81–82; Combs, "Review of *Starman*," 163; Anthony Scott King, "Film Review: On the Set of *Starman*," *Starlog* 89 (December 1984): 59.

42. Carl G. Jung, "Psychotherapists or the Clergy," in *Modern Man in Search of a Soul*, trans. W. S. Dell and Cary F. Baynes (San Diego, CA: Harcourt Brace Jovanovich, 1990), 234–35.

43. Lowry, "Robert Hays: *Starman* About Town," 19; Werkley, *The Starman Episode Synopsis*, 7.

44. Jeff Jarvis, "Television Program Review: *The Pretender*," *TV Guide* 45 (25–31 January 1997): 17.

45. Iaccino, *Psychological Reflections on Cinematic Terror*, 129–45; Pearson, *Hero Within*, 86.

46. Steven Reddicliffe, ed., "Review of *The Pretender*: NBC's Saturday Night Line-Up," *TV Guide* 44 (14–20 September 1996): 15.

47. Jarvis, "Television Program Review: *The Pretender*," 17.

48. Carl G. Jung, "The Dual Mother," in *Symbols of Transformation: The Collected Works*, trans. R.F.C. Hull (Princeton, NJ: Princeton University Press, 1990), 337.

49. Jung, "The Origin of the Hero," in *Symbols of Transformation*, 177–78.

50. Jung, "The Self," in *Aion*, 30–31; Jung, "The Shadow," in *Aion*, 9.

51. Jung, "Archaic Man," in *Modern Man in Search of a Soul*, 126–30.

52. *Jarod's Notebooks*, http://www.intex.net/~perridox/pretender/notebook.html (1997): 5.

53. Carl G. Jung, "The Relations Between the Ego and the Unconscious. Part Two: Individuation. II. Anima and Animus," in *The Basic Writings of C. G. Jung*, trans. R.F.C. Hull (Princeton, NJ: Princeton University Press, 1990), 182.

54. Ibid., 183; Carl G. Jung, "The Masculine in Women: From Esther Harding's Notebooks," in *Aspects of the Masculine*, trans. R.F.C. Hull (Princeton, NJ: Princeton University Press, 1989), 112.

55. Jung, "The Syzygy: Anima and Animus," in *Aion*, 16.

56. *Jarod's Notebooks*, 8.

57. Jung, "The Syzygy: Anima and Animus," in *Aion*, 11–12.

58. Carl G. Jung, "The Psychological Aspects of the Kore," in *The Archetypes and the Collective Unconscious: The Collected Works*, trans. R.F.C. Hull (Princeton, NJ: Princeton University Press, 1990), 188.

59. Jung, "Psychological Aspects of the Mother Archetype," in *The Archetypes and the Collective Unconscious*, 88.

60. *Jarod's Notebooks*, 10.

61. Jung, "Christ, A Symbol of the Self," in *Aion*, 57; Jung, "The Fish in Alchemy," in *Aion*, 147.

62. Emma Jung and Marie-Louise von Franz, "The Suffering Grail King," in *The Grail Legend*, trans. Andrea Dykes (Boston: Sigo Press, 1986), 209–10.

Final Remarks

It would certainly seem to be the case that Jungian archetypes are alive and well and residing in the world of the cinema. From *Star Wars*' space-fathers and *The Omen*'s demon children to *Star Trek* creators and *Planet of the Ape* shadows, stories continue to unfold their powerful, primordial contents on the screen each and every decade. It is hoped that the reader will come away with a new perspective on film analysis and will recognize, at the very least, two facts that operate in his (or her) perceived reality: (1) Jungian archetypes have shaped a significant number of creative works since the earliest moments of our history, and (2) the realm of the collective unconscious has found (and continues to find) expression in any story depicting the human condition, whether it be written, oral, or visual. We have just scratched the surface with respect to Jungian interpretations in film, but the start of such ventures is necessary and even justified if we are ever going to address our species' commonalities in a practical way. Though there might be critics of this text who would have wanted to see other film genres (e.g., detective, Western, or romance) discussed at length, this author does not consider it his responsibility to provide the requested analyses. Rather, it is up to those scholars to assume the helm and research their own areas of interest in depth. If I have provided a base for their investigations, however, then I feel that my work has succeeded in showing others that the Jungian model is applicable to a diverse range of media.

Due to page restrictions and time constraints, I was limited in how much

I could adequately cover in one book. Thus, certain archetypes were omitted from Parts One, Two, and Three. I should briefly mention those images should anyone want to study them further. Films like the *Phantasm* trilogy, *Stargate*, and *Independence Day* highlight the less than perfect mandalas which open the door to killing as well as mass destruction. Likewise, a theme evidenced in our modern era and portrayed in numerous science-fiction and fantasy movies (from *The Lawnmower Man* and *Species* to *Jurassic Park*) deals with the perverted products of science which are sometimes inflated to monstrous proportions. Television archetypes that were being considered include the following: shadow government conspiracies (*X-Files, Earth 2, La Femme Nikita*), sinister doppelgangers (*Sliders, Two*), alien collectives (*Babylon 5, Dark Skies, War of the Worlds*), fractured personae (*Dr. Who, Quantum Leap*), and prototypical swashbucklers (*Hercules, Sinbad,* and *Xena*). I would personally like to devote an entire book to Jungian archetypes on the small screen to cover not only the aforementioned images but others as well. Perhaps this dream of mine can become a reality in the not too distant future.

The journey is truly far from over as we further explore our cinematic environment according to the Jungian archetypal perspective. I can only wish you well in your future travels and hope that you are as intrigued as I am by the way in which contemporary films continue to express age-old images in exciting and novel ways as the millennium rapidly approaches. "May you live long, prosper, and be one with these archetypes, always" (Kenobi and Spock, date unknown).

Appendix: Science-Fiction and Fantasy Filmography

The science-fiction and fantasy films listed below are discussed at length in the text. For the reader's convenience, information on each film's availability in video is provided along with the appropriate chapter number in which it is referenced.

The following key is used: Dir = director(s); Prod = producer(s); Exec Prod = executive producer(s); Assoc Prod = associate producer(s); Scr = screenplay writer(s); St = Star(s); [#] = chapter number.

Back to the Future. MCA/Universal, 1985. Dir: Robert Zemeckis. Prod: Bob Gale and Neil Canton. Exec Prod: Steven Spielberg, Frank Marshall, and Kathleen Kennedy. Scr: Bob Gale and Robert Zemeckis. St: Michael J. Fox, Christopher Lloyd, Crispin Glover, Lea Thompson, and Thomas F. Wilson. On video. 115 min. [5]

Back to the Future Part II. MCA/Universal, 1989. Dir: Robert Zemeckis. Prod: Bob Gale and Neil Canton. Exec Prod: Steven Spielberg, Frank Marshall, and Kathleen Kennedy. Scr: Bob Gale. Based on a story by Robert Zemeckis and Bob Gale. St: Michael J. Fox, Christopher Lloyd, Lea Thompson, and Thomas F. Wilson, Claudia Wells. On video. 107 min. [5]

Back to the Future Part III. MCA/Universal, 1990. Dir: Robert Zemeckis. Prod: Bob Gale and Neil Canton. Exec Prod: Steven Spielberg, Frank Marshall, and Kathleen Kennedy. Scr: Bob Gale. Based on a story by Robert Zemeckis and Bob Gale. St: Michael J. Fox, Christopher Lloyd, Mary Steenburgen, Thomas F. Wilson, Lea Thompson. On video. 118 min. [5]

Batman: The Movie. Warner Brothers, 1989. Dir: Tim Burton. Prod: Jon Peters and Peter Guber. Exec Prod: Benjamin Melniker and Michael Uslan. Scr: Sam Hamm and Warren Skaaren. Based on a story by Sam Hamm. St: Michael Keaton, Jack Nicholson, Kim Basinger, Michael Gough, Billy Dee Williams, Jack Palance, and Pat Hingle. On video. 126 min. [6]

Batman Forever. Warner Brothers, 1995. Dir: Joel Schumacher. Prod: Tim Burton and Peter Macgregor-Scott. Exec Prod: Benjamin Melniker and Michael E. Uslan. Scr: Lee Batchler, Janet Scott Batchler, and Akiva Goldsman. Based on a story by Lee Batchler and Janet Scott Batchler. St: Val Kilmer, Tommy Lee Jones, Jim Carrey, Nicole Kidman, Chris O'Donnell, Michael Gough, and Pat Hingle. On video. 122 min. [6]

Batman Returns. Warner Brothers, 1992. Dir: Tim Burton. Prod: Denise Di Novi and Tim Burton. Exec Prod: Jon Peters, Peter Guber, Benjamin Melniker, and Michael Uslan. Scr: Daniel Waters. Based on a story by Daniel Waters and Sam Hamm. St: Michael Keaton, Danny DeVito, Michelle Pfeiffer, Christopher Walken, Michael Gough, and Pat Hingle. On video. 126 min. [6]

Battle for the Planet of the Apes. Twentieth-Century Fox, 1973. Dir: J. Lee Thompson. Prod: Arthur P. Jacobs. Assoc Prod: Frank Capra, Jr. Scr: John William and Joyce Hooper Corrington. Story by Paul Dehn. Based on characters created by Pierre Boulle. St: Roddy McDowall, Natalie Trundy, Austin Stoker, Claude Akins, Paul Williams, and Severn Darden. On video. 86 min. [3]

Battlestar: Galactica (Pilot movie). MCA/Universal Television, 1978. Dir: Richard A. Colla. Prod: John Dykstra and Leslie Stevens. Exec Prod: Glen A. Larson. Scr: Glen A. Larson. St: Richard Hatch, Dirk Benedict, Lorne Greene, Herbert Jefferson, Jr., Maren Jensen, Terry Carter, John Colicos, and Jane Seymour. Edited version on video. 152 min. [4]

Battlestar: Galactica, "War of the Gods" (Parts 1 and 2). MCA/Universal Television, 1979. Dir: Daniel Haller. Prod: David J. O'Connell. Assoc Prod: Donald Bellisario. Story by Glen A. Larson. St: Richard Hatch, Dirk Benedict, Lorne Greene, Patrick Macnee, and Anne Lockhart. Not available on video. 94 min. [4]

Beneath the Planet of the Apes. Twentieth-Century Fox, 1970. Dir: Ted Post. Prod: Arthur P. Jacobs. Assoc Prod: Mort Abrahams. Scr: Paul Dehn and Mort Abrahams. Based on characters created by Pierre Boulle. St: James Franciscus, James Gregory, Kim Hunter, Maurice Evans, Linda Harrison, and Charlton Heston. On video. 108 min. [3]

Conquest of the Planet of the Apes. Twentieth-Century Fox, 1972. Dir: J. Lee Thompson. Prod: Arthur P. Jacobs. Assoc Prod: Frank Capra, Jr. Scr: Paul Dehn. Based on characters created by Pierre Boulle. St: Roddy McDowall, Don Murray, Natalie Trundy, Hari Rhodes, and Ricardo Montalban. On video. 86 min. [3]

Damien—Omen II. Twentieth-Century Fox, 1978. Dir: Don Taylor. Prod: Harvey Bernhard. Assoc Prod: Charles Orme. Scr: Stanley Mann and Michael Hodges. Based on a story by Harvey Bernhard with characters created by David Seltzer. St: William Holden, Lee Grant, Jonathan Scott-Taylor, Lew Ayres, Sylvia Sidney, Robert Foxworth, Lance Henriksen, and Lucas Donat. On video. 107 min. [8]

The Empire Strikes Back. Twentieth-Century Fox, 1980. Dir: Irvin Kershner. Prod: Gary Kurtz. Exec Prod: George Lucas. Scr: Leigh Brackett and Lawrence Kasdan. Based on a story by George Lucas. St: Mark Hamill, Harrison Ford, Carrie Fisher, Anthony Daniels, and David Prowse. On video. 124 min. [1]

Escape from the Planet of the Apes. Twentieth-Century Fox, 1971. Dir: Don Taylor. Prod: Arthur P. Jacobs. Assoc Prod: Frank Capra, Jr. Scr: Paul Dehn. Based on characters created by Pierre Boulle. St: Roddy McDowall, Kim Hunter, Sal Mineo, Bradford Dillman, Natalie Trundy, Eric Braeden, and Ricardo Montalban. On video. 98 min. [3]

The Final Conflict—Omen III. Twentieth-Century Fox, 1981. Dir: Graham Baker. Prod: Harvey Bernhard. Exec Prod: Richard Donner. Scr: Andrew Birkin. Based on characters created by David Seltzer. St: Sam Neill, Rossano Brazzi, Lisa Harrow, Don Gordon, and Barnaby Holm. On video. 108 min. [8]

The Fugitive, "The Final Judgment," (Parts 1 and 2). United Artists Television, 1967. Dir: Don Medford. Prod: William Schiller. Exec Prod: Quinn Martin. Assoc Prod: George Eckstein. Story by George Eckstein and Michael Zagor. Created by Roy Huggins. St: David Janssen, Barry Morse, Bill Raisch, Richard Anderson, Jacqueline Scott, Diane Baker, Joseph Campanella, Michael Constantine, and J. D. Cannon. On video. 104 minutes. [9]

Galactica 1980, "The Night the Cylons Landed" (Parts 1 and 2). MCA/Universal Television, 1980. Dir: Barry Crane. Prod: Frank Lupo. Exec Prod: Glen A. Larson. Story by Glen A. Larson. St: Kent McCord, Barry Van Dyke, Lorne Greene, Robyn Douglass, Roger Davis, and Lara Parker. Edited version on "Battlestar: Galactica—Conquest of Earth" video. 94 min. [4]

Galactica 1980, "The Return of Starbuck. " MCA/Universal Television, 1980. Dir: Ron Satloff. Prod: Frank Lupo. Exec Prod: Glen A. Larson. Story by Glen A. Larson. St: Dirk Benedict, Judith Chapman, Rex Cutter, and Lorne Greene. Complete version on "Battlestar: Galactica—The Return of Starbuck" video. 47 min. [4]

Highlander. Thorn EMI Screen Entertainment, 1986. Dir: Russell Mulcahy. Prod: Peter S. Davis and William N. Panzer. Exec Prod: E. G. Monell. Scr: Gregory Widen, Peter Bellwood, and Larry Ferguson. Based on a story by Gregory Widen. St: Christopher Lambert, Sean Connery, Roxanne Hart, and Clancy Brown. On video. 110 min. [7]

Highlander: The Final Dimension. Dimension Films, 1995. Dir: Andy Morahan. Prod: Claude Leger. Exec Prod: Guy Collins and Charles L. Smiley. Scr: Paul Ohl. Based on a story by William Panzer and Brad Mirman. St: Christopher Lambert, Mario Van Peebles, Deborah Unger, and Mako. On video. 99 min. [7]

Highlander II: The Quickening. Lamb Bear Entertainment, 1990. Dir: Russell Mulcahy. Prod: Peter S. Davis and William N. Panzer. Exec Prod: Guy Collins and Mario Sotela. Assoc Prod: Stephen Kaye. Scr: Peter Bellwood. Based on a story by Brian Clemens and William Panzer. St: Christopher Lambert, Virginia Madsen, Michael Ironside, and Sean Connery. On video. 90 min. [7]

The Incredible Hulk (Pilot movie). Universal Television, 1977. Dir: Kenneth Johnson. Prod: Kenneth Johnson. Assoc Prod: Craig Schiller. Story by Kenneth Johnson. Based on the Marvel Comics Group character. St: Bill Bixby, Lou Ferrigno, Jack Colvin, and Susan Sullivan. On video. 94 min. [9]

The Incredible Hulk, "Mystery Man" (Parts 1 and 2). Universal Television, 1979. Dir: Frank Orsatti. Prod: Nicholas Corea. Exec Prod: Kenneth Johnson. Story by Nicholas Corea. Based on the Marvel Comics Group character. Developed for television by Kenneth Johnson. St: Bill Bixby, Lou Ferrigno, Jack Colvin, Victoria Carroll, and Don Marshall. Not available on video. 94 min. [9]

The Incredible Hulk, "Prometheus" (Parts 1 and 2). Universal Television, 1980. Dir: Kenneth Johnson. Prod: Robert Bennett Steinhaeur, Karen Harris, and Jill Sherman. Exec Prod: Kenneth Johnson. Story by Kenneth Johnson. Based on the Marvel Comics Group character. Developed for television by Kenneth Johnson. St: Bill Bixby, Lou Ferrigno, Jack Colvin, Laurie Prang, Monte Markham, Carol Baxter, and Whit Bissell. Not available on video. 94 min. [9]

The Incredible Hulk, "Proof Positive." Universal Television, 1980. Dir: Dick Harwood. Prod: Robert B. Steinhauer and Jeff Freilich. Assoc Prod: Stephen P. Caldwell and Alan Cassidy. Story by Karen Harris and Jill Sherman. Based on the Marvel Comics Group character. Developed for television by Kenneth Johnson. St: Jack Colvin, Lou Ferrigno, Caroline Smith, Walter Brooke, and Charles Thomas Murphy. Not available on video. 47 min. [9]

Indiana Jones and the Last Crusade. Paramount, 1989. Dir: Steven Spielberg. Prod: Robert Watts. Exec Prod: George Lucas and Frank Marshall. Scr: Jeffrey Boam. Based on a story by George Lucas and Menno Meyjes. St: Harrison Ford, Sean Connery, Denholm Elliott, Alison Doody, John Rhys-Davies, and Julian Glover. On video. 129 min. [7]

Indiana Jones and the Temple of Doom. Paramount, 1984. Dir: Steven Spielberg. Prod: Robert Watts. Exec Prod: George Lucas and Frank Marshall. Assoc Prod: Kathleen Kennedy. Scr: Willard Huyck and Gloria Katz. Based on a story by George Lucas. St: Harrison Ford, Kate Capshaw, Ke Huy Quan, and Amrish Puri. On video. 118 min. [7]

Logan's Run. Metro-Golden-Mayer, 1976. Dir: Michael Anderson. Prod: Saul David. Scr: David Zelag Goodman. Based on the novel by William F. Nolan and George Clayton Johnson. St: Michael York, Jenny Agutter, Richard Jordan, Peter Ustinov, and Roscoe Lee Brown. On video. 120 min. [4]

Logan's Run (Pilot movie). Metro-Golden-Mayer Television, 1977. Dir: Robert Day. Prod: Leonard Katzman. Exec Prod: Ivan Goff and Ben Roberts. Scr: William F. Nolan, Saul David, and Leonard Katzman. Based on the novel by William F. Nolan and George Clayton Johnson. St: Gregory Harrison, Heather Menzies, Donald Moffat, Randy Powell, and Morgan Woodward. Not available on video. 76 min. [4]

Logan's Run "Carousel." Metro-Golden-Mayer Television, 1977. Dir: Irving J. Moore. Prod: Leonard Katzman. Exec Prod: Ivan Goff and Ben Roberts. Assoc

Prod: William O. Cairncross. Teleplay by D. C. Fontana and Richard L. Breen, Jr. From a story by Richard L. Breen, Jr. Based on the novel by William F. Nolan and George Clayton Johnson. St: Gregory Harrison, Heather Menzies, Donald Moffat, Randy Powell, Ross Bickell, and Morgan Woodward. Not available on video. 47 min. [4]

Logan's Run, "The Judas Goat." Metro-Golden-Mayer Television, 1977. Dir: Paul Krasny. Prod: Leonard Katzman. Exec Prod: Ivan Goff and Ben Roberts. Assoc Prod: William O. Cairncross. Story by John Meredyth Lucas. Based on the novel by William F. Nolan and George Clayton Johnson. St: Gregory Harrison, Heather Menzies, Donald Moffat, Nicholas Hammond, Lance LeGault, and Morgan Woodward. Not available on video. 47 min. [4]

The Omen. Twentieth-Century Fox, 1976. Dir: Richard Donner. Prod: Harvey Bernhard. Exec Prod: Mace Neufeld. Assoc Prod: Charles Orme. Scr: David Seltzer. St: Gregory Peck, Lee Remick, Billie Whitelaw, David Warner, Patrick Troughton, and Harvey Stephens. On video. 110 min. [8]

Omen IV: The Awakening. Twentieth-Century Fox Television, 1991. Dir: Martin Fuhrer. Prod: Harvey Bernhard. Exec Prod: Mace Neufeld. Assoc Prod: Robert Anderson. Scr: Brian Taggert. Based on a story by Harvey Bernhard and Brian Taggert with characters created by David Seltzer. St: Asia Vieria, Faye Grant, Michael Woods, Michael Lerner, Madison Mason, Ann Hearn, and Jim Byrnes. On video. 94 min. [8]

Planet of the Apes. Twentieth-Century Fox, 1968. Dir: Franklin J. Shaffner. Prod: Arthur P. Jacobs. Assoc Prod: Mort Abrahams. Scr: Michael Wilson and Rod Serling. Based on the novel *Monkey Planet* by Pierre Boulle. St: Charlton Heston, Roddy McDowall, Kim Hunter, Maurice Evans, and Linda Harrison. On video. 112 min. [3]

The Pretender (Pilot). MTM Television, 1996. Dir: Rick Wallace. Prod: Sascha Scheinder. Exec Prod: Steven Long Mitchell and Craig W. Van Sickle. Story by Steven Long Mitchell and Craig W. Van Sickle. St: Michael T. Weiss, Andrea Parker, Patrick Bauchau, Steven Tobolowsky, Peter Michael Goetz, L. Scott Caldwell, and Dylan Provencher. Not available on video. 47 min. [9]

The Pretender, "The Better Part of Valor." MTM Television, 1997. Dir: Anson Williams. Prod: Harvey Frand and Marianne Canepa. Exec Prod: Craig W. Van Sickle and Steven Long Mitchell. Assoc Prod: Tommy Thompson. Story by Javier Grillo-Marxuach. St: Michael T. Weiss, Andrea Parker, Patrick Bauchau, Michael O'Neill, Anthony Starke, Isabel Glasser, Jon Gries, and Jon Pennell. Not available on video. 47 min. [9]

The Pretender, "The Dragon House" (First season finale). MTM Television, 1997. Dir: Fred K. Keller. Prod: Harvey Frand and Marianne Canepa. Exec Prod: Craig W. Van Sickle and Steven Long Mitchell. Assoc Prod: Ian Toynton and Tommy Thompson. Story by Steven Long Mitchell and Craig W. Van Sickle. St: Michael T. Weiss, Andrea Parker, Patrick Bauchau, Jeffrey Donovan, Harve Presnell, Linda Carlson, James Tolkan, Kim Meyers, and Jon Gries. Not available on video. 94 min. [9]

The Pretender, "Keys." MTM Television, 1997. Dir: Terrence O'Hara. Prod: Harvey Frand and Marianne Canepa. Exec Prod: Craig W. Van Sickle and Steven Long Mitchell. Assoc Prod: Tommy Thompson. Story by Steven Long Mitchell and Craig W. Van Sickle. St: Michael T. Weiss, Andrea Parker, Patrick Bauchau, Harve Presnell, Jeremy Roberts, Leslie Jordan, Richard Marcus, and Jon Gries. Not available on video. 47 min. [9]

The Pretender, "Ranger Jarod." MTM Television, 1997. Dir: Ian Toynton. Prod: Harvey Frand and Marianne Canepa. Exec Prod: Craig W. Van Sickle and Steven Long Mitchell. Assoc Prod: Ian Toynton and Tommy Thompson. Story by Steven Long Mitchell and Craig W. Van Sickle. St: Michael T. Weiss, Andrea Parker, Patrick Bauchau, Elpidia Carrillo, John Posey, Jack Kehler, Christopher James Williams, and Jon Gries. Not available on video. 47 min. [9]

The Pretender, "A Virus Among Us." MTM Television, 1996. Dir: Fred Keller. Prod: Harvey Frand and Marianne Canepa. Exec Prod: Craig W. Van Sickle and Steven Long Mitchell. Assoc Prod: Tommy Thompson. Story by Lawrence Meyers. St: Michael T. Weiss, Andrea Parker, Patrick Bauchau, Jon Polito, David Spielberg, Raphael Sbarge, Brenda Varda, and Jon Gries. Not available on video. 47 min. [9]

Raiders of the Lost Ark. Paramount, 1981. Dir: Steven Spielberg. Prod: Frank Marshall. Exec Prod: George Lucas and Howard Kazanjian. Scr: Lawrence Kasdan. Based on a story by Philip Kaufman and George Lucas. St: Harrison Ford, Karen Allen, Denholm Elliott, Paul Freeman, and John Rhys-Davies. On video. 115 min. [7]

Return of the Jedi. Twentieth-Century Fox, 1983. Dir: Richard Marquand. Prod: Howard Kazanjian. Exec Prod: George Lucas. Scr: Lawrence Kasdan and George Lucas. Based on a story by George Lucas. St: Mark Hamill, Harrison Ford, Carrie Fisher, Billy Dee Williams, and Anthony Daniels. On video. 132 min. [1]

Starman. Columbia, 1984. Dir: John Carpenter. Prod: Larry J. Franco. Exec Prod: Michael Douglas. Assoc Prod: Barry Bernardi. Scr: Bruce A. Evans and Raynold Gideon. St: Jeff Bridges, Karen Allen, Charles Martin Smith, and Richard Jaeckel. On video. 115 min. [9]

Starman, "Fever." Columbia Television, 1986. Dir: Bill Duke. Prod: Mike Gray and John Mason. Exec Prod: James Henerson, James Hirsch, and Michael Douglas. Story by Tom Lazarus. Based on characters created by Bruce A. Evans and Raynold Gideon. St: Robert Hays, C. B. Barnes, Michael Cavanaugh, Marta Dubois, and Dabbs Greer. Not available on video. 48 min. [9]

Starman, "Grifters." Columbia Television, 1987. Dir: Claudio Guzman. Prod: Mike Gray and John Mason. Exec Prod: James Henerson, James Hirsch, and Michael Douglas. Assoc Prod: Joel Chernoff. Story by Steven Hollander. Based on characters created by Bruce A. Evans and Raynold Gideon. St: Robert Hays, C. B. Barnes, Michael Cavanaugh, David Doyle, Eric Server, and Bill Macy. Not available on video. 48 min. [9]

Starman, "The Return." Columbia Television, 1986. Dir: Charles S. Dubin. Prod: Mike Gray and John Mason. Exec Prod: James Henerson, James Hirsch, and

Michael Douglas. Story by James Henerson and James Hirsch. Based on characters created by Bruce A. Evans and Raynold Gideon. St: Robert Hays, C. B. Barnes, Michael Cavanaugh, and Mimi Kuzyk. Not available on video. 48 min. [9]

Starman, "Society's Pet." Columbia Television, 1986. Dir: Claudio Guzman. Prod: Mike Gray and John Mason. Exec Prod: James Henerson, James Hirsch, and Michael Douglas. Story by Ross Hirshorn. Based on characters created by Bruce A. Evans and Raynold Gideon. St: Robert Hays, C. B. Barnes, Michael Cavanaugh, Janet Leigh, and Katherine Moffat. Not available on video. 48 min. [9]

Starman, "Starscape" (Parts 1 and 2). Columbia Television, 1987. Dir: Claudio Guzman. Prod: Mike Gray and John Mason. Exec Prod: James Henerson, James Hirsch, and Michael Douglas. Assoc Prod: Joel Chernoff. Story by James Henerson and James Hirsch. Based on characters created by Bruce A. Evans and Raynold Gideon. St: Robert Hays, C. B. Barnes, Michael Cavanaugh, Erin Gray, Joshua Bryant, and Marilyn Lightstone. Not available on video. 96 min. [9]

Star Trek Generations. Paramount, 1994. Dir: David Carson. Prod: Rick Berman. Exec Prod: Bernie Williams. Scr: Ronald D. Moore and Brannon Braga. Based on a story by Rick Berman, Ronald D. Moore, and Brannon Braga. St: Patrick Stewart, William Shatner, Jonathan Frakes, Brent Spiner, and LeVar Burton. On video. 117 min. [2]

Star Trek: The Motion Picture. Paramount, 1980. Dir: Robert Wise. Prod: Gene Roddenberry. Scr: Harold Livingston. Based on a story by Alan Dean Foster. St: William Shatner, Leonard Nimoy, DeForest Kelley, James Doohan, George Takei, and Nichelle Nichols. On video. 132 min. [2]

Star Trek II: The Wrath of Khan. Paramount, 1982. Dir: Nicholas Meyer. Prod: Robert Sallin. Exec Prod: Harve Bennett. Scr: Jack B. Sowards. Based on a story by Harve Bennett and Jack B. Sowards. St: William Shatner, Leonard Nimoy, DeForest Kelley, Ricardo Montalban, and Bibi Besch. On video. 113 min. [2]

Star Trek III: The Search for Spock. Paramount, 1984. Dir: Leonard Nimoy. Prod: Harve Bennett. Exec Prod: Gary Nardino. Scr: Harve Bennett. St: William Shatner, Leonard Nimoy, DeForest Kelley, Mark Lenard, and Christopher Lloyd. On video. 105 min. [2]

Star Trek IV: The Voyage Home. Paramount, 1986. Dir: Leonard Nimoy. Prod: Harve Bennett. Exec Prod: Ralph Winter. Scr: Harve Bennett and Nicholas Meyer. Based on a story by Leonard Nimoy and Harve Bennett. St: William Shatner, Leonard Nimoy, DeForest Kelley, Catherine Hicks, Mark Lenard, and Jane Wyatt. On video. 119 min. [2]

Star Trek V: The Final Frontier. Paramount, 1989. Dir: William Shatner. Prod: Harve Bennett. Exec Prod: Ralph Winter. Scr: David Loughery. Based on a story by William Shatner, Harve Bennett, and David Loughery. St: William Shatner, Leonard Nimoy, DeForest Kelley, David Warner, and Laurence Luckinbill. On video. 107 min. [2]

Star Trek VI: The Undiscovered Country. Paramount, 1991. Dir: Nicholas Meyer. Prod: Ralph Winter and Steven-Charles Jaffe. Exec Prod: Leonard Nimoy. Scr: Nicholas Meyer and Denny Martin Flinn. Based on a story by Leonard Nimoy, Lawrence Konner, and Mark Rosenthal. St: William Shatner, Leonard Nimoy, DeForest Kelley, Kim Catrall, David Warner, and Christopher Plummer. On video. 113 min. [2]

Star Wars. Twentieth-Century Fox, 1977. Dir: George Lucas. Prod: Gary Kurtz. Exec Prod: George Lucas. Scr: George Lucas. St: Mark Hamill, Alec Guinness, Carrie Fisher, Harrison Ford, and Peter Cushing. On video. 119 min. [1]

Superman: The Movie. Warner Brothers, 1978. Dir: Richard Donner. Prod: Pierre Spengler. Exec Prod: Ilya Salkind. Scr: Mario Puzo, David Newman, Leslie Newman, and Robert Benton. Based on a story by Mario Puzo. St: Christopher Reeve, Margot Kidder, Marlon Brando, Susannah York, Gene Hackman, Glenn Ford, and Ned Beatty. On video. 142 min. [6]

Superman II. Warner Brothers, 1981. Dir: Richard Lester. Prod: Pierre Spengler. Exec Prod: Ilya Salkind. Scr: Mario Puzo, David Newman, and Leslie Newman. Based on a story by Mario Puzo. St: Christopher Reeve, Margot Kidder, Gene Hackman, Ned Beatty, Terence Stamp, Sarah Douglas, Jack O'Halloran, and Susannah York. On video. 127 min. [6]

Superman III. Warner Brothers, 1983. Dir: Richard Lester. Prod: Pierre Spengler. Exec Prod: Ilya Salkind. Scr: David Newman and Leslie Newman. St: Christopher Reeve, Richard Pryor, Robert Vaughan, Annette O'Toole, and Pamela Stephenson. On video. 124 min. [6]

Superman IV: The Quest for Peace. Warner Brothers, 1987. Dir: Sidney J. Furie. Prod: Menahem Golan and Yoram Globus. Exec Prod: Michael J. Kagan. Assoc Prod: Michael Kagan and Graham Easton. Scr: Lawrence Konner and Mark Rosenthal. Based on a story by Christopher Reeve, Lawrence Konner, and Mark Rosenthal. St: Christopher Reeve, Mariel Hemingway, Gene Hackman, Jon Cryer, Mark Pillow, and Margot Kidder. On video. 89 min. [6]

Bibliography

MOVIE REVIEWS

Adler, Renata. "*Planet of the Apes*." *New York Times*, 9 February 1968, 55: 2.

Alleva, Richard. "*Batman Returns*: 'Meow!' She Roared." *Commonweal* 119 (14 August 1992): 29–30.

Ansen, David. "*The Final Conflict*." *Newsweek* 100 (30 October 1981): 83.

———. "*Starman*: At Long Last?" *Newsweek* 104 (17 December 1984): 80–82.

Asahina, Robert. "*The Empire Strikes Back*." *New Leader* 63 (2 June 1980): 20.

———. "*Return of the Jedi*." *New Leader* 66 (30 May 1983): 19.

———. "*Superman III*." *New Leader* 66 (27 June 1983): 22.

Benson, Sheila. "*Back to the Future Part II*." *Los Angeles Times*, 22 November 1989, Calendar, 1.

———. "*Starman*." *Los Angeles Times*, 13 December 1984, Calendar, 1.

———. "*Superman II*." *Los Angeles Times*, 18 June 1981, Calendar, 1.

———. "*Superman III*." *Los Angeles Times*, 17 June 1983, Calendar, 1.

Bibby, Bruce. "*Batman Forever*: Riddle Me This, Batman." *Premiere* 8 (May 1995): 52–59.

Billson, Anne. "*Superman IV: The Quest for Peace*." *Monthly Film Bulletin* (September 1987): 283.

Blake, Richard. "*Batman Returns*: Menagerie à Trois." *America* 163 (22 August 1992): 89.

———. "Knight Errand: *Indiana Jones and the Last Crusade*." *America* 160 (17–24 June 1989): 591.

Brown, Georgia. "*Indiana Jones and the Last Crusade*." *Village Voice* 34 (30 May 1989): 57–58.

Buckley, Michael. "*Indiana Jones and the Temple of Doom*." *Films in Review* 35 (August-September 1984): 426–27.

Canby, Vincent. "*Battle for the Planet of the Apes*." *New York Times*, 13 July 1973, 19: 1.

———. "*Damien—Omen II*: Born Unto a Jackal." *New York Times*, 8 June 1978, Section C6: 5.

———. "*Damien—Omen II*: On Keeping the Scenery in Its Place." *New York Times*, 18 June 1978, Part II: 17: 4.

———. "*Logan's Run*." *New York Times*, 24 June 1976, 25: 1.

———. "*The Omen*: Hollywood Has an Appealing New Star—Old Gooseberry." *New York Times*, 25 July 1976, Part II: 13: 1.

———. "*Star Wars*—A Trip to a Galaxy That's Fun and Funny." *New York Times*, 26 May 1977, Section C18: 1.

———. "*Superman*: Nothing 'Went Wrong.' " *New York Times*, 24 December 1978, Part II: 11: 1.

———. "*Superman*: Super Cast." *New York Times*, 15 December 1978, Section C15: 1.

Champlin, Charles. "*The Empire Strikes Back*." *Los Angeles Times*, 18 May 1980, Calendar, 1.

Combs, Richard. "*The Final Conflict—Omen III*." *Monthly Film Bulletin* (October 1981): 198.

———. "*Starman*." *Monthly Film Bulletin* (May 1985): 163–64.

Corliss, Richard. "Keeping the Customer Satisfied: *Indiana Jones and the Temple of Doom*." *Time* 123 (21 May 1984): 82–83.

Cramer, Barbara. "*Batman Returns*." *Films in Review* 43 (October 1992): 337–38.

Denby, David. "*Back to the Future*." *New York* 18 (15 July 1985): 64.

———. "*Batman Returns*." *New York* 25 (13 July 1992): 63–64.

———. "*Batman the Movie*." *New York* 22 (17 July 1989): 45–46.

———. "*Indiana Jones and the Temple of Doom*: Lost in the Thrill Machine." *New York* 17 (4 June 1984): 72–74.

———. "*Star Trek III: The Search for Spock*." *New York* 17 (11 June 1984): 67.

———. "*Superman II*." *New York* 14 (22 June 1981): 49–50.

Edelstein, David. "*Star Trek III: The Search for Spock*." *Village Voice* 29 (5 June 1984): 65.

Eder, Richard. "Screen Review: *Omen* Is Nobody's Baby." *New York Times*, 26 June 1976, 16: 1.

Gelmis, Joseph. "*The Final Conflict*." *Newsday*, 20 October 1981, Part II: 10.

Grant, Edmond. "*Back to the Future Part II*." *Films in Review* 41 (March 1990): 165.

Greenspun, Roger. "*Escape from the Planet of the Apes*." *New York Times*, 29 May 1971, 10: 1.

Hanke, Ken. "*Batman The Movie*." *Films in Review* 40 (October 1989): 480–81.

Hoberman, J. "*Back to the Future*." *Village Voice* 30 (2 July 1985): 48–49.

———. "*Back to the Future Part II*." *Village Voice* 34 (5 December 1989): 117–18.

———. "*Starman*." *Village Voice* 30 (25 December 1984): 67.

Holden, Stephen. "*Highlander: The Final Dimension.*" *New York Times*, 28 January 1995, 16.

Kael, Pauline. "*Batman: The Movie*: The City Gone Psycho." *New Yorker* 10 (July 1989): 83–85.

———. "*Indiana Jones and the Temple of Doom*: A Breeze, a Bawd, a Bounty." *New Yorker* 60 (11 June 1984): 100–106.

Kermode, Mark. "*Omen IV: The Awakening.*" *Sight and Sound* (December 1991): 44–45.

King, Anthony Scott. "On the Set of *Starman*." *Starlog* 89 (December 1984): 58–60, 66.

Kopkind, Andrew. "*Indiana Jones and the Temple of Doom.*" *The Nation* 238 (9 June 1984): 713–14.

Kroll, Jack. "*Batman Forever*: Lighten Up, Dark Knight!" *Newsweek* 125 (26 June 1995): 54.

———. "*Indiana Jones and the Temple of Doom*: Indy Strikes Again." *Newsweek* 103 (4 June 1984): 78–79.

Maslin, Janet. "Space Operetta: *Battlestar Galactica.*" *New York Times*, 18 May 1979, Section C12: 1.

Mason, M. S. "*Back to the Future Part III.*" *Christian Science Monitor* 82 (22 June 1990): 10–11.

McGrady, Mike. "*Batman The Movie.*" *Newsday*, 23 June 1989, Part III: 3.

———. "*Superman IV: The Quest for Peace.*" *Newsday*, 25 July 1987, Part II: 7.

Moore, Suzanne. "*Back to the Future Part II.*" *New Statesman & Society*, 1 December 1989, 42.

———. "*Star Trek V: The Final Frontier.*" *New Statesman & Society*, 27 October 1989, 40.

Murray, Will. "*Batman Forever*: Riddler Forever?" *Starlog* 218 (September 1995): 27–30.

Nangle, John. "*Starman.*" *Films in Review* 36 (March 1985): 182–83.

Newman, Kim. "*Batman Returns.*" *Sight and Sound* (August 1992): 48–49.

———. "*Star Trek V: The Final Frontier.*" *Monthly Film Bulletin* (November 1989): 346.

Novak, Ralph. "*Batman Forever.*" *People Weekly* 43 (26 June 1995): 21.

———. "*Indiana Jones and the Temple of Doom.*" *People Weekly* 21 (4 June 1984): 12.

O'Brien, Tom. "Facts of (Ghetto) Life: *Do the Right Thing* and *Indiana Jones and the Last Crusade.*" *Commonweal* 116 (14 July 1989): 402–3.

———. "*Indiana Jones and the Temple of Doom.*" *Commonweal* 111 (15 June 1984): 374–75.

Postone, Moishe, and Elizabeth Traube. "*Indiana Jones and the Temple of Doom.*" *Jump Cut* 30 (March 1985): 12–16.

Pulleine, Tim. "*Highlander.*" *Monthly Film Bulletin* (August 1986): 236.

Rainer, Peter. "*Back to the Future Part III.*" *Los Angeles Times*, 25 May 1990, Calendar, 1.

Reed, Rex. "*Starman.*" *New York Post*, 14 December 1984, 43.

Rickey, Carrie. "*The Final Conflict.*" *Village Voice* 26 (25–31 March 1981): 38.

———. "*Star Trek II: The Wrath of Khan.*" *Village Voice* 27 (22 June 1982): 54.

Roegger, Berthe. "*Batman Forever*: Batman Reborn." *Sci-Fi Entertainment* 2 (June 1995): 41–47.

Rozen, Leah. "*Highlander: The Final Dimension*." *People Weekly* 43 (13 February 1995): 27–28.

———. "*Highlander 2: The Quickening*." *People Weekly* 36 (25 November 1991): 22.

Sarris, Andrew. "*Superman II*." *Village Voice* 26 (10–16 June 1981): 51.

Seligsohn, Leo. "*Starman*." *Newsday*, 14 December 1984, Part III: 9.

Shapiro, Marc. "Battle of the Immortals: *Highlander 2*." *Starlog* 185 (December 1992): 32–35.

———. "The Immortal Man: *Highlander 2*." *Starlog* 174 (January 1992): 48–51, 71.

———. "*Batman Forever*: Robin Forever." *Starlog* 217 (August 1995): 27–30.

Solman, Gregory. "*Return of the Jedi*." *Films in Review* 34 (June–July 1983): 369.

Sterritt, David. "*The Final Conflict*." *Christian Science Monitor* 73 (7 May 1981): 19.

———. "*Raiders of the Lost Ark*." *Christian Science Monitor* 73 (18 June 1981): 18–19.

———. "*Starman*." *Christian Science Monitor* 76 (31 December 1984): 18.

———. "*Star Trek VI: The Undiscovered Country*." *Christian Science Monitor* 83 (12 December 1991): 14.

Strick, Philip. "*Indiana Jones and the Temple of Doom*." *Films and Filming* 358 (July 1984): 18–20.

———. "*Return of the Jedi*." *Monthly Film Bulletin* (July 1983): 181.

Thomas, Kevin. "*Star Trek II: The Wrath of Khan*." *Los Angeles Times*, 3 June 1982, Calendar, 1.

———. "*Star Trek III: The Search for Spock*." *Los Angeles Times*, 1 June 1984, Calendar, 1.

———. "*Star Trek V: The Final Frontier*." *Los Angeles Times*, 9 June 1989, Calendar, 1.

Thompson, Howard. "*Conquest of the Planet of the Apes*." *New York Times*, 30 June 1972, 24: 1.

Travers, Peter. "*Batman Returns*: Bat Girls on the Line." *Rolling Stone*, 9 July 1992, 109.

———. "*Batman Returns*." *Rolling Stone*, 23 July 1992, 111.

———. "Movie Reviews of Heroes: Macho Under Fire." *Rolling Stone*, 19 October 1989, 27–30.

Tunney, Tom. "*Highlander 3: The Sorcerer*." *Sight and Sound* (March 1995): 37–38.

Turner, Jenny. "*Highlander 2: The Quickening*." *Sight and Sound* (June 1991): 47–48.

Ward, John Paul. "*The Final Conflict*." *Films in Review* 32 (May 1981): 312.

Weiler, A. H. "*Beneath the Planet of the Apes*." *New York Times*, 29 May 1970, 16: 1.

Wilmington, Michael. "*Star Trek IV: The Voyage Home*." *Los Angeles Times*, 26 November 1986, Calendar, 1.

Winsten, Archer. "*The Final Conflict*." *New York Post*, 20 October 1981, 41.

Yakir, Dan. "Raising Kane: *Highlander 3.*" *Starlog* 210 (January 1995): 36–39,
    66.
Zehme, Bill. "*Batman: The Movie.*" *Rolling Stone*, 29 June 1989, 38–42.

BOOKS AND JOURNAL ARTICLES

Aronstein, Susan. "Not Exactly a Knight: Arthurian Narrative and Recuperative
    Politics in the *Indiana Jones* Trilogy." *Cinema Journal* 34 (Summer 1995):
    3–30.
Benton, Mike. *Superhero Comics of the Golden Age: The Illustrated History*. Dal-
    las: Taylor Publishing, 1992.
———. *Superhero Comics of the Silver Age: The Illustrated History*. Dallas: Taylor
    Publishing, 1991.
Biskind, Peter. "Blockbuster: The Last Crusade." In *Seeing Through Movies*, edited
    by Mark Crispin Miller, 112–49. New York: Pantheon Books, 1990.
Black, Campbell. *Raiders of the Lost Ark*. New York: Ballantine Books, 1981.
Boichel, Bill. "Batman: Commodity as Myth." In *The Many Lives of the Batman:
    Critical Approaches to a Superhero and His Media*, edited by Roberta E.
    Pearson and William Uricchio, 4–17. London: BFI Publishing, 1991.
Bonanno, Margaret W. *Star Trek Probe*. New York: Pocket Books, 1992.
Bookbinder, Robert. *The Films of the Seventies*. New York: Carol Publishing
    Group, 1993.
Boulle, Pierre. *Planet of the Apes*. New York: New American Library, 1963.
Brode, Douglas. *The Films of the Eighties*. New York: Carol Publishing Group,
    1991.
Brody, Michael. "*Batman*: Psychic Trauma and Its Solution." *Journal of Popular
    Culture* 28 (Spring 1995): 171–78.
Collins, Jim. "*Batman The Movie*: Narrative and the Hyperconscious." In *The
    Many Lives of the Batman: Critical Approaches to a Superhero and His
    Media*, edited by Roberta E. Pearson and William Uricchio, 164–81. Lon-
    don: BFI Publishing, 1991.
Dallek, Robert. *Ronald Reagan: The Politics of Symbolism*. Cambridge: Harvard
    University Press, 1984.
David, Peter. *Batman Forever*. New York: Warner Books, 1995.
Dillard, J. M. *Star Trek Generations*. New York: Pocket Books, 1994.
———. *Star Trek V The Final Frontier*. New York: Pocket Books, 1989.
———. *Star Trek VI The Undiscovered Country*. New York: Pocket Books, 1992.
Eder, Bruce. "Videodisc Review: *Logan's Run.*" *Video Magazine* 16 (August 1992):
    44.
Edinger, Edward F. *Ego and Archetype: Individuation and the Religious Function
    of the Psyche*. London: Penguin Books, 1972.
Eisler, Riane. *The Chalice and the Blade: Our History, Our Future*. San Francisco:
    Harper & Row, 1987.
Eramo, Steven. "Barry Morse: Space Refugee." *Starlog* 221 (December 1995): 47–
    51, 64.
Everson, William K. *More Classics of the Horror Film: Fifty Years of Great Chillers*.
    New York: Carol Publishing Group, 1990.

Filmer, Kath. *Scepticism and Hope in Twentieth Century Fantasy Literature*. Bowling Green, OH: Bowling Green State University Popular Press, 1992.

Fordham, Frieda. *An Introduction to Jung's Psychology*. London: Penguin Books, 1966.

Gardner, Craig Shaw. *Back to the Future Part II*. New York: Berkley Books, 1989.

———. *Back to the Future Part III*. New York: Berkley Books, 1990.

———. *Batman Returns*. New York: Warner Books, 1992.

Gerrold, David. *Battle for the Planet of the Apes*. New York: Award Books, 1973.

Gipe, George. *Back to the Future*. New York: Berkley Books, 1985.

Glut, Donald F. *Star Wars: The Empire Strikes Back*. New York: Ballantine Books, 1997.

Goldenson, Leonard H., with Martin J. Wolf. *Beating the Odds*. New York: Charles Scribner's Sons, 1991.

Hall, Calvin S., and Vernon J. Nordby. *A Primer of Jungian Psychology*. New York: New American Library, 1973.

Henderson, Jason. *Highlander: The Element of Fire*. New York: Warner Books, 1995.

Hopcke, Robert H. *A Guided Tour of the Collected Works of C. G. Jung*. Boston: Shambhala, 1992.

Horton, Scot W. "Review of *Phantasm*." *Phantasm LP Soundtrack* (Back Record Sleeve). Burbank, CA: Varese Sarabande Records, 1979.

Howard, Joseph. *Damien—Omen II*. New York: Signet, 1978.

Iaccino, James F. "Jungian Archetypes in American Superhero Comic Strips: The Hero's Shadow Side." In *Understanding the Funnies: Critical Interpretations of Newspaper Comic Strips Worldwide*, edited by Ken Nordin and Gail Pieper, 62–76. Lisle, IL: Procopian Press, 1997.

———. *Psychological Reflections on Cinematic Terror: Jungian Archetypes in Horror Films*. Westport, CT: Praeger Publishers, 1994.

Inchausti, Robert. "The Superhero's Two Worlds." In *The Hero in Transition*, edited by Ray B. Browne and Marshall W. Fishwick, 66–73. Bowling Green, Ohio: Bowling Green University Popular Press, 1983.

Jacobs, Will, and Gerard Jones. *The Comic Book Heroes: From the Silver Age to the Present*. New York: Crown, 1985.

Jacoby, Mario A. *Longing for Paradise: Psychological Perspectives on an Archetype*. Translated by Myron B. Gubitz. Boston: Sigo Press, 1980.

Jankiewicz, Pat. "*The Incredible Hulk*: Time of the Green." *Starlog* 204 (July 1994): 72–76.

Jarod's Notebooks. http://www.intex.net/~perridox/pretender/notebook.html (1997): 1–10.

Jarvis, Jeff. "Television Program Review: *The Pretender*." *TV Guide* 45 (25–31 January 1997): 17.

Jung, Carl G. *Aion: Researches into the Phenomenology of the Self: The Collected Works*. Translated by R.F.C. Hull. Princeton, NJ: Princeton University Press, 1990.

———. *The Archetypes and the Collective Unconscious: The Collected Works*. Translated by R.F.C. Hull. Princeton, NJ: Princeton University Press, 1990.

———. *Aspects of the Masculine*. Translated by R.F.C. Hull. Princeton, NJ: Princeton University Press, 1989.

————. *The Basic Writings of C. G. Jung*. Translated by R.F.C. Hull. Princeton, NJ: Princeton University Press, 1990.

————. *Civilization in Transition: The Collected Works*. Translated by R.F.C. Hull. Princeton, NJ: Princeton University Press, 1990.

————. *Flying Saucers: A Modern Myth of Things Seen in the Skies*. Translated by R.F.C. Hull. Princeton, NJ: Princeton University Press, 1991.

————. *Freud and Psychoanalysis: The Collected Works*. Translated by R.F.C. Hull. Princeton, NJ: Princeton University Press, 1989.

————. *Memories, Dreams, Reflections*. Edited by Aniela Jaffe and translated by Richard Winston and Clara Winston. New York: Vintage, 1989.

————. *Modern Man in Search of a Soul*. Translated by W. S. Dell and Cary F. Baynes. San Diego, CA: Harcourt Brace Jovanovich, 1990.

————. *The Practice of Psychotherapy: The Collected Works*. Translated by R.F.C. Hull. Princeton, NJ: Princeton University Press, 1990.

————. *Psychological Types: The Collected Works*. Translated by R.F.C. Hull. Princeton, NJ: Princeton University Press, 1990.

————. *Psychology and Alchemy: The Collected Works*. Translated by R.F.C. Hull. Princeton, NJ: Princeton University Press, 1991.

————. *Symbols of Transformation: The Collected Works*. Translated by R.F.C. Hull. Princeton, NJ: Princeton University Press, 1990.

————. *Synchronicity: An Acausal Connecting Principle*. Translated by R.F.C. Hull. Princeton, NJ: Princeton University Press, 1991.

Jung, Carl, and C. Kerenyi. *Essays on a Science of Mythology: The Myth of the Divine Child and the Mysteries of Eleusis*. Translated by R.F.C. Hull. Princeton, NJ: Princeton University Press, 1993.

Jung, Emma, and Marie-Louise von Franz. *The Grail Legend*. Translated by Andrea Dykes. Boston: Sigo Press, 1986.

Kahn, James. *Indiana Jones and the Temple of Doom*. New York: Ballantine Books, 1984.

————. *Star Wars: Return of the Jedi*. New York: Ballantine Books, 1997.

Kahn, Jenette. "Tribute." *Detective Comics* 599 (April 1989).

Kaminsky, Stuart M. *American Film Genres*. Chicago: Nelson-Hall, 1988.

Kaminsky, Stuart M., and Jeffrey H. Mahan. *American Television Genres*. Chicago: Nelson-Hall, 1988.

Kilworth, Garry. *Highlander: The Movie*. London: HarperCollins, 1996.

Larson, Glen A., and Ron Goulart. *Battlestar Galactica 9: Experiment in Terra*. New York: Berkley Books, 1984.

Larson, Glen A., and Robert Thurston. *Battlestar Galactica*. New York: Berkley Books, 1978.

Larson, Glen A., and Nicholas Yermakov. *Battlestar Galactica 7: War of the Gods*. New York: Berkley Books, 1982.

Le Guin, Ursula. *A Wizard of Earthsea*. New York: Bantam Books, 1968.

Lowry, Brian. "Robert Hays: *Starman* About Town." *Starlog* 114 (January 1987): 17–19, 71.

Lucas, George. *Star Wars The Special Edition: A New Hope*. New York: Ballantine Books, 1997.

Luthman, Shirley G. *Energy and Personal Power*. San Rafael, CA: Mehetabel, 1982.

MacGregor, Rob. *Indiana Jones and the Last Crusade*. New York: Ballantine Books, 1989.

Marriott, John. *Batman: The Official Book of the Movie*. New York: Bantam Books, 1989.

Matthews, John. *At the Table of the Grail: Magic and the Use of Imagination*. New York: Routledge and Kegan Paul, 1987.

———. *The Elements of the Grail Tradition*. Rockport, MA: Element Books, 1990.

Matthews, John, and Marian Green. *The Grail Seeker's Companion: A Guide to the Grail Quest in the Aquarian Age*. Wellingborough, Northhamptonshire, England: Aquarian Press, 1986.

McGill, Gordon. *The Final Conflict*. New York: Signet, 1980.

———. *Omen IV—Armageddon 2000*. New York: Signet, 1982.

McIntyre, Vonda N. *Star Trek The Wrath of Khan*. New York: Pocket Books, 1982.

———. *Star Trek III The Search for Spock*. New York: Pocket Books, 1984.

———. *Star Trek IV The Voyage Home*. New York: Pocket Books, 1986.

Medhurst, Andy. "Batman, Deviance and Camp." In *The Many Lives of the Batman: Critical Approaches to a Superhero and His Media*, edited by Roberta E. Pearson and William Uricchio, 149–63. London: BFI Publishing, 1991.

Meyers, Richard. *The Great Science Fiction Films*. New York: Carol Publishing Group, 1990.

Newell, Mindy. *Catwoman* 1–4 (New York: DC Comics, 1989).

Nolan, William F., and George Clayton Johnson. *Logan's Run*. New York: Bantam Books, 1976.

Orr, Philip. "The Anoedipal Mythos of Batman and Catwoman." *Journal of Popular Culture* 27 (Spring 1994): 169–82.

Pearson, Carol S. *Awakening the Heroes Within: Twelve Archetypes to Help Us Find Ourselves and Transform Our World*. San Francisco: HarperCollins, 1991.

———. *The Hero Within: Six Archetypes We Live By*. San Francisco: Harper-Collins, 1989.

Pearson, Carol S., and Katherine Pope. *The Female Hero in American and British Literature*. New York: R. R. Bowker, 1981.

Pearson, Roberta, and William Uricchio. "Notes from the Batcave: An Interview with Dennis O'Neil." In *The Many Lives of the Batman: Critical Approaches to a Superhero and His Media*. edited by Roberta E. Pearson and William Uricchio. London: BFI Publishing, 1991.

Peterson, Don E. "*Alien Nation*: Bright Horizon." *Sci-Fi Entertainment* 2 (February 1996): 48–53, 79.

Phipps, Maurice. "The Myth and Magic of *Star Wars*: A Jungian Interpretation." *Educational Resources Information Center*. 1983: 2–12 (ERIC Document Reproduction Service No. ED315–833).

Rathwell, Mark. *The Incredible Hulk FAQ Version 2.4*. http://www.uoguelph.ca/%7Emrathwel/Hulk/faq.html (1996): 1–19.

Reddicliffe, Steven, ed. "*The Pretender*: NBC's Saturday Night Line-Up." *TV Guide* 44 (14–20 September 1996): 14–15.

Reynolds, Richard. *Super Heroes: A Modern Mythology*. Jackson: University Press of Mississippi, 1992.

Roberson, Jennifer. *Highlander: Scotland the Brave*. New York: Warner Books, 1996.

Robertson, Ed. *The Fugitive Recaptured: The 30th Anniversary Companion to a Television Classic*. Los Angeles: Pomegranate Press, 1993.

Roddenberry, Gene. *Star Trek The Motion Picture*. New York: Simon and Schuster, 1979.

Rohr, Richard. *Quest for the Grail*. New York: Crossroad Publishing, 1994.

Romanko, Karen A. "Where No Librarian Has Gone Before . . . The 10 Best *Star Trek* Episodes on Video." *Emergency Librarian* 21 (1993): 24–26.

Ronan, Margaret. "Television Program Review: *Starman*." *Scholastic Update* 119 (23 February 1987): TE8.

Roth, Lane. "Death and Rebirth in *Star Trek II: The Wrath of Khan*." *Educational Resources Information Center* 1990: 2–13 (ERIC Document Reproduction Service No. ED311–515).

———. "Vraisemblance and the Western Setting in Contemporary Science Fiction Film." *Educational Resources Information Center*. 1990: 1–12 (ERIC Document Reproduction Service No. ED312–708).

Sassienie, Paul. *The Comic Book: The One Essential Guide for Comic Book Fans Everywhere*. London: Chartwell Books, 1994.

Scheuer, Steven H. *Movies on TV and Videocassette*. New York: Bantam Books, 1991.

Seltzer, David. *The Omen*. New York: Signet, 1976.

Shatner, William, with Chris Kreski. *Star Trek Movie Memories*. New York: HarperCollins, 1994.

Stuckey, Mary. *Playing the Game: The Presidential Rhetoric of Ronald Reagan*. New York: Praeger, 1990.

Trungpa, Chogyam. *The Sacred Path of the Warrior*. Boston: Shambhala, 1978.

Uricchio, William, and Roberta Pearson. "I'm Not Fooled by That Cheap Disguise." In *The Many Lives of the Batman: Critical Approaches to a Superhero and His Media*, edited by Roberta E. Pearson and William Uricchio, 182–213. London: BFI Publishing, 1991.

Werkley, Vicki Hessel. *The Starman Episode Synopsis*. http://www.calweb.com/~smccrory/stepguide.html (1993): 1–7.

Index

wonder in nature, 25, 27. *See also*
Jungian archetypes
Gotham City. *See Batman* films
grail myths, 121–23, 182. *See also*
Holy Grail archetype
Grayson, Dick, 112, 114–15
Green, Marian, 126
Greene, Lorne, 65
Gregory, James, 40
Guiness, Alec, 3, 5

Hackman, Gene, 95, 97, 104
Hamill, Mark, 3
Hamm, Sam, 107
Harrison, Gregory, 61
Harrow, Lisa, 155
Hatch, Richard, 65
Hayden, Jenny. *See Starman*
Hayden, Scott. *See Starman*
Hays, Robert, 174, 176
Henerson, James, 176
Hercules, 188
Hercules, xiii
hero, 55, 82, 121, 138; Caesar in
Planet of the Apes, 48–50; Clark
Kent in *Superman,* 100–101; Com-
mander Adama in *Battlestar Galac-
tica,* 68–69; Indiana in *Indiana
Jones,* 124–26, 130–32; Kirk in *Star
Trek,* 27; Logan-5 in *Logan's Run,*
58–60, 64; Luke in *Star Wars,* 10–
11; MacLeod in *Highlander,* 135–36;
Marty in *Back to the Future,* 82–83,
87; Spock in *Star Trek,* 20. *See also*
fairy tale archetypes
Herod, 43–44
Heston, Charleton, 36, 38, 41
Highlander movies, 79, 121, 133–41,
191–92; *Highlander,* 133–36; *Highlander: The Final Dimension,* 139–
41; *Highlander 2: The Quickening,*
136–39; *Highlander 3: The Sorcerer,*
137, 139; *Highlander 4,* 141. *See
also* Holy grail archetype
Highlander: The Television Series, 137,
141
Hirsch, James, 176
Hitler, Adolf, 40, 126
Holden, William, 151

Holy grail archetype, 121–45; anti-
grails, 133; as the Ark of the Covenant, 123–24, 126; Belloq as the
knight's shadow counterpart, 124–
26; the Camelot story, 122; and the
dark self, 128–29; the exploits of a
knight, 123; and fatherless heroes,
130–31; the Fisher King legend, 121–
22; greatest grail of all, 130–33; the
Highlander films, 133–41, 191–92;
the *Indiana Jones* trilogy, 123–33,
192, 194; inheriting the prize, 134–
36; Kane as trickster, 140; Keeper of
the Grail, 133; Kurgan as Black
Knight, 134–35; MacLeod's troubled
opus, 137; Marion as revered object,
125; metamorphosis into a hero,
124–25; mystery of, 139, 141; Parsifal, 121–22, 128, 134–35; the
pre-knight's journey towards, 123–
26; Professor Jones' quest of spiritual enlightenment, 130, 133;
Ramirez as Merlin, 134; rebirth into
immortality, 138–39; rejuvenation of
a wasteland, 126–29; relationship
with Jungian synchronicity, 127–28;
resurrection of Conner, 135–36; as a
sacred stone, 127–28; and sacrifice
for the greater good, 139; search for
loved ones, 125, 129, 141; and significance of the sword, 138, 140; the
three tests of, 132; and urges of fortune and glory, 128–29, 130, 132
Hopcke, Robert, 6
Howard, Joseph, 154
Huggins, Roy, 166
Hugo, Victor, 166
Hunter, Kim, 37
hysteric, 45

Iaccino archetypes: alchemic traveler,
79–89; creator, 15–34; demon child,
147–61; divided superhero, 93–119;
evolving shadow species, 35–53;
Holy grail, 121–45; shadow destroyer, 55–75; shadow pursuer, 165–
83; space father, 3–12
Iblis, Count, 69–71
Immortal, The, 167

About the Author

JAMES F. IACCINO is Professor of Psychology at Benedictine University in Lisle, Illinois. His extensive publications in psychology include *Psychological Reflections on Cinematic Terror* (Praeger, 1994) and his comprehensive physiological text, *Left Brain-Right Brain Differences: Inquiries, Evidence, New Approaches* (1993).

ISBN 0-275-95048-4

90000>

9 780275 950484

HARDCOVER BAR CODE

EAN